Realism and Naturalism

The Novel in an Age of Transition

Richard Lehan

The University of Wisconsin Press

The University of Wisconsin Press
1930 Monroe Street
Madison, Wisconsin 53711

www.wisc.edu/wisconsinpress/
3 Henrietta Street
London WC2E 8LU, England

1   3   5   4   2

Printed in the United States of America

Library of Congress Cataloging-in-Publication Data
Lehan, Richard Daniel, 1930–
Realism and naturalism: The novel in an age of transition /
Richard Lehan.
p.   cm.
Includes bibliographical references and index.
ISBN 0-299-20870-2 (hardcover: alk. paper)—
ISBN 0-299-20874-5 (pbk.: alk. paper)
1. Fiction—19th century—History and criticism.
2. Fiction—20th century—History and criticism.
3. Realism in literature.
4. Naturalism in literature.   I.   Title.
PN3500.L44   2005
809.3′912—dc22   2004024548

To

Edward F. Callahan

Bon Ami

And the Memory of

David Nelson Lehan
(1935–2001)

"I use the [realistic/naturalistic] method because, like every one else, I have to respond to world currents. At this time the world current flows to realistic representation, and will for some time do so more and more. In time, however, it will turn back to romanticism."

Interview with Theodore Dreiser in the *New York Evening Post*, 15 November 1911.

"The Naturalists for all their faults were embarked on a bolder venture than those other writers whose imaginations can absorb nothing but legends already treated in other books, prepared and digested food. They tried to seize the life around them, and at their best they transformed it into new archetypes of human experience. We look for Studs Lonigan in the Chicago streets as our grandfathers looked for Leatherstocking in the forest. Just as Cooper had shaped the legend of the frontier and Mark Twain the legend of the Mississippi, so the naturalists have been shaping the harsher legends of an urban and industrial age."

Malcolm Cowley, "Not Men: A Natural History of American Naturalism," *The Kenyon Review* (Summer 1947).

"The nineteenth century dislike of Realism is the rage of Caliban seeing his own face in a glass.
The nineteenth century dislike of Romanticism is the rage of Caliban not seeing his own face in a glass."

"All art is at once surface and symbol.
Those who go beneath the surface do so at their own peril.
Those who read the symbol do so at their own peril."

Oscar Wilde, preface to *The Picture of Dorian Gray*.

Contents

Preface

In its extended coverage of realism and naturalism, this book offers an in-depth consideration of an important phase of the European and American novel. It also serves to supply an enlarged critical context for those in the field who might welcome a historical perspective on this literary material. I have written it because it is the kind of book I was looking for when I first became interested in this field. I know of no other book that treats realism and naturalism together, text and context, as part of a historical moment.

The aim here is to supply a comprehensive treatment of the major works of these international movements that dominated the literary world from about 1850 in Europe to 1950 in America—although earlier novels will be treated by way of explaining the origins of and transformations within these movements. In its look at narrative from Cervantes to DeLillo, it is in part a history of the novel. In seeing the romantic vision as anachronistic, the romance as inadequate, and realism/naturalism as necessary to a depiction of the new commercial-industrial reality, it offers a new context for the consideration of realism/naturalism. And in seeing realism/naturalism as a vortex through which the novel passed before it became modernism, it offers a new way of reconceptualizing both realism/naturalism and the modern novel.

One of my goals is to reveal the cultural preoccupations of realistic and naturalistic fiction; another is to display its historical insights and richness, an aspect of it less acknowledged today than I think justified; and a third is to suggest the need for an expanded critical context, one that brings text and context into focus. In bringing dozens of primary and secondary texts into common play, it reconsiders the familiar and much of its originality lies in its unfolding.

Most critical studies work vertically—that is, they see the work independent of a totalizing context, are concerned selectively with the formal properties of a work, or with the text as a system of discourse, or with describing the genesis of a work, or with recording a reader's response. This study, on the other hand, works horizontally— postulating a sequence of elements that are part of a larger continuum, a period of time that is both the product and catalyst of change and that creates an intellectual climate that in turn informs literary reality.

The method here rests on the assumption that the writer possesses a concept of history that precedes the text and a concept of the text that precedes the actual writing of the novel. Thus the "idea" of the text is larger than the text itself: naturalism as a narrative mode brings together a group of texts that speak to each other. Each novel is pretextualized—that is, comes off a larger model of realism/naturalism—and each is different from but connected to the other novels that make up the sequence and establish parallels between the literary and the historical event. Just as ideas today are marshaled in the name of postmodernism, ideas from the past can be marshaled to suggest the meaning that realism and naturalism had to their contemporaries.

In working back and forth between historical context and text, this study revises the idea of literary influence, demonstrating that a changing culture involved changes in the novel itself. A major assumption informing this idea stems from the belief held by writers in the early nineteenth century that the romantic view of nature was inadequate to the new city with its commercial and industrial institutions. Realism/naturalism was the first corrective to this anachronistic view. As a result, subject matter and narrative technique were drastically changed. The romance did not do justice to the new reality. Plots could no longer be resolved in sentimental terms. If there were contradictions in the idea of realism and naturalism, they were the contradictions of a new age.

My intention here is not to argue for a concept of the Novel so generic that individual difference is lost. But neither is it to settle for a belief that novels contemporary with each other cannot share meaning. The attempt is to find common ground between these conflicting positions—to read fiction in terms of the movement that produced it, along a spectrum of meaning that preserves the uniqueness of the text at the same time that it allows for a more general illumination of intellectual and literary history.

This method involves seeing realism/naturalism as a response to an era of transition—specifically, to the new commercial and, later, industrial society, the influence of the new city, the inception of Darwinian and other biological thought as well as cosmic and political theory, leading to the rise of a secular society undergoing great intellectual and moral change. Every era is a time of change, which is why it is an "era." But the late nineteenth century and early twentieth century was an especially volatile period of change. Two themes dominate this study. The first involves the myth of the land, the belief that the land is infused with spiritual meaning. A challenge to this claim came in the form of questioning the innocence of human nature especially as expressed in the town. The other theme involves the transforming power of the city. The rise of a consumer, urban culture created material desire and continued sense of a narcissistic concept of self—elements that informed the novel of this era.

There may be no Reality in the sense of an essential meaning outside of us that can be universally grasped. And there may be no History separate from an interpretation of the past that is equally subjective. But all supposition is not equal; paradigms wait to be tested by judgment and experience; our sense of history and reality is weighted. Moreover, the order of fiction is different from the order of life. Fiction creates its own reality through narrative conventions that reflect historical concerns, suppositions that can be tested against our sense of experience and shared by engaged readers. My theory of narrative modes assumes that works can share an inherent meaning, a similar content—all of which point toward narrative commonality rather than formal difference. Literature and history inform each

other. Their workings involve process: literary evolution and historical change, the unfolding of historical narratives often expressed as
literary subgenres.

The revision as well as the resistance to history stemmed from
several sources. Americans had long thought of their country as
"new," the product of a break from rather than continuity with a European past. Second, the historical emphasis in America tended to
look west toward the frontier rather than east toward Europe. Third,
the old historicism put the emphasis upon national identity, a search
for indigenous meaning as called forth by Emerson that eventually
led to the creation of academic disciplines like American Studies.
And last, formalist critics maintained that historical concerns inter-
fered with artistic integrity, the self-contained purity of the literary
work. I am more interested in the shared assumptions of European
and American thought, with the continuity that produced literary
movements rather than in futilely trying to exhaust the meaning of
an individual text; more interested in the forces that produced an era
than in the work as aesthetic object. As critics diverse as Georg
Lukács, Lucien Goldman, and Kenneth Burke have told us, history itself is a form of consciousness; its imaginative ordering subsumes
literary movements like realism and naturalism. Such movements reinforced historical purpose: they supplied the means of going beyond anachronistic visions and coming to terms with postromantic
reality.

The emphasis here is on the changes that were reflected in the
literary subgenres of realism and on the themes and conventions of
literary naturalism—that is, changing attitudes toward land and
money; the rise of urbanism, which generated slums and social outcasts; the restraints that social conventions put on individual, especially sexual, behavior; the coming of a commodity culture that produced a narcissistic "me now" philosophy; the materialized self that
fragmented into the multi-self containing a compulsive, hidden persona. These concerns inform realism/naturalism and supply a critical background, a means of anticipating narrative content. As we
move back and forth from text to context, we can better understand
the makeup of the realistic/naturalistic novel and how directly this
fiction depended on the social and intellectual events of its era.

A major assumption of this book is that Darwinian thought and post-Darwinian commentary revised a preceding "reality," undermining both a Christian and Enlightenment sense of order: realistic and naturalistic fiction is written against this lost order. Darwinism begins with certain universal assumptions stemming from a belief in evolution. But such evolution involves adaptation rather than progress: evolution assumes the ability of a species to adjust to its environment. If the hemisphere should heat up, certain molecules will die; if the hemisphere should cool down, a different group of molecules will die. One group of molecules is not "better" than the other—just more capable of survival under different environmental circumstances.

A related issue involves the distinction between civilization and culture. Civilization moves a step beyond biological evolution, accommodates a belief in progress, and justifies a sense of universal right and wrong. Civilization is the product of human advances through history—first, through a hunter-gatherer stage, then an agriculture stage, and finally an urban stage, marked by the rise of markets, trade, and systems of law that allow commerce even with strangers (that is, those who are outside the family and tribe) and in which cooperation replaces aggression and violence. Put differently, civilization is the product of fixed codes that are held together by financial, legal, medical, and educational institutions and whose primary function is to restrain behavior. Combined with forms of technology, such institutions accommodate adaptation and supply the building blocks of human advancement. Civilization sets moral limits, disavowing such practices as, say, cannibalism, incest, and slavery. Culture, on the other hand, involves historical accident, the communal beliefs and customs of a people at a certain point in time and place. The practices of culture might justify cannibalism, moral limits giving way to moral relativism. In academia, humanistic scholars study the civilization side of this divide, focusing on the universal truths that arise out of, say, human tragedy, while multicultural scholars study the other, emphasizing the totems and taboos of a specific people. Literary naturalism examined both sides of this equation, moving back and forth between opposed assumptions, bringing fixed theories of heredity and history into focus with the variables of environment.

Recently, the culture-civilization debate has morphed into the primitivism-civilization debate. Those who favor primitivism have turned against advanced forms of technology, repudiated the industrial (sometimes even the agricultural) revolution(s), and advocated a modern anarchism. We will not turn back the industrial clock short of global apocalypse—a fact acknowledged by most naturalist writers, who were more concerned with depicting how new forms of technology changed the nature of human thinking—of human adaptation—than with eliminating the machine.

In assuming a concept of literature as representation (the capacity of a work to reflect physical reality), I also assume the idea of narrative "re-presentation" (the capacity of a work to become a model for another work and to thus function within heuristic or interpretive categories). By so doing, I suggest the philosophical, political, and social context that made realism/naturalism possible in the first place. During the roughly one hundred years that realism/naturalism prevailed, it offered a powerful way of seeing the physical world—a way that still has the value of historical importance. In this context, realism and naturalism can still be read as viable modes of narrative, even in a postmodern age in which language is thought of as self-referential and reality unstable.

RDL

Acknowledgments

Since this book is in some ways a continuation of my recent and past writing on literary realism and naturalism, I should acknowledge the connection here with my books on Theodore Dreiser (1969), *The City in Literature* (1998), and my monograph on *Sister Carrie* (2001). In these studies and in my other books, I have been concerned with the evolution of narrative modes, primarily in combination with forms of intellectual evolution. This in turn has involved a study of how institutions—cultural and literary—were transformed by historical change. I have treated some of this material in different terms in past essays cited in the bibliography, especially "Realism/Naturalism: The European Background" (1995) and "American Literary Naturalism: The French Connection" (1984).

The writing here is in part the result of past research and reading made possible by the Guggenheim Foundation and the University of California for a President's Research Fellowship, both of whom I have previously thanked. I am also grateful to stipends from the Research Committee of the Academic Senate at UCLA.

I should like to thank several people who read and commented on this study: Donald Pizer, Jerome Loving, and Louis Budd. They are not to be held responsible for my own critical pronouncements. Pizer, for example, believes that realism/naturalism is more an indigenous American movement than I do, better subjected to formal than historical analysis.

Thanks also to Jeanette Gilkison and Doris Wang of the UCLA English Department for help of many kinds, and to Juan Tan and

Steve Lee at UCLA and Craig Binney at Stonehill College for computer help. My continued thanks to the staff of the Young Research Library at UCLA for their years of help and assistance. My debt to both the staff of the English department and the library goes far beyond mere acknowledgement; this staff makes UCLA into one of the most accommodating research environments a scholar could hope for.

While naturalism often stresses the negative, my dedication acknowledges the positive: a friend of many years and a brother, no longer living; their friendship gives meaning to the illusive pursuit of stability, allowing constancy to triumph over a fleeting sense of permanence. Once again, thanks to Ann for love, companionship, and encouragement.

Introduction

This study is a history of the rise and fall of a literary idea: it offers suppositional explanations for major changes in the direction of fiction in the late nineteenth and early twentieth century. In its broad scope, it offers a brief history, an anatomy, of the novel from its origins in comic realism and romance before it gave way to the modern and then the modern to postmodern novelists like Don DeLillo.

Three concerns order its divisions. The first chapter treats realism and naturalism as an expression of their times. In this context, I examine the historical background of and the connection between realism and naturalism. The second considers how realism became a narrative mode, moving beyond its origins and then beyond both the comic and romantic modes of realism that dominated the novel form from Fielding to Dickens, Hugo to Balzac, Gogol to Dostoyevsky. I then discuss realism in relation to prevailing subgenres and to the historical circumstances that created their generic need. The discussions of individual authors are not intended be exhaustive, but they do offer an overview and suggest how the major works of the leading novelists established a narrative mode, becoming the literary models of their times. The emphasis here is on the way a narrative mode creates its own order of reality.

The next four chapters describe the way realism gave way to naturalism under the influence of commercial-industrial change as well as that of the new science, the first of which led to a new urban reality and the second to radical revision in the concept of self. Here I treat the Darwinian revolution, Zola and the rise of the experimental novel, the confluence of French and American literary naturalism, and the themes and narrative conventions that naturalism spawned. I consider how naturalism encouraged fields of force (biological, cosmic, and political) and how Darwinian assumptions were modified by the anti-Darwinism of such commentators as Samuel Butler. The movement from Darwin's theory of adaptation to Butler's theory of a directing mind paralleled the transformation of literary naturalism into literary modernism.

Chapters 8 and 9 explore the rise and fall of literary realism/naturalism and the literary criticism that accompanied it. Just as this was an era influenced by the idea of evolution, this study involves what might be called literary evolution. I argue that naturalism evolved out of realism and that naturalism eventually gave way to modernism with its various interior movements such as neorealism and existentialism. The claims of the naturalists to an objective reality were supplanted by the interest in the workings of consciousness and memory of the modernists. Discussed also is how these modes differed from romance and melodrama, how a mechanistic text differs from an organic, and how a residue of literary naturalism remained after World War II.

Most of the books that cover this subject begin with a literary discussion and allow background aspects to emerge from the critiques of individual works. Reversing this approach, I supply first the historical background that informed these texts on the assumption that realism emerged from a particular era—from a transformed and transforming culture that needs to be understood at the outset. There are radical differences between the reality of the nineteenth century and the reality of today. We have moved from a commercial and industrial to information and service age, from early theories of race to their transformation, from a scientific base that first accepted naturalistic assumptions, then rejected them, and then adopted a new set of assumptions resembling those of naturalism based on genetic theory.

Literary naturalism is the hinge between forms of realism and modernism. It took as its subject the matter of atavism (ancestral influence as a product of genetic recombination) and a universe of force (cosmic or political) that was almost always subterranean and

disruptive. The moral complexity of the age was reflected in the social complexity of a new literature. The moral center of the old realism was emptied and the realist novel left in its place a vacuum that
was then filled by a new form composed of both cosmic and social
questions.

Realism/naturalism did away with the authority of sentiment that
had held the novel in place from Fielding to Dickens. In America, it
went hand-in-glove with the Progressive movement and the investigative journalists ("muckrakers") who exposed corruption in business and politics in the aftermath of the Civil War. Its plots held out
the illusion of hope to its fictional subjects while it showed the realm
of opportunity becoming smaller and smaller and the gulf between
the rich and the poor widening. A spiritual resolution was discounted on the assumption that as products of a natural environment we cannot go beyond it.

Realism/naturalism challenged a false idealism. The New World
offered Europe new hope, as did the American frontier—but at
the expense of its first inhabitants. There was opportunity to create
gigantic wealth—but such wealth would only arise out of agrarian slavery in the South and industrial slavery (the slums) in the
North. America was both physically beautiful and rich in natural
resources—but preserving its beauty meant foregoing the mining of
its resources and mining its resources meant destroying its beauty.
America was the product of an Enlightenment vision—but that new
definition of individual liberty competed with a willingness to exploit both the people and the nation's resources. Built into an idealized vision of a New World were all the contradictions of the land,
and no fiction came to a better understanding of those contradictions than realism/naturalism.

Recent literary criticism has allied naturalism with other narrative forms—such as the romance and gothic fiction. That such a connection would be made was perhaps predictable because like the romance the naturalistic novel often depicted extreme behavior, and
like gothic fiction it sometimes treated the mysterious and the hidden. But realism/naturalism gradually eliminated the fantasy elements it shared with the romance from its plots and began depicting
a more ordinary reality. Rider Haggard gave way to Rudyard Kipling,

Kipling to Jack London, London to Joseph Conrad, Conrad to Ernest
Hemingway, Hemingway to the noir reality of a James M. Cain—
each new form of the mode moving it further away from forms of
the romance.

Since the link between naturalism and the romance stemmed
in part from shared cosmic concerns, there were as many differences
as similarities, and naturalism in all its manifestations was self-
contained enough to preserve a sense of difference from other narrative modes. Unlike the romance with its largely heroic and epic character, naturalism treated mostly the ordinary before it gave way to
the extraordinary. Unlike the gothic, which appealed to the supernatural and the element of the unknown, naturalism usually attempted to give the machinations of its plots a pluralistic explanation, grounding their twists and turns in material and empirical
reality before introducing the ironic. And unlike both the romance
and melodrama, realism/naturalism emptied the novel of a moral
center, except in some cases in which it gave expression to a political
philosophy that generally leaned toward the Left or toward other
forms of power politics and hope.

Darwinism held to universal assumptions tempered by historical
change. For example, the difference between the jungle and civilization was more a matter of institutional transformation than a change
in a residually consistent human nature. Human nature is a given,
not purely the product of a nation state or a specific culture: what is
debased functions globally; a feral element is continuously displayed
both conspicuously and inconspicuously. Thus the stock market involves "killings," bears and bulls in an arena of winning and losing.
The handsomely packaged meat in the supermarket belies the animal
slaughter that produced it. Contact sports like football, hockey, and
boxing—sublimated forms of more aggressive behavior—are popular spectator events. Modern institutions like court trials conceal
the confrontational nature of humanity and substitute for physical
combat. Cult behavior is often antisocial and aggressively expressed.
And while only one percent of those convicted of murder are executed, capital punishment exists to soothe our primitive fears. The
lore, the fiction, and the films involving the werewolf testify to the
long-held belief (an assumption in place long before Darwin) that

human and animal natures are interchangeable, an assumption that Frank Norris brings to *Vandover and the Brute* (1914). The zoos we find in every major city throughout the world testify to our compatibility with the animal realm. There the beauty and seeming docility of animals like the mountain lion conceal its killer instinct—a superficial placidity it sometimes shares with the human animal as the universality of war demonstrates. Jack London traces the transformation back and forth between the tamed and wild sled dog. The riddle of sexuality—especially the compulsions of sex—has an equally naturalistic explanation. Obsessions with love and money have their origins in a residual, naturalistic self. And the courting process involves a ritual that human males, competing for female favor, share with males of the animal kingdom. Road rage, soccer mayhem, and urban riots reveal a primitive violence at the core of civilized life.

Human behavior is altered by social practices, as primitive instincts remain much the same. Once destabilized by forms of revolt, a nation is subject to internal chaos—a seemingly natural state. Modern technology has increased destructive capacity: every era has been bloody but none more so than the twentieth century. Every day human kindness encounters human malice—a contradiction that is on continued display. Literary naturalism revealed that civilization is the jungle or wilderness in disguise. A thin line separates the two, and is often crossed in naturalistic fiction, as in Conrad's journey up the Congo or Jack London's into the Yukon.

The evolutionary interface between the animal and the human realm leads to what I have called "the stranger in the mirror." This second self expresses itself variously: it can intuit the beautiful and sublime amid ugliness; it can reveal hidden human impulses; it can expose the contradictions that exist between natural impulses and social conventions; it can show generosity and display self-indulgence; and it can reveal both generate and degenerate forms.

Initially the doubled self was embodied in two different persons—Dickens's Joe Gargery and Orlick or Dostoyevsky's Stavrogin and Kirillov—but soon came to be embodied in one, as in Conrad's Kurtz. From Stevenson's Hyde to Wilde's Dorian Gray, from Zola's Jacques Lantier to Dreiser's Clyde Griffiths, from Twain's pauper to

Conrad's secret sharer, this second self exposes the idealism often built into social conventions or takes on separate, often atavistic, life in which the irrational side of the character takes control.

The Enlightenment substituted natural rights for birthrights, creating a sense of individual opportunity. Darwinism put emphasis on the idea of life as combat by transforming Enlightenment ideals into a process of natural selection and a struggle for adaptation and survival. Literary naturalism called attention to the social forces that worked against the individual in an era where the industrial scale diminished the human scale. Most realistic/naturalistic fiction functioned within this duality—between the idea that individual opportunity was unlimited and the knowledge that there were counterforces that worked against such personal fulfillment. This opposition supplied a conflict in fiction from George Eliot to Emile Zola to Joyce Carol Oates. While the intensity of this conflict varied from author to author, its nature remained the same.

In addition to supplying a literary, intellectual, and cultural history of the late nineteenth and early twentieth century, this book also offers a modal rather than formal reading of the major works of realism and naturalism. A theory of modes assumes narrative similarity, a commonality, and is more generic than a theory of form. In a formal reading, form and history are considered to be separate entities; in a modal reading, text and history inform each other. In a modal reading, the historical background is meant to serve as a frame of reference, the organizing principle, out of which the "reality" of the fiction emerges. There is thus no attempt to reduce meaning to an individual text as we might find in a more formal reading. In an autotelic reading, the focus is usually on one text; in a modal reading, the focus is on narrative realms like realism and naturalism. The historical and literary background given here is meant to inform realism/naturalism as movements, not just the individual texts that make up their canon, and the several accounts I offer of the origins of realism/naturalism are necessary for an understanding of the evolution of the novel from comic realism to modernism and beyond.

Progression here is both chronological and thematic. After a statement of purpose (introduction) and consideration of background information (chapter 1), my concern is with realism as a major narrative mode (chapter 2) and as a series of subforms that evolve in relation to historical events (chapter 3). In my examination of naturalism, I show how Zola put biological Darwinian thought to narrative use, and discuss the confluence of Darwin's thought and Zola's narrative practices that led to American literary naturalism (chapter 4). I then treat the naturalistic response to scientific theories of the cosmic (chapter 5) and to political philosophy (chapter 6). I then explore the distinct set of themes and narrative conventions this material provided when considered as a whole (chapter 7). I also treat the transition from realism/naturalism to modernism (chapter 8), assess the major literary criticism associated with realism/naturalism (chapter 9), and provide a summary of key ideas (conclusion).

While the approach of demonstrating progression through na-tional literatures might suggest the indigenous nature of these works, my assumption is that in the Western world—under the influence of the industrial revolution, of the new urbanism, and of shared intel-lectual beliefs—what transpired in one nation-state eventually oc-curred in another. The French Revolution, for example, challenged both the landed and the aristocratic privileges as did the Puritan Revolution in seventeenth-century England and the Civil War in nineteenth-century America. Since a modal reading examines the work in terms of the reality it creates, it moves beyond the text to other works that evoke a similar sense of reality—that is, to intertex-tuality and to historical matters that inform the text. As a study in intertextuality, this book examines one work talking to or respond-ing to another: Dreiser's *Sister Carrie* (1900) to Zola's *Nana* (1884); Norris's *McTeague* (1899), Crane's *Maggie* (1893), or Sinclair's *The Jungle* (1906) to Zola's *L'Assommoir* (1887); Norris's *Octopus* (1901) to Zola's *Germinal* (1885), *La Terre* (1887), or *La Bête humaine* (1890). Moreover, as narrative modes changed, so did the reputation of var-ious popular authors. This study suggests why the reputation of such writers as Kipling, London, and Sinclair has been revised in recent criticism.

As a study in narrative modes, this book examines the novel at the crossroads of romantic realism and modernism, tracing the ev-olution of realism and naturalism in the context of other narrative modes. I specify five dominant modes: comic realism, romantic realism, naturalism, modernism, and postmodernism. Realism/ naturalism drastically changed the nature of comic and romantic realism and was changed in turn by literary modernism before it gave way to postmodernism. Comic realism involved a moral center (often the world of the estate, where we find the man or woman of sentiment who embodies the power of the human heart to do good). Romantic realism superimposed symbolic meaning on a usually urban landscape. Modernism, the second stage of romantic realism, put the emphasis on mythic symbolism, cyclical history, and Bergsonian consciousness. Postmodernism collapsed that consciousness into the culture itself.

In the aftermath of deconstruction, one must confront the charge that there is no authority that locks reality in place, that the return of the repressed leads to textual instability in the largest sense of what we mean by text. A sense of the absolute finds its limits in every discipline from literature to architecture. But the realm of limits is subject to its own limits, and every proposition is weighted with evidence, which may not lead to the absolute but which allows preferential interpretations, a preponderance of meaning. Zola's scientific observer has given way to a more introspective narrator: unreliability is a modern and postmodern phenomenon. But to dismiss Zola on theoretical grounds is to miss his historical insights and the weight of the political, social, and moral understanding that he brought to his times.

Until the eighteenth century, literature was thought of as mimetic or representational in function. Under the influence of romanticism and later modernism, literature came to be thought of as expressive in function—as an expression of first the artist's sensibility and later of language itself. Once narrative meaning was reduced to the workings of language, discourse took the place of realism. In emphasizing the representational aspect of language, I do not mean to deny its subjective import. Under the influence of aestheticism and later structuralism, language became its own reality. While the only way into a text is obviously through its language, such language infuses and complements rather than replaces reality. Language is a social construction, a means of representing reality and not a substitute for it. To move from the idea of self-reflexive to representational language is to move from one narrative assumption to another—and to establish a context that the realist authors took for granted. The move from the representation of an outer to inner reality changed the very nature of the novel. The naturalist believed the novel stemmed from the observations of a scientific observer, the modernists from a realm of subjectivity. How we went from one view to the other is a consideration of this book.

The postmodern agenda does not carry the authority today that it did between 1960 and 1990. Structuralism and deconstructionism have gone into the same abyss as existentialism. But critical practice today still gives preference to "formalist" or "constructed" readings, encourages those who question the international nature of realism/naturalism, and supports those who allow a theory of discourse to absorb the meaning of terms like "realism" and "naturalism." All of these matters are contested by this study, which offers an alternative to existing, mainstream commentary.

Chronology

1846   Balzac's *Splendeurs et misères des courtisanes.*

1847–48 Balzac's *La Cousine Bette.*

1848   On 10 December Louis Napoleon Bonaparte is elected president of the republic, replacing Louis Philippe. Revolutions in France, Austria, Italy. Marx and Engels's *Communist Manifesto.* Dickens's *Dombey and Son.*

1851   On 2 December Louis Napoleon dissolves the Legislative Assembly and declares himself president. He later declares himself Napoleon III, Emperor of the Second Empire, with a new constitution of 14 January 1853.

1852   Dickens's *Bleak House.* Melville's *Pierre.*

1853   Arthur de Gobineau's *Essai sur l'inégalité des races humanines.*

1854   Dickens's *Hard Times.*

1855   Spencer's *First Principles.*

1855–57 Dickens's *Little Dorrit.*

1857   Flaubert's *Madame Bovary.* Baudelaire's *Les Fleurs du Mal.*

1859   Darwin's *On the Origin of Species by Means of Natural Selection.* George Eliot's *Adam Bede.*

1860   Eliot's *The Mill on the Floss.* Hawthorne's *The Marble Faun.*

1860–61 Dickens's *Great Expectations.*

1861–65 American Civil War.

1861   Eliot's *Silas Marner.*

1862   Spencer's *Synthetic Philosophy.* Victor Hugo's *Les Misérables.* Flaubert's *Salammbô.* Dostoyevsky's *The House of the Dead.* Turgenev's *Fathers and Sons.*

1864   Edmond and Jules Goncourt's *Germinie Lacerteux.*

1864–65 Dickens's *Our Mutual Friend.*

1865   Dostoyevsky's *Crime and Punishment.*

1865–69 Tolstoy's *War and Peace.*

1867   Marx's *Capital.* Zola's *Thérèse Raquin.*

1869   Flaubert's *L'Education sentimentale.* Twain's *The Innocents Abroad.*

1870   Zola begins *Rougon-Macquart* series.

1870–71 France declares war on Prussia on 19 July. On 2 September France is defeated at Sedan, ending the Second Empire. The Third Republic is proclaimed on 4 September.

1871   The Paris commune (21–28 May). Darwin's *The Descent of Man*. George Eliot's *Middlemarch*. Dostoyevsky's *The Possessed*. Twain's *Roughing It*. Nietzsche's *Birth of Tragedy*.

1871–93   Zola's *Rougon-Macquart* novels.

1872   Zola's *La Curée*. Butler's *Erewhon*.

1873   Zola's *Le Ventre de Paris*. Pater's *The Renaissance*. Twain's *The Gilded Age* (with Charles Dudley Warner).

1874   First impressionist exhibition in Paris. Impressionists exhibited their work outside official salons: Monet (1840–1926), Renoir (1841–1919), and Pissarro (1830–1903) worked out of doors, often painting urban scenes. Manet (1832–1883) and Degas (1834–1917), and Cezanne (1839–1906) joined the group. Flaubert's *La Tentation de Saint Antoine*. Hardy's *Far from the Madding Crowd*.

1875–77   Tolstoy's *Anna Karenina*.

1876   Twain's *The Adventures of Tom Sawyer*.

1877   Zola's *L'Assommoir*. James's *The American*.

1878   Butler's *Life and Habit*. Hardy's *The Return of the Native*.

1879   Butler's *Evolution, Old and New*. James's *Daisy Miller*. Ibsen's *A Doll's House*.

1880   Zola's *Le Roman expérimental*. Dostoyevsky's *The Brothers Karamazov*. Henry Adams's *Democracy*.

1881   Flaubert's *Bouvard et Pécuchet*. James's *The Portrait of a Lady*. Howells's *A Modern Instance*. Verga's *The House by the Medlar Tree*.

1883   Zola's *Au bonheur des Dames*. Maupassant's *A Woman's Life*. Twain's *Life on the Mississippi*.

1884   Zola's *Nana*. Nietzsche's *Thus Spake Zarathustra*. Daudet's *Sappho*. Huysman's *A Rebours*. Twain's *Adventures of Huckleberry Finn*.

1885   Pater's *Marius the Epicurean*. Zola's *Germinal*. Howells's *The Rise of Silas Lapham*. Leopold II, King of Belgium, takes possession of the Congo.

1886   Zola's *L'Oeuvre*. Van Gogh (1853–1890) settles in France—along with Gaugin (1848–1903), which marks the rise of expressionism. Haymarket riot in Chicago. Stevenson's *Dr. Jekyll and Mr. Hyde*. Hardy's *The Mayor of Casterbridge*.

James's *The Bostonians*. James's *The Princess Casamassima*. Gissing's *Demos*.

1887   Haggard's *She*.

1888   Strindberg's *Miss Julie*. Bellamy's *Looking Backward*. Gissing's *The Nether World*.

1889   Twain's *A Connecticut Yankee in King Arthur's Court*.

1890   Zola's *La Bête humaine*. Howells's *A Hazard of New Fortunes*. James's *The Tragic Muse*. Knut Hamsun's *Hunger*. Ignatius Donnelly's *Caesar's Column*. Wilde's *The Picture of Dorian Gray* (unauthorized American edition containing only thirteen chapters). Doyle's *The Sign of Four*.

1891   Zola's *L'Argent*. Hardy's *Tess of the D'Urbervilles*. George Gissing's *New Grub Street*. William Morris's *News from Nowhere*. Wilde's *The Picture of Dorian Gray* (first authorized edition in book form, published in England, containing twenty chapters).

1892   Stevenson's *The Beach of Falesa*. Zola's *La Débâcle*. Hauptmann's *The Weavers*. Gilman's "The Yellow Wallpaper."

1893   Max Nordau's *Degeneration*. Crane's *Maggie: A Girl of the Streets*.

1894   Dreyfus affair divides France. Hardy's *Jude the Obscure*. Moore's *Esther Waters*.

1895   Kipling's "The Brushwood Boy." Wells's *The Time Machine*. Crane's *The Red Badge of Courage*.

1896   Bergson's *Matter and Memory*. Gustave Le Bon's *The Crowd: A Study of the Popular Mind*. Hardy's *Jude the Obscure*. Wells's *The Island of Dr. Moreau*.

1897   Kipling's *Captains Courageous*.

1898   Zola's *J'Accuse*. Norris's *Moran of the Lady Letty*. Conrad's *The Nigger of the Narcissus*.

1899   Haeckel's *Riddle of the Universe*. Wells's *When the Sleeper Wakes*. Conrad's *Youth* (in serialized form). *Heart of Darkness* appears in Blackwells. Norris's *McTeague*. Chopin's *The Awakening*. Veblen's *Theory of the Leisure Class*.

1900   Jacques Loeb's *Physiology of the Brain and Comparative Psychology*. Conrad's *Lord Jim*. Dreiser's *Sister Carrie*.

1901   Norris's *The Octopus*. Mann's *Buddenbrooks*.

Realism and Naturalism

1

Realism and Naturalism as an Expression of an Era

1

Realism, naturalism, symbolism—from 1848 to 1914 in Europe, these were three major movements in literary history, corresponding roughly to three generations of writers. Realism lasted approximately from 1848 to 1871, naturalism from 1871 to the early 1890s, and symbolism from about 1890 to 1914. In America, realism took hold after the Civil War and lasted until the turn of the century when it was forced to compete with literary naturalism. Literary naturalism in American fiction lasted until the end of World War II. Symbolism marked the transition away from realism/naturalism toward modernism.

Realism involved the literary attempt to write an objective narrative, to depict the outside world as honestly and truthfully as possible. Naturalism carried realism one step further, added a biological and philosophical component to the writing of fiction, and stressed the connection between literature and science. Naturalism presumed that a theory of environment and heredity along with Darwinian and post-Darwinian theories of evolution would ground the literary work in a factual and scientific context.

Realism was the bridge between the romance and the naturalistic novel. The realist wanted to depict middle-class reality, the life of ordinary people, and was critical of the heightened—often symbolic, even allegorical—characters who made up the romance. And yet the novels of Mark Twain sometimes depicted members of the lower classes and the novels of Henry James almost always members of the

3

higher, so the representation of a certain social class is not a hard and fixed attribute of realism.

While it is impossible to define realism on the basis of a few novels, a pretextualized sense of realism as a system of historical concerns allows a wide enough range to accommodate definition. In order to locate such a context, we must work outward from the text toward historical representation. The death of an agrarian society and the birth of an industrial one produced a change both in the subject matter and technique of the novel. The heroic was diminished; the capacity for unqualified good was questioned; conflict could no longer be resolved by sentiment; the banal competed with the extraordinary; contradictions prevailed. Despite the variation among texts, a number of elements remained constant: realism and, later, naturalism involved a plot that turned on cause-and-effect events—acts that had consequences, like the stealing of money in plots by Howells or Dreiser. In the realist novel, these acts usually turned on a moral choice—the moral dilemmas that Huck Finn or Silas Lapham faced. But by the time we get to Henry James, the moral choice becomes more ambiguous, the moral center of the novel more difficult to determine. The decisions that Huck and Silas made—one intuitively, the other more reflectively—are less fraught and ambivalent than the decisions made by characters in James's fiction.

Increasingly, the realists moved away from depicting characters who acted according to idealized values toward depicting ones who tested their values against their own sense of experience. Ernest Hemingway once said that American literature began with *Huckleberry Finn,* an overstatement to be sure, but one that nonetheless revealed his identification with Twain and characters like Huck Finn. Unlike Tom Sawyer who gets his ideas from books, Huck responds directly to his own sense of right and wrong. When Hemingway's Lt. Henry makes his "separate peace" and tells us that abstract words only embarrassed him, he is echoing Twain's sense of truth—an idea of it that results from testing values experientially and an idea that, as it came to inform the novel, carried it toward pragmatic reality.

Photography encouraged a sense that reality was transparent. We know now that the photographer can create "reality" as well as the artist, that photography has a subjective component. But the photograph, especially when it reinforced the facticity of the daily newspaper, gave the illusion of reality. Many of the new realists—for example, Stephen Crane, Frank Norris, Harold Frederic, Theodore Dreiser, and Ernest Hemingway—began as newspaper reporters and were used to recording daily events and concentrating on the here-and-now experience. And many of the plots in this era came from events reported at length in the newspapers—for example, the criminality of Charles Yerkes (1837–1905) or the Grace Brown-Chester Gillette case that became the basis for Dreiser's *Trilogy of Desire* (*The Financier* [1912]; *The Titan* [1914]; *The Stoic* [1947]) and *An American Tragedy* (1925).

In America, this newspaper activity was supplemented by what today we would call investigative reporting. A group of journalists known as "muckrakers" exposed the corruption inherent in big business and city-state and federal politics. While most of the group wrote for popular media such as *McClure's* magazine, much of their writing ended up in book form. Ida Tarbell wrote an exposé of Standard Oil (*The History of Standard Oil* [1904]); Lincoln Steffens wrote on political corruption in the city (*The Shame of the Cities* [1904]); and David Graham Phillips, the author of the naturalist novel *Susan Lenox* (1917), wrote on senatorial corruption (*The Treason of the Senate,* first published in book form in 1964).[1] The muckrakers successfully agitated for important legislation such as the federal Pure Food and Drug Act, the Meat Inspection Act, and the Hepburn (railroad regulation) Act—all in 1906.

The muckrakers were especially influential between 1902 and 1912, and their writing complemented the realists/naturalists' disgust with unregulated capitalism and their sympathy for the poor. Even earlier, such sympathy characterized Jacob Riis's *How the Other Half Lives* (1890). The growing gulf between rich and poor, the idea of conspicuous consumption, and the effect in general of money on the culture were the subjects of Thorstein Veblen's *Theory of the Leisure Class* (1899). While social conventions were often variously received, there was general outrage at the abuses that accompanied capitalism. On the other hand, the values of the genteel tradition were preserved in magazines like *Scribner's, Harpers,* and the *Century.* The more radical critics like Van Wyck Brooks, Randolph

Bourne, and Floyd Dell published elsewhere—as did such left-wing journalists as Max Eastman and John Reed.

While realist writers varied in matters of style and literary technique, they all portrayed the individual struggling for identity in a hostile society. Literary naturalism deepened this depiction by making the individual less resilient and the environment more hostile. Naturalism as a narrative mode involved the everyday. But superimposed on the commonplace—especially in the works of Emile Zola and Frank Norris—were the sensational and the extraordinary. Frank Norris insisted that terrible things had to happen in naturalistic fiction: characters must be twisted away from the ordinary and brought to the edge of violence and sudden death in a heightened plot that worked itself out in an unleashing of passion. A force larger than human beings acts on the ordinary, transforming it into the monstrous. A second self made conventional life unpredictable. Such stories gave rise to the uncanny feeling that life was charged with atavistic energy, a sense that the ordinary could quickly become strange, and that just beneath the surface of common life was a volcano of violence waiting to erupt. The civilized concealed the primitive, by which it was tested. Civilized values proved tenuous: order was threatened by chaos, the literal competed with the ironic, and the generative eventually gave way to the degenerative.

A new philosophy demanded new forms of expression. Zola, Dreiser, and other naturalists depicted the new artist, whose craft allowed insight into the workings of nature. Naturalism helped qualify the transcendental aspect of romantic aestheticism. The romantics believed that beauty stemmed from the God-like creation of the universe. Coleridge's secondary imagination "dissolves, diffuses, dissipates" in order to re-create. The artist employed the secondary imagination to replicate God's primary imagination. Beauty was truth; truth, beauty. Unlike romanticism, which idealized life and valued imagination over fact, naturalism represented life as a harsh affair, relying on principles of objectivity based on detailed observation and insisting on the existence of external forces, especially heredity and environment, which were subject to laws of the natural universe. Naturalism saw art emerging from life, thought of it as the product of observation informed by craft, and believed that life ought to be the subject of art everywhere. Zola and Dreiser depicted the artist who could find beauty in the street. Like so much in the naturalistic realm, beauty contained the mystery of life even as it was referred back to physical reality—not to some transcendent realm. The naturalistic novel thus depicted a range of hierarchically-ordered physical states. The look into nature revealed a destructive element, to use Conrad's phrase, as well as a sublime order. In between was the placidity of the everyday, in which the turbulent and the common, the predictable and the ironic, could meet, as in the fiction of Stephen Crane. The tensions between a submerged turbulence and a residual beauty revealed the complexity of nature's extremes.

Naturalism also served as a social corrective, forcing a reevaluation of cultural "truths." In America, for example, there were three major historical movements, a residue of each of which could be found in established values: Puritanism with its God above, the Enlightenment with its belief in natural rights over birth rights, and romanticism with its belief in heroic action and sentimental love. A novelist like Frank Norris found the Puritan God wanting in a world of residual violence. Dreiser questioned the superiority of a tale of sentimental love to one about the needs of the kept woman; he also demonstrated that a belief in natural rights did not guarantee the good life and that there was a thin line between success and failure. Stephen Crane questioned the very idea of the heroic in war, seeing bravery as more an instinctual reaction to the threat of death than a matter of willed behavior. Crane also questioned the code of the West and explored the sentiment of love, the workings of chance, and the nature of cosmic play. And almost all of the naturalists doubted the integrity of capitalism, even as they stood in awe of it, questioning the manipulation and the chicanery that influenced the marketplace.

While the naturalists sometimes depicted the upper class, they more often descended the social ladder to portray the world of the poor and the outcast, taking a stark look at what before were forbidden subjects. The naturalists felt that the more attention that was given to lower or deviant aspects of life—to poverty, alcoholism, degeneration, and the dysfunctional family—the more "realistic" the writing would be. They specifically took as their subject the working class (a subject frowned on by many of the earlier novelists), and they depicted sexuality with an explicitness that many readers found offensive. In fact, while they often took on middle-class concerns, the naturalists wrote mainly against the moral grain of the middle class, and from Zola to Dreiser there was an attempt to censor the sexual aspect of their novels.

One of the major differences between literary realists/naturalists and the romancers who preceded them was that while the latter tended to set their stories in the distant historical past, the former were inclined to locate their tales in the more immediate historical present. More contemporary problems were foregrounded in naturalism. Zola, for example, whose writing career spanned the years 1870–90, concentrated on the years of the Second Empire (1851–70). Every one of his novels dealt with topical issues. He chronicled the peasantry's greed for land, the eventual economic shift from the provinces to the city, the fate of the urban worker, the corruption of the high-society prostitute, the rise of the department store, and the workings of the urban market. He depicted the struggle for survival of the new industrial worker, the rise of the steam engine and the railroad system, and the fate of a degenerating France as it prepared for war with Germany. Zola viewed history through a biological prism that was constituted in great part by Darwinian thought.

2

Despite a common assumption otherwise, Darwinian evolution was not progressive but adaptive. Darwin's (1809–1882) theory of evolution was based on the ability of a species to adapt to its environment, not go beyond it. Darwin's theory was progressive only so far as it postulated that a species tended to move toward greater adaptability—not toward a more idealized form. The claim that evolution was moving the human species onward and upward came from Herbert Spencer (1820–1903). Moreover, to Darwin's theory of adaptation, Spencer added the phrase "the survival of the fittest." Out of these ideas came social Darwinism, a radically new form of laissez faire: the belief that those who cannot adapt to their physical environment are unfit to survive. Altruism thus found itself competing with a rugged individualism.

Another theory that was extrapolated from the new science was positivism. August Comte (1798–1857), the father of positivism, was also the father of sociology. Comte saw a connection between physical and social laws. Just as "truths" were available in the physical universe, corresponding truths were available in the social realm. One simply had to pay attention to the data in order to generalize from it. Comte looked on Buffon's 44-volume *Natural History* (1749–1804) and Charles Lyell's *Principles of Geology* (1830–33) as models of how empirical data could be organized to reveal natural laws. He then held that the laws that governed society could be discovered in the same way.

Comte rejected the Enlightenment mode of reason. He questioned the belief that reason linked man and nature, arguing that the two were not identical: reason had a being of its own, separate from nature. He also questioned the belief that certain truths were "self-evident." Nothing was self-evident: "truth" had to be abstracted from empirical data. Reason was not more powerful than natural or social laws, which functioned according to their own necessities. While one could discover these laws, one could not change them, just as one could not change the law of gravity.

Comte believed that we had progressed through various periods of thought. The religious period saw the world as governed by some form of God. The philosophical period gave up God for forms of controlling abstractions (as in Hegel's work, for example). The positivist era introduced the idea that a belief should be accepted only after it had been tested empirically, an idea that anticipated American pragmatism. In relating "truth" to the empirical realm, Comte helped validate the new literary realism and, later, literary naturalism. It was only a matter of time—as the ideas of Comte and social Darwinism proved—before theories designed to explain the physical universe were extrapolated from and applied to the social realm.

3

Despite the sense of progress built into Comte's ideas, and despite the Spencerian belief that the species was evolving upward, the naturalists also believed that the laws of nature worked to produce chaos and disorder. The law of entropy held that when an enclosed system lost heat, it also lost its capacity to do work. When heated molecules become random, there is a loss of energy. The naturalists believed that the tendency toward disorder was so strong that degredation was the eventual lot of all human life. They gave universal consent to the principle of degeneration.

The idea of heat-death was connected to the belief that the sun was cooling—connected to a fear of cosmic entropy. *Untergang des Abendlandes,* the German title of Spengler's magnus opus (1918–22), literally means "the sunset of the Occident" (not "the decline of the West," as it is standardly translated). Anatole France also used the sun—which he represented as white in its youth, yellow in its middle realm, and red before it dies—as a metaphor for human growth and decline, and H. G. Wells used the red sun as an image of heat-death in *The Time Machine* (1893).[2]

The idea that sun was indeed dying was reinforced by a belief in cultural decline. In *Degeneration* (1893), Max Nordau saw the fin de siècle as the dead end of decadence. Nordau attacked Zola, even as he agreed with him that the city was producing a survival of the unfittest—an emotionally exhausted overclass and a bestial under-class. Nordau was distressed by the loss of individual autonomy, and he believed that the personal breakdown revealed a cultural break-down: at stake was the loss of a vision coming from a cohesive people with an organic sense of the land controlling their destiny. Despite the fact that he was the object of Nordau's attack, Zola and the other naturalists shared his theory of degeneration.[3]

4

Along with the idea of degeneration, the naturalists were obsessed with the idea of race. Darwin's theory of evolution encouraged an interest in racial identity. Race became an important issue because it was used to justify imperialist policies, especially European rule in the colonies. Race was also an issue when it came to establishing a lower class that could supply cheap industrial and agrarian labor or when it came to establishing a "superior" class that could serve as a rationale for nationalism.

Johann Friedrich Blumenbach (1752–1840), the founder of anthropology, began the process of classifying the existing races in 1775. Relying primarily on the difference in skin color, he established five races: Caucasian (white), Mongolian (yellow), Ethiopian (black), Native American (red), and Malaysian (brown). Another theory of race stemmed from separating communities geographically. Norway became representative of the Nordic race; Switzerland of the Alpine race; and southern Italy of the Mediterranean race. But such distinctions proved too vague and arbitrary, confusing the racial identities of people living on or between these boundaries. Later, physical traits were added to the classification system and, still later yet, language systems, which led to the idea of the "Aryan race," the "Anglo-Saxon race," the "Semitic race," and others.

In Germany, Friedrich Max Mueller (1823–1900) studied linguistic roots, hoping to discover in them a basis for racial distinctions that would justify the superiority of the Aryan nations. The Aryan people originally lived in what today is Iran (hence the name), but eventually migrated into northern Europe. Mueller tracked how the language of the Aryan people changed as a result of their migration into England and Germany, arguing that the new environment further strengthened the inherent racial character of the Aryan people. In France, Maurice Barrès (1862–1923) used a similar argument to advance the superiority of the Gauls and Celts. Such thinking connected ideas of race with the land and the idealization of the rural life. The assumption was that the life force came from the land, which embodied the past and was the source of racial vitality.

These ideas were codified by racist thinkers like Arthur de Gobineau (1816–1882) in works such as *Essai sur l'inégalité des races humains* (*The Inequality of the Human Race* [1853–55; Engl. tr. 1915]). Gobineau argued that racial decline sets in when a people lose contact with the life force that stems from their racial (that is, national) roots. At first Gobineau claimed the English as the most Aryan of countries, but after 1871 he shifted emphasis to the Germans, who, after the Franco-Prussian War, were united into a powerful new nation. Under Gobineau's influence, Germany became the center of such racial thinking. His ideas were picked up by Houston Stewart Chamberlain (1855–1927), writing from Germany, who reduced the struggle to two factions—the "superior" Germans and the "inferior" Jews. This division played into the distinctions made between the land (and a nationalized citizenry) and the city (with its large Jewish population) as well as between an Aryan and Semitic people.[4] Hitler would build his racial theories on these kinds of distinctions.

These racial theories have been disproved by modern theories of genetics. The father of modern genetics was Gregor Mendel (1822–1884), an Austrian botanist-monk, whose laws of heredity (1865) were not recognized until about 1900. Mendel worked with the garden pea plant, addressing the question of why different varieties of the plant produced hybrids. Mendel anticipated the idea of dominant and recessive genes with each gene producing a trait. Edwin Chargaff (1905–2002) made advances in hereditary theory after he read the 1944 report by Oswald Avery that identified DNA as the hereditary material. Chargaff's study led to an understanding of the four bases, or chemical groups, of which DNA was composed— adenine, cystosine, guanine, and thymine. He noticed that in extracted DNA, the amount of adenine and thymine were almost the same, as were the amounts of cystosine and guanine.

The explanation of this phenomenon was supplied by James D. Watson (1928–) and Francis H. C. Crick (1916–2004), working in 1953 at Cambridge University. They discovered that a DNA molecule is a double helix, consisting of two long strings coiled around one another. The strings are composed of Chargaff's nitrogen elements, which they called nucleotides. Each nucleotide connects to a corresponding nucleotide in the other string, which explained Chargaff's corresponding ratios. There are normally forty-six chromosomes in the human body, the father and mother each contributing twenty-three. The chromosomes consist of the DNA molecules and contain the genes that determine biological traits. Thus, even in the same family, no two siblings (except identical twins) will have the same genetic makeup, just as each shuffle of a deck of cards will typically produce a different hand.

As individuals differ, so do the races. David Barash argues that "people of different races *are* different . . . members of any race seem likely to share more genes with each other than with individuals of a different race."[5] These assertions have generated a ready reply, especially from cultural theorists who believe behavior is learned, not genetically transmitted. Feminists have contested the idea that women by nature are more passive than men, and the Left has balked at the idea of a genetic base to race. The argument at its most focused was carried out between two Harvard biologists: Edward O. Wilson, arguing the sociobiologist position, and Stephen Jay Gould, arguing the culturist position. Thus, while we have moved far beyond nineteenth-century biological assumptions, the debate over whether we are mostly determined or free still goes on.

5

Biological evolution supplied the model for transformations in the natural world. Historical evolution supplied the model for change in the social realm. After Napoleon was defeated at Waterloo in 1815, the old European regime was reconstituted, but not for long. A major uprising in Germany in 1848 followed a minor uprising in France in 1830. Karl Marx (1818–1883) and Freidrich Engels (1820–1895) saw these events as the basis for a new political vision. Out of this came the *Communist Manifesto* (1848) in which Marx rendered Hegel a dialectic materialist, arguing that the struggle between capital and labor would be resolved by the rise of a communist state. This did not happen in 1848. In 1870, however, after the defeat at the hands of Bismark, Emperor Napoleon III abdicated; at this time, Parisian workers rose up against Louis-Adolphe Thiers (1797–1877), who had replaced Napoleon III, becoming head of the new republic. Thiers defeated the Communards in the street, shooting the rest against the Mur des Fédérés in Père-Lachaise cemetery on 28 May 1871, an incident Zola describes in detail in *La Débâcle* (1892). While Zola's hope for a new order resided elsewhere, Marx's hope for a new order lay in exacting retribution for this massacre, and when Marx died in 1883, V. I. Lenin (1870–1924) took up his cause.

While there is no direct connection between literary naturalism and Marxist's philosophy, there are affinities. Marx substituted social and historical evolution for biological evolution—that is, he saw in history a process analogous to biological growth, a phenomenon in which history moved in stages through a primitive communism, to

feudalism, to capitalism, and eventually to modern communism in which the worker would have control of the industrial process. The assumption was that communism—with its concern for the industrial worker—was better suited to industrial nations like England, France, or Germany. But the middle (propertied) class in these countries with their established institutions prevented communism from displacing capitalism. Moreover, Marx believed that when the time came the workers of the world would unite and throw off their capitalist lords. However, when World War I occurred, the workers from England and France went to war against the workers from Germany and Austria: nationalism proved to be stronger than worker solidarity. But when the czars of Russia were toppled, it left a political vacuum. Lenin, among others, led the Bolsheviks' uprising over Alexander Kerensky's (1881–1970) provisional government, forsaking the ideology of Marx, who believed in the necessity of an interim government that would bridge a bourgeois and a communist state. Instead he brought communism—based on the councils (soviets) of workers, peasants, and soldiers—directly to Russia in 1917.

After the worldwide depression of the early thirties, communism had an appeal in the West, including America. Many of the naturalists saw it as an alternative to the abuses of capitalism. Jack London and Upton Sinclair saw socialism as a corrective; Edward Bellamy had a theory of distribution based on a technology plan that came close to socialist doctrine; Dreiser, who visited Communist Russia in 1927, returned to America sympathetic to and later engaged in Communist causes; John Dos Passos and Edmund Wilson also paid homage to communism by visiting Russia to determine firsthand the state of this new world experiment; and Richard Wright and Nelson Algren were at one time members of the American Communist Party: the last part of Wright's *Native Son* (1940) offers a communist explanation of Bigger Thomas's ordeal.

There are, however, inconsistencies between Marxist philosophy and Darwinian theories of evolution. Marx believed that inevitably, as the source of industrial production was taken over by the worker, there would be a classless society. For Darwin, the process of adaptation was such that there would always be a social hierarchy with some in the species—such as the alpha animal in the pack—succeeding and others failing. Also Darwin believed that consciousness (a product of adaptation) informed environment while Marx thought that environment (the workings of capitalism and industrialism) informed consciousness. Darwin's philosophy was open-ended and adaptive; Marxist's philosophy, especially when it became socialist realism, was teleological and inseparable from an idealized sense of communism as a kind of utopian destiny. Lastly, Marx's interest in the industrial world was based on the means of production and the differences among the classes, while Darwin's interest in the physical world was based on the adaptive nature of biological species.

The industrial revolution changed the relationship of the individual to society. Organized around the farm, the agrarian order encouraged the need for the family as well as its stability. A sense of clan created a familiar world. Organized around the office or factory, the commercial-industrial world broke down the traditional family, led to less personal gratification at work (especially when the fruits of labor were produced by an assembly line), and allowed the strange (as in a personal stranger as well as the unknown) to dominate the familiar.

The world became a bit less friendly—more uncanny. One sees this phenomenon at work in literary naturalism. Georg Lukács (1885–1971) contends that social relationships in a capitalistic culture tend to become mechanical. He points to a Dos Passos novel to suggest how characters begin to share a similar consciousness. Relationships become reified—each character takes on the same material traits of another, embodying the meaning of the capitalist system itself.[6] Perhaps that is why there is a strange disjunction in literary naturalism between life on the land and life in the city. The two realms produce different states of mind—different social values.

6

Another analogue to literary naturalism was the old historicism. Just as a theory of race was dependent on supposedly scientific assumptions, so it was claimed that theories of history and society were based on scientific principles. And central to any history of this movement is the subject of history itself. Historians put greater emphasis on the accumulation of facts and the idea of historical force to explain the past.

Most significant here are such historians as Leopold von Ranke (1795–1886) and Jacob Burckhardt (1818–1897), who combined Hegelian assumptions with an empirical method. They insisted that a period of time (the Italian Renaissance) or a spatial entity (the German nation) had a geist or spirit or identity that, provided enough data could be found, illuminated the period or entity. Ranke's culminating work, *Weltgeschichte*, a nine-volume study, published between 1881–88, and Burkhardt's famous study of the Italian Renaissance, published in 1860, which shared a worldview with that of literary naturalism, exemplify this approach.

This method underwrote the social theories of Thorstein Veblen (1857–1929), the folk and fairly-tale studies of the Brothers Grimm (Jacob, 1785–1863, and Wilhelm, 1786–1859), the old philology, and, in the realm of scientific research, the mechanistic theories of Ernst Haeckel (1834–1919) and Jacques Loeb (1859–1924). This naturalistic discourse thus cut across many fields, manifesting itself in the work of the physical sciences, cultural history, urban sociology, literary naturalism, folklore, and philology. It became the basis for the seminar method of teaching used in German universities and first introduced in America at Johns Hopkins University and later used in creating such disciplines as American Studies.[7] As a methodology, it was materially grounded, despite its belief in national or cultural identity. It depended on a belief in the linearity of history, the necessity of cause and effect, and the idea of a verifiable narrative—that is, a narrative that could prove itself among other narratives by the weight of the physical evidence that it presented.

Frederick Jackson Turner (1861–1932), who was trained at Hopkins and then went on to teach at Wisconsin and later Harvard, was the leading American historian in this era. His frontier thesis, which dominated the historical view of America during the progressive period, reinforced the belief in the superiority of the land over the city. He carried this idea over to a study of sectional America: North versus South, East versus West.

From Twain to the moderns (Pound, Faulkner, Fitzgerald, Dos Passos), the literary imagination gave consent to the Jeffersonian pastoral view long after it no longer remained viable. Thorstein Veblen, born on the agricultural frontier of Wisconsin, was the product of the agrarian unrest of the 1870s and 1880s. He was sympathetic to the utopian socialist ideas that led to the Populist attacks against the railroads and the Eastern establishment. He attacked the robber barons in his *Theory of the Leisure Class*. There he defined "conspicuous leisure" and "conspicuous consumption"; both activities lacked material productivity and therefore were a form of waste.

Even at the end of the twenties, Vernon L. Parrington (1871–1929) was making the Jeffersonian vision the key idea on which American thought turned in his influential three-volume *The Main Currents of American Thought* (1927–30). Such a belief died hard despite the obvious fact that the forces at work turned on commercial and industrial axles and that the new world would inevitably be both industrial and urban.

Turner's predominant place in the practice of American history eventually gave way to that of Charles A. Beard (1874–1948) and James Harvey Robinson (1863–1936), the former factoring the commercial city into the historical equation, the latter informing the discussion with intellectual history. Their use of social history was extended by Arthur M. Schlesinger Sr. (1888–1965). When Walter P. Webb published *The Great Frontier* (1952), pushing the idea of a frontier back to Europe, the study of American history—like the study of American literary naturalism—came full circle; it now had a social dimension and had moved from believing in the European-American connection, to emphasizing indigenous matters, back to acknowledging a link between European and American history.

But this is only half the story. Eventually historicism, with its deterministic assumptions, gave way to historical relativism, especially in America under the influence of Beard and then Carl Becker (1873–1945), who had studied under Turner at Wisconsin and under Beard and Robinson at Columbia. Becker's theory of history involved the needs of what he called Everyman—a hypothetical person whose identity depended on memory. By extrapolation, history becomes a consideration of the past in terms of the ongoing needs of a society. Out of this theory came the idea of history as a "usable" past—a pragmatic sense of history involving what a society needs to function, to control the environment, and to motivate people.[8] This moved history away from the historicist's assumptions that ideas like national destiny were built into time and that historical process involved rise and fall, progress and entropy.

The various theories of history were part of an attempt to come to terms with an era of change, one that saw the transformation from an agrarian to an industrial economy. And the movement from a history of force locked into determinism to a pragmatic history that accommodated a usable past paralleled the move (as we shall see in chapter 8) from naturalism to neorealism.

7

The transition from a landed to an urban economy brought with it the rise of the middle class and the inclination for more republican forms of government. The city created an enclosed space, a compressed realm of shared desire, in which the struggle to succeed could be observed on an individual (that is, realistic) scale. This upheaval was founded on empirical and scientific assumptions, encouraged an emphasis on physical reality, and coupled itself to a new technology that promoted a literary sense of photographic reality. In the fine arts, the impressionists—especially Monet, Renoir, and Pissarro—began to make use of the urban setting, depicting street scenes and painting such public spaces as railroad stations.

The marketplace with its new forms of money, creating new kinds of banks and credit theories, had replaced feudalism. The new state was based on the consent of the governed; later, it would be defined by nationalism, and even later still by imperialism. In this context, the Puritan Revolution (1642–60), the French Revolution (1789–99), and the American Civil War (1861–65) had the same historic function: each (albeit occurring at different times) marked the transition from a feudal and aristocratic to a commercial/ industrial and bourgeois world. Defoe and Dickens observed this phenomenon in England; Balzac and Zola in France; and Twain and Dreiser in America.

The nineteenth century was marked by the rise of a new power. The new capitalists took on a heroic character, replacing explorers,

military leaders, and men of state as role models. The new industri-
alist left their imprint on the literary imagination—Charles Yerkes
on Theodore Dreiser, James J. Hill on F. Scott Fitzgerald. These men
were the new heroes or the new villains or a bit of both, at least as
they were depicted in the naturalistic novel. Their rise took place
from the end of the Civil War to the turn of the century, the same
period that saw the rise of realism/naturalism in America.

As these changes distanced a people from the land, the urban
world appeared, as we have seen, more grotesque and uncanny:
the familiar suddenly became strange. The urban experience would
eventually lead to a sense of reality so distorted that it was antirealis-
tic; in fiction, this nightmarish quality of city life would be reflected
in the expressionism of Kafka—the desire to go beyond mere representation to find the symbolic equivalent or inner reality of things.
Such technique eventually moved toward deliberate distortion, but
at the outset it was about a fresh way of seeing reality. Dickens in particular depicted the grotesque reality that came with the new commercial process. Zola began where Dickens left off, eschewing sentiment for a hard-hearted examination of the industrial world of
modern Paris.

The starting place for the study of Zola' works is the July Monarchy of 1830, which occurred ten years before his birth, when Louis
Philippe took power in France in the name of the Second Republic.
One historian tells us: "It was not long before liberals came to see
that their idealism was misplaced; the system of divine right and
ultra royalism had been driven out, only to be replaced by a regime of
landlords and capitalists with a bourgeois monarch. There was not
much to choose between the two."[9]

Under Louis Philippe, France became a commercial, urban, and
industrial country.[10] The transition in December of 1848 from Louis
Philippe to Louis Napoleon Bonaparte was smooth. Three years
later, however, on 2 December 1851, Louis Napoleon's troops occu-
pied Paris, and one year later he became Napoleon III, Emperor of
the Second Empire, with a new constitution of 14 January 1853 codifying his powers. Once again a liberal revolution gave way to a conservative reign.

Zola later saw these events as the betrayal of liberalism. But many historians have pointed to the enlightened aspect of Napoleon III's regime. Baron Georges Haussmann (1809–1891) demolished medieval Paris, built boulevards and city parks, and created vistas that spatially connected landmark buildings.[11] Canals and rivers were dug or widened, preserving what were the best transportation systems in Europe. Paris became the center of Europe with six great railroad lines converging on the capital. But the splendors of the new architecture competed with the sordidness of the industrial slums. In America, Frank Norris, who was influenced by Zola, and Theodore Dreiser, who was not, depicted the same historical transformations—using the same dichotomy—in New York, Philadelphia, Chicago, and San Francisco.

8

What was happening in France after the French Revolution had its historical parallels in America after the Civil War. Both a new physical reality and a state of mind came into being as the country became more industrialized. These changes rendered obsolete the romantic view of reality and established the need for a new way of seeing.

One change brought about by industrialization was the birth of a new-money class. As previously suggested, this was the age of the new tycoon, often referred to as the "robber baron." J. P. Morgan was amply rewarded when he helped finance the new railway system; Andrew Carnegie made a fortune in the new steel industry, as did John D. Rockefeller by refining oil. People used kerosene to light their homes, but kerosene was limited by its expense. A breakthrough occurred when it was discovered that petroleum oil could be refined and used for such purposes as well as for lubricating industrial machinery; Rockefeller made a fortune by setting up such refineries. Another breakthrough involved turning iron ore into the much stronger steel by baking out the carbon content of the ore; Andrew Carnegie opened up such a refinery at Homestead, Pennsylvania, just outside Pittsburgh. He would later sell his holdings to J. P. Morgan for an estimated twenty-five billion dollars (in today's dollars) in a deal that led to the birth of U.S. Steel. The new industry, which combined science and technology, spawned efficiency experts like Frederick W. Taylor (1856–1915). Before Taylor, each man brought his own shovel to work; Taylor experimented, however, until he found the right-size shovel for each job at the Bethlehem Iron Company, inventing fifteen kinds of shovels and decreasing the number of men needed to do the same work from 600 to 140.

Other changes were wrought by the new technology that had created the new industrial system—they transformed the very environment, brought into being a new physical world: the electric light, telephone, telegraph, and automobile appeared within a decade of each other. The genius of new inventions was Thomas A. Edison (1847–1931), whose "invention factory" produced a light bulb that used a carbonized thread in a vacuum as a filament, allowing it to replace oil lamps and the fire signs that Dreiser described. Dreiser's Robert Ames, an electrical engineer, is modeled, at least in part, on Edison. Ames (aims?) points Carrie toward more idealized pursuits. Like Ames, Edison never missed an opportunity: he added the phonograph to his list of inventions, and later the "kinetoscope," which went beyond photography and supplied "moving" pictures.

The end result of these transformations was the rise of a consumer culture. More goods, less expensively produced, were available. Farmers, for example, could buy a variety of goods at lower prices through the revolutionary mail-order system of A. Montgomery Ward, the success of which was duplicated by Richard Sears and his partner Alvah Curtis Roebuck. If the average family kept a Bible in the living room, it kept a Sears or Ward catalog in the kitchen. In the city, the mail-order system was supplemented by the rise of the department store, where Drouet impresses Carrie with its assortment of goods in Dreiser's Sister Carrie (1900).

The new industrial-consumer culture led in turn to the need for a transcontinental railroad system to supplement transportation by river and canal. Because there were fewer navigable rivers west of the Mississippi River, that region depended almost solely on the railroad for transporting people and commerce. In the 1880s as many miles of track were laid as in the forty-two years from 1828 to 1870. The first transcontinental railroad was completed in 1869, reducing the time it took to cross the country from one month to one week. In the next twenty-five years, four more transcontinental railroads were built. These railroads received 131 million acres of land from Congress and 49 million acres of land from the states. This land increased enormously in value after the tracks were laid and after the farmers and ranchers had worked the land. At this time many of the railroads reclaimed the improved land, driving off the farmers and ranchers, a situation depicted by Frank Norris in *The Octopus* (1901).

The new transportation system brought with it a new wave of migration: westward, to settle the Great Plains, and to the city, the new center of gravity for the nation. The cities attracted laborers from Europe: a total of twenty-five million immigrants came to the United States between the Civil War and World War I, an average of five-hundred thousand a year for over fifty years. Also on the move was a black population from the South, giving rise to pockets of ethnicity like Harlem in New York. Such migrations created great urban slums, embodied by the tenement house, six or seven stories high, with few windows and little ventilation. When steel replaced wrought iron and when the elevator came into being, the new steel-framed skyscraper transformed the eighteenth-century brick city.

This new urban/ industrial reality depended on a more detached way of seeing, which in turn led to a new fiction. The romantic sublime gave way to the grotesque of realism/ naturalism. A material reality competed with the transcendental; sentiment, the power of the human heart to do good, was not relevant in a realm of industrial force; the power of nature now had to be seen through the lens of the industrial city, transforming the whole idea of what is art and what is the function of the artist.

9

Naturalism revealed the biological transformations involved in the move from country to city, away from the rhythms of the land, away from craft to factories, away from the farmhouse or the ranch and cottage to the townhouse and tenement. In Europe, the city speculator replaced the lord of the manor; the high bourgeoisie replaced the aristocracy. Urban life was more hectic, more rushed, and more anxiety-inducing. Crowded, noisy, and untidy tenements warehoused the poor, who were needed for industrial work.

There was no American novelist who covered the panorama of economic and historical activity depicted by Zola. But collectively there were hundreds of novels that did for America after the Civil War what Zola did for the Second Empire.[12] This postwar period witnessed the rapid growth of cities, the rise of corporate businesses, the influx of immigrant labor, and the development of wretched working conditions. As one commentator has put it: "The result was an all but incredible skyrocketing of industrial production. . . . Correspondingly, the number of cities of 8,000 or more inhabitants at least trebled."[13]

Many of the American writers depicted this economic transition from the point of view of the upper classes, and thus their position differed from that of Zola, who was sympathetic to the peasants and the emerging working class. But even among the more conservative American writers, there was an increasing sympathy for the hardships of the new, working poor and a growing distrust of big business.

There were two major political movements near the end of the century: the Populist movement under the leadership of William Jennings Bryan, which reached its peak in the 1890s, and the Progressive movement, which was spearheaded by investigative journalists and was influential from about 1900 to 1917. Bryan's Populism was keyed to the agrarian myth that promoted the idea of the vitality of the land and the superiority of the farmer. The myth had worldwide adherents, but in America it rested on a Jeffersonian agrarianism. Bryan was opposed to the gold standard because it worked against cheaper money and hence the well-being of the farmer whose interest he believed preceded that of the big-city banks. In 1896 he won the Democratic Party nomination for the presidency. At the convention in Chicago, he gave his "cross-of-gold" speech, in which he said, "You shall not press down upon the brow of labor this crown of thorns. You shall not crucify mankind upon a cross of gold." To an electrified audience, he continued, "The great cities rest upon our broad and fertile prairies. Burn down your cities and leave our farms, and your cities will spring up again as if by magic; but destroy our farms, and the grass will grow in the streets of every city in the country." Bryan won the nomination twice more, but he was never elected president.[14]

Bryan's Populism gave way to Progressivism with its corrective legislation. Stephen Crane's *Maggie* (1893), Jack London's *The People*

of the Abyss (1903), and Upton Sinclair's *The Jungle* (1906) sympathetically addressed the plight of the poor. But, as Theodore Dreiser's Cowperwood trilogy illustrates, the disdain for big business was
often accompanied by an awe at the power that these new capitalists
commanded. There was in the Western world, especially in America,
an ongoing conflict between the idea that individual opportunity
was limitless and the idea that the individual's freedom was in fact
severely constrained by the ruthless exploitation of the new com-
mercial/industrial forces. Thus Jack London could write in the same
year (1903) *The People of the Abyss*, a sympathetic treatment of the
poor, and *The Call of the Wild*, a celebration of the natural order in
which only the strongest survive.

Darwinism and literary naturalism expressed sentiments for the
poor along a spectrum ranging from deeply felt sympathy to utter
disdain. In America the reform movements assisted the poor, as did
the big-city political machines like Tammany Hall.[15] Out of this ambivalent world came altruistic politicians like Al Smith in New York.
Franklin Delano Roosevelt had been a Smith supporter: he had
placed Smith's name in nomination at the 1924 national presidential
Democratic convention. While Roosevelt was not connected with
Tammany Hall, and while Smith never endorsed the welfare state, the
politics of the big-city machine had rubbed off on him and became,
in part, the basis for the New Deal, instilling in him the idea of an active federal government that would supply social relief. This involved
a radically new interpretation of the Constitution, one that relaxed
the Founding Fathers' suspicion of a strong, central government im-
posed from afar in Britain. Populism, Progressivism, and the new
politics all worked in tandem, anticipating the New Deal. Literary
naturalism created sympathy for the downtrodden that helped carry
these movements forward. Not everyone, however, saw these movements as forms of progress.

10

Among those who saw history as an entropic process was Henry
Adams (1838–1918): in his autobiography he discussed the progression away from mythic centers, representing history as decline and

lamenting the displacement of modern (especially aristocratic) man in a world where the establishment was giving way. The Dynamo, physical force, replaced the Virgin, mythic order—and brought with it moral relativism and religious doubt, chaotic change, and distrust in institutions that were suppose to be the source of imaginative order. *The Education of Henry Adams* (privately printed 1907, published 1918) is his attempt to find meaning and belief in the face of naturalistic history. It is the story of a patrician, the great-grandson of one American president and the grandson of another, who tries unsuccessfully to find his place in a world that will no longer accommodate his class. *Education* begins with Adams telling us that "the [old] universe was thrown into an ash heap and a new one created."[16] Adams discovers that his eighteenth-century education with its faith in reason cannot resolve the problems of a New World transformed by the industrial revolution and Darwinism.

As he struggled to find something that he could believe in, Adams pared away at his self until it was devoid of illusion. Adams became disillusioned with the Quincy of his childhood; saw Boston being invaded by a new financial class and by Irish immigrants; distrusted Washington politics and resented the Free Soil Party; disdained Harvard and its genteel education and Berlin University with its dreary lecture system; and was angered by England's pro-Confederate sympathies during the Civil War. He could not come to terms with a Darwinism that promulgated an adaptability he could not recognize, and he had only guilt regarding his own teaching at Harvard when he could not answer his own questions.

The corruption of the Grant administration embodied for him what America was becoming. Adams saw history as polarized into the unified domain of the Virgin and the discontinuous multiplicity of the Dynamo. The Virgin as icon could supply the illusion of meaning to the Middle Ages, become the imaginative means by which a mythical unity centripetally pulled an age together. The Dynamo offered no such syncretistic resolution for modern man: Adams saw it as a symbol of centrifugal force, of what the culture was throwing off, a force that left the fragmented self caught in a process of motion that the mind could neither arrest nor give meaning to. Moreover, since the Dynamo ran on fossil fuel and such fuels were physically limited, depletion and exhaustion were built into the modern system itself. Naturalism supplied a pessimism that challenged the idea of Enlightenment progress.

11

While Adams saw history as a runaway force, others saw history in terms of a usable past—that is, saw it as supplying an agenda that would meet with the needs of a nation. After World War I Europe was in shreds. The Treaty of Versailles divided Europe in such a way as to guarantee World War II. Hitler would take advantage of this political situation, reminding Germans of the German-speaking territory that they had lost after World War I and of the national destiny that lay waiting. (The Third Reich was supposedly the third historical movement in the achievement of Germany's destiny, building on the glory of the Holy Roman Empire and the reign of Frederick the Great.) Hitler saw that once a charismatic leader took control of the masses he would have the means to take a nation in any direction that he wanted. Hitler's move toward totalitarianism involved consolidating the power of the big corporations, making labor unions illegal, and creating a national myth that would both solidify and energize the masses at the same time as it would create a realm of outsiders (Jews, homosexuals, gypsies) who could be demonized. Once his reign was in place Germany, Hitler moved to bring all of Europe under his control.

In America, the move was toward the other end of the political compass. As mentioned previously, three ideological movements had dominated America. Puritanism dominated the colonial period. Enlightenment values dominated the national period. And a romanticism that encouraged sentimental love and the ideal of heroic action dominated the early to mid-nineteenth century. Near the end of the nineteenth century and into the modernist period a fourth movement would be added to this list—pragmatism.

Pragmatism came into being simultaneously with realism/naturalism; indeed it could be considered an offshoot of naturalism. Both movements helped extend religious and political freedom and create a more secular society. Pragmatism mediated between organism and environment. Truth could be justified only as the fulfilling of experiential conditions. The same ideas could change meaning if they changed context. The emphasis was on what worked. Truth was goal directed; beliefs were confirmed empirically and subject to revision; knowledge was instrumental. Concepts were habits of belief or plans for action. Problems were solved ad hoc, as they arose, and not in terms of some preexistent, absolute religious or political system. Apropos of democracy, there was no appeal to a higher or final authority. As in American realistic fiction, the emphasis was on the individual resolution of a problem.

C. S. Peirce (1839–1914), as a member of the Metaphysical Club in Cambridge, Massachusetts, formulated the basic idea of pragmatism in the early 1870s.[17] Other members of the club advanced his ideas. William James (1842–1910) promulgated the philosophy in his 1898 address to the Philosophical Union at the University of California at Berkeley. And Oliver Wendell Holmes Jr. (1841–1935), later Supreme Court Justice, formulated a pragmatic theory of law. Independent of the club was the work of John Dewey (1859–1952), at the University of Chicago and later Columbia, whose belief in community-oriented education, based on developmental growth and the needs of a democratic citizenry, was the basis for progressive education. In a 1909 lecture at Columbia, John Dewey called *The Origin of Species* "the greatest dissolvent in contemporary thought of old questions."[18] Dewey wanted philosophy to move away from absolutes, arguing that the religious comfort they may bring does not outweigh the need to resolve problems by shifting the responsibility of such problems to a "transcendent cause." Ernest Hemingway's Jake Barnes gives us another version of this same idea when he says, "I did not care what it was all about. All I wanted to know was how to live in it."[19]

The pragmatist's emphasis on the concrete as the source of truth was also probably the origin of Hemingway's literary belief that all values must be tested against one's sense of experience. This was an idea that Hemingway may have gotten from Gertrude Stein, who was William James's student at Harvard and Hemingway's "tutor" during his Paris years. Pragmatism caught an aspect of the American character in its discounting of the past and its emphasis on the present. Unlike the world of, say, William Faulkner, where everything is mediated through the past, pragmatism put the emphasis on the immediate, know-how present. Such an interest in the foreground of life accommodated literary realism.

An outgrowth of positivism and naturalism, pragmatism was primarily an empirical method. Again, like naturalism, it mediated between philosophy and science, theory and practice. Chauncey Wright, who championed Darwin, established the connection between naturalism and pragmatism. Pragmatism is closer to naturalism than is often thought, and the two became even more closely linked when naturalism took up the idea of adapting to the environment. As a cold response to an often hostile world, pragmatism opened up problems that welcomed any solution, thereby promoting relativism. Such a limited ethic led Bertrand Russell (1872–1970) to suggest that pragmatism could lead to cosmic impiety, if not fascism. Many commentators have found this criticism unfair, insisting that pragmatism was the logical philosophy of a democracy, that it accommodated legislative debate and the working out of problems issue by issue. But such thinking allowed "solutions" from both ends of the political spectrum. In this context, pragmatism opened up an ethical vacuum that—given the power system in which laws came into being—was easily filled by corporate or national interests. At times, the political compass seemed to point from different ends in the same direction.

12

In America, the initial response to European naturalism was not one of enthusiasm. Even William Dean Howells could not accommodate *Sister Carrie*. But Howells's reservations were mild compared to those of the neohumanists such as Irving Babbitt, Paul Elmer More, and Stuart Sherman. But in time no one took very seriously the old charges that the novels of Dreiser and Dos Passos were explosions in a cesspool, to refer to one famous phrase.

Besides Howells and the neohumanists, Hamlin Garland, T. S. Perry, and H. H. Boyesen all had reservations about the new subject matter. Their response led some later critics to dismiss realism/naturalism as descriptive terms—a move that belied a shared sense of meaning by Stephen Crane, Frank Norris, and Theodore Dreiser. These writers not only defined the new realism but also consciously rebelled against the genteel tradition, which held an earlier realism in place. A new social reality had spawned a new literary reality, which was reinforced by the cultural writings of Van Wyck Brooks, Randolph Bourne, Lewis Mumford, and Vernon L. Parrington, who helped establish naturalism as a heuristic category. Such works were supplemented by the critical writing of Maxwell Geismar, Alfred Kazin, Malcolm Cowley, and Willard Thorp. Other critics—Everett Carter in *Howells and the Age of Realism* (1954), E. H. Cady in *The Light of Common Day* (1971), and Harold H. Kolb in *The Illusion of Life* (1969)—helped to secure the idea of realism as a literary category. Carter, for example, located the source of Howells's realism in Comte and Taine.

13

One of the more ambitious attempts to come to terms with the American novel was Richard Chase's *The American Novel and its Tradition* (1957). Chase believed the American novel derived mainly from British fiction until about 1880 or 1890, when it turned toward French and Russian models. He further believed that American fiction was a product of its cultural contradictions as well as a divergence between the novel and romance. The contradictions involved a sense of solitariness in a democratic nation; a Manichean play of good and evil in the face of Puritanism; and an intellectual allegiance to both the Old and the New World. These thematic elements found expression in both the romance and the novel. But the European novel engaged social institutions and class conflict, while the romance focused on the isolated individual struggling through a symbolic universe devoid of social restraints. The novel, according to Chase, emphasized character, creating a complexity of temperament and motives, giving rise to a plausibility of circumstance. The romance, on the other hand, emphasized action over character, producing two-dimensional, abstract or symbolic characters, whose involvement with others, if deep, was also narrow. The romance, in other words, rejected verisimilitude, continuity of plot, and a social context in which characters bigger than life experience radical forms of alienation. One critic has contrasted Chase's asocial world of the romance with the novel of social responsibility that makes up "the great tradition" of F. R. Leavis's book by that title.[20]

Chase traces the difference between novel and romance back to the pronouncements of Henry James in his prefaces. James came to terms with the idea of romance when he admitted the implausibility of his plot in *The American* (1877). Chase argues: "'Disconnected and uncontrolled experience' . . . is the essence of romance." James believes "that the novel does not find its essential being until it discovers . . . the circuit of life among extremes or opposites, the circuit that passes through the real and the ideal, through . . . the mysterious or the indirectly known."[21]

Chase is helpful in distinguishing between the novel and the romance. But his reducing that difference to Henry James's metaphor of the circuit and his giving priority to the romance over the novel in American fiction is arbitrary. Chase's theory would have more validity if he saw how literary naturalism mediated between his two forms, how it added another dimension to the novel but still retained aspects of the romance by moving through the ordinary to the extraordinary, by placing common characters in extreme but not necessarily symbolic situations.

A number of other more recent critics have been caught up in this novel versus romance debate. Charles Walcutt, for example, maintained that naturalism went back to the transcendental ideas of the romantics.[22] And Eric Sundquist also believed that the naturalistic novel accommodated the romance. In a far-reaching essay entitled "The Country of the Blue," Sundquist argued that American realism failed as "realism" because of the conflict between the realm of imagination and the realm of the times and because of the pervasive influence of the romance with its rejection of verisimilitude.[23]

The question here of the connection between the romance and realism/naturalism is central to any discussion of the subject. There are always traces of previous narrative forms in new modes. Elements of both the romance and transcendentalism can be found in the realist/naturalistic novel—especially the American version: Norris's *The Octopus,* Dreiser's last novels *The Bulwark* (1946) and

The Stoic (1947), Steinbeck's *The Grapes of Wrath* (1939), the ending of Hemingway's *For Whom the Bell Tolls* (1940) offer obvious examples. But nonetheless there are differences between romance and realism/naturalism.

We can chart the gradations in the transition of the novel from romance to forms of realism as we move from the pure fantasies of Bram Stoker and Rider Haggard, to the more realistic fantasies of Kipling and Stevenson, to the naturalism of London and Norris, to the neorealism of Hemingway and Dos Passos, to the noir realism of Raymond Chandler and James M. Cain.[24] The handling of both theme and plot content helps to establish this taxonomy. For example, the British anxiety over the consequences of imperialism was often the basis for the popular fantasies of Rider Haggard before realists like Joseph Conrad rewrote them for a less popular audience. Secondly, the realist/naturalist did at times append a philosophy of hope, usually political but sometimes philosophical, to the story to counter the bleak reality of a text, but seldom was this appeal consistent with the logic of the work itself. Thirdly, such romantic elements as there were in realist/naturalist fiction often stemmed from the realist/naturalist's tendency to reference cosmic phenomena (as, for example, the cosmic symbolism of Herbert Spencer's philosophy) rather than from a belief in allegorical characters or pure vitalism. And lastly, confusion arose from the fact that until "naturalism" became the precise word of choice, the term "romance" was used in its place. Frank Norris, for example, in essays entitled "Zola as a Romantic Writer" and "A Plea for Romantic Fiction," used the term "romantic" when he was clearly discussing what would later be called naturalistic fiction.

A further consideration of the difference between romance and realism involves four ideas of reality: that of absolute essence as claimed by the transcendentalists; that of a reality unique to an individual, such as that experienced by a hero, or outside of time, as in Proust's time spots; that which inheres in external reality; and that which inheres in a relationship between external reality and human consciousness.[25] While the romance works the first two ideas of reality, realism and naturalism repudiate them; realism in the broadest sense stems from the third notion; and psychological realism is a

product of the fourth. There is thus a different notion of reality separating the romance from naturalism and built into the problem of
defining realism/naturalism is a material resistance to conflating it
and the romance.

14

Recently there has been an attempt to discredit both the meaning of
history and literary realism. The assumption is that the past is unknowable and that literary realism is simply a convention of fiction.
But as Laurence Lerner has pointed out, the first assumption disregards the connection between history and social evidence—the way
Friedrich Engels, for example, was able to deepen the meaning of
Manchester by informing it with evidence of industrial abuse; and
the second assumption ignores the volatility of conventions—the
way an author like George Eliot changed the conventional meaning
of a milkmaid like Hetty Sorrel in *Adam Bede* (1859) by infusing a
pastoral stereotype with modern life. Such reality also informs language, creating a bridge between history and fiction, a bridge those
working in the realm of realism/ naturalism took for granted.[26]

In *Romantic Imperialism* (1998), Saree Makdisi points out that in
The Prelude (1805) Wordsworth's way of seeing nature does "not
work in London"[27]: the city cannot be understood from the perspective of romantic nature. I believe that one of the reasons realism/
naturalism came into being was to provide a way of comprehending
this new reality, the modern city and the institutions that came with
it. Zola, Crane, and Dreiser were dealing with a different order of
reality and had to see it differently from how Wordsworth saw his
reality—that "difference" is what we mean by realism. While the individual imagination may have rendered variations within the mode,
realism/naturalism taken together gave us a sustained if not coherent
view of the new city, the continued presence of the frontier, and the
friction between American and European culture.

Naturalism separated itself from the romance altogether when it
abandoned the superstructure that had forged a link between them,
and, moving to the other end of the spectrum, gave rise to a neorealism that made use of naturalistic elements without naturalistic

commentary as in James M. Cain's *The Postman Always Rings Twice* (1934), Hemingway's *A Farewell to Arms* (1929), or F. Scott Fitzgerald's *The Beautiful and Damned* (1922). What differentiates a mode from the works that precede it is a new way of handling of narrative elements, which eventually a number of writers adopt, thus achieving a critical mass. At some point, as narrative weight shifts, we are no longer talking about the same order of fiction. Literary realism/naturalism modified the romance and transcendental literature before literary modernism transformed it in turn.

15

Realism and later naturalism depicted a conflicted reality. In ideality, the individual was free to realize his or her potential, but in reality the large migration of people from rural areas to the city created a mob situation in which the individual found it difficult to set himself or herself apart from the crowd and usually ended up being exploited as cheap labor. There was thus a tension between the ideal and the real, between the expectation and the reality, between promise and achievement. The new novel depicted conflicted characters, men and women who strove for success in the face of failure, desired to be human despite the machine, and strove for order while surrounded by chaos. Their human potential was subject to physical limits. Often obsessed by sex or the desire for money, they intuited higher truths but were held back by their compulsions.

Naturalism as a philosophy of life caught the nineteenth-century struggle between ideal and material realms, between a belief in progress and entropy, religion and science, aesthetics and decadence, human growth and degeneration, order and chaos, and democracy and totalitarianism. As a cultural and historical point of view, it was better at defining the dialectic than offering a synthesis, better at revealing a divided state of mind than supplying a resolution, better at depicting a displaced population than in offering social solutions.

2

Realism as a Narrative Mode

The novel had its origins in the middle class. The old romance was the narrative of the medieval aristocracy, celebrating the world of the manor and the heroics and love rituals of a knightly class. The bourgeoisie wanted a fiction of its own, and the novel gave expression to the fate of the individual in a New World. A new reading class came into being that was interested in the rituals of courtship, marriage, family, commerce and exchange, and the conflicts built into the new pursuits of money and success. Before the realistic novel could take effect, however, it had to displace the romance. Cervantes did this in Spain, Defoe in England, Balzac in France, and Twain in America.

Once the novel began concentrating on the pursuits of the individual, its depiction of the community changed as well. The comic realism of Fielding and Jane Austen still celebrated the world of the estate with its moral presence. But by the time we get to George Eliot, the idea of community has radically changed: the town actually works against the well being of Dorothea Brooke. The fiction of both Dickens and Twain began as a sentimental treatment of contemporary events before it turned dark and somber at the end of their careers. Comic realism gave way to romantic realism: the individual took precedence over community; myth and symbol infused an urban reality as in Melville's *Pierre* (1852) and Hugo's *Les Misérables* (1862).

At this point realism/naturalism modified romantic realism by emptying it of moral content, making the individual choice more ambiguous (as in realism) or more determined (as in naturalism). That did not mean there was no sense of right and wrong (as Sinclair proved when he attacked the meat-producing industry in *The Jungle* [1906]), only that the opposition between good and evil became harder to discern in the realistic novel and that in naturalistic fiction good and evil were more pronounced, although narrative resolution, where "evil" often triumphed, made the distinction between the two virtually meaningless. Modernism changed the direction of the novel, giving us time-bound stories held together by memory and consciousness. Postmodernism collapsed that consciousness into the culture itself, transforming Descartes' distinction between subject and object, eliminating Zola's scientific observer, and concealing the point where self ends and culture begins.

These narrative modes created their own "version" of reality. There is no *Realism* (with a capital "R"), only *realisms*, which are brought into being by changing narrative conventions that are in turn the product of a changing historical reality. Naturalism is another form of realism—a sterner realism. A survey of the rise and fall of realism/naturalism thus provides a historical overview as well as an explanation of the transition from romantic realism to modernism.

1

Don Quixote (Part 1, 1605; Part 2, 1615) has been seen by many as a parody of chivalric romance. Undoubtedly Cervantes intended to discredit books of chivalry. But *Don Quixote* ultimately does more than that. The problem of the novel is also the problem of the Renaissance: what is the nature of reality? Out of his search for the truly real comes Don Quixote's vision. This vision demands that the ideal be seen in relation to the physical world. The quest becomes a road test of his new idea of reality. The outcome of this test leads to a conflict between the knight-errant and the caballero: it is a conflict of a Renaissance man with a gothic soul who attempts to bridge two worlds.

In *Don Quixote,* parts 1 and 2, Cervantes takes us from romance to realism, from chivalric adventure to the everyday reality, from untested ideals to experience as a form of reality.[1] In many ways, Cervantes's novel parallels the history of prose narrative from the medieval to the modern world. Cervantes completed in fiction what his era completed as history: the move from the chivalric world in which feudalism reigned to the more material world of commerce. As a product of the Renaissance, Cervantes still believed in a world of correspondences—that worldly matters had their heavenly parallels. He locked reality into this dualism, giving a realistic foundation to what was otherwise symbolic, even allegorical. Later novelists, like Defoe, would undo this typology and create a more purely realistic novel. But Cervantes took an important step toward, indeed instituted, a modern realism. No other novelist was so prescient in anticipating the evolution of the realistic novel.

Realism, in demanding a new way of seeing, challenged both romanticism and the romance. The view that Wordsworth brought to *The Prelude* (1805) was, as far as the realists were concerned, inadequate to depicting the new, commercial, industrialized city with its slums and dysfunctional families. Wordsworth, like most of the romantics, was a visionary poet. He wanted to reconcile the human mind with the sublimity of nature. Behind Wordsworth's agenda was the poetry of John Milton with its intent to "justify the ways of God to men" by considering the Biblical revelation of the first to last things. Wordsworth had set himself the task of going beyond Milton by humanizing Milton's poetics. He would give natural dimension to Milton's supernatural agenda.[2] His poetry was like a celebration of spring, when new natural life emerged from a moribund world. Although Wordsworth had lost confidence in the liberating power of the French Revolution, he never lost confidence in the power of human consciousness to bring about radical social change. It is here that literary realism and naturalism break with romanticism. No longer is the individual mind or the power of sentiment enough to undermine the degenerative effects of the industrial revolution. From Balzac to Zola the emphasis will be on depicting a fallen world rather than on a vision of its resurrection.

A transformation in the Miltonic agenda had preceded Wordsworth and the romantics. Daniel Defoe had not only gone beyond Milton; he had gone beyond what Wordsworth would later claim as a new vision. Defoe marks the beginning of modern realism. He abandons the placeless world of Sidney and Lodge and the symbolic, at times allegorical, world of Cervantes for the concrete world of eighteenth-century London. Defoe takes us step-by-step through history. The story of Robinson Crusoe duplicates the story of man's transition from the primitive wilderness to tool maker, to farmer, to lord of his manor, to finally being a member of a social order based on a contract theory of political rule and a new commercial process. In Defoe's novel, birthrights give way to natural rights—the right to create oneself and to go beyond a worldly father, even as one looks for signs of approval from a heavenly Father.

But if Defoe reconciles the physical and the spiritual, his world is not typological. As Ian Watt points out, "Defoe and Richardson are the first great writers in our literature who did not take their plots from mythology, history, legend or previous literature." In Defoe's novels, time moves slower, more mechanically, and the use of place is more specific.[3] Defoe is the first major realist. Crusoe never looks to the Bible for literal correspondences but for signs that can be evaluated and interpreted in the physical context of his own situation. Unlike Milton, Defoe eschews myth and legends of the past and creates his own realistic narratives.

The modification of the typological at this time helps explain the rise of realism: one must now create models based on the here and now. In creating a narrative that relies heavily on a sense of place and of individual development, Defoe was consolidating various kinds of subgenres—such as the tour book, the diary, the memoir, and the biography and the autobiography in both their secular and spiritual manifestations. In many ways, Defoe's history of an individual is the basis of the modern, realistic novel.

But it was up to others to bring this narrative mode to true fulfillment. Dickens, Balzac, and Dostoyevsky mark the advance of literary realism. Each novelist depicted the transformation of culture: Dickens the rise of industrial England, Balzac money-obsessed Parisian society, and Dostoyevsky the movement away from a peasant-based society in Russia. Dickens exposed corrupt institutions, especially Chancery and the legal system. His world turned on the ability of those of good heart to right social wrongs, at least until late in his career when his novels turned more bleak and he seemed to repudiate personal forms of redemption. Balzac treated the demise of the French aristocracy and the rise of the young-men-from-the-provinces who make Paris their battleground. Balzac was among the first to depict the Napoleonic character who felt unrestrained by conventional laws. Balzac looked deeply into the changes in the psyche that came with a new commercial society, especially the all-compelling desire for money that led to the extremes of adventure capitalism or the insecurity of miserliness. Balzac was the bridge between the comic realism of Dickens and the naturalism of Zola. Dostoyevsky took the novel beyond social concerns to religious and moral matters. Redemption was inseparable from suffering in a community of like selves that took its meaning from the land. Dostoyevsky also added a psychological component to the novel that anticipated literary modernism.

2

Henry Fielding (1707–1754) defined the novel as "a comic epic in prose." He believed that like the classical epic, the novel should have a sweep. But he felt that unlike the classical epic, the novel should treat common people, not the heroic or people of high estate. The idea of the commonplace was built into the comic, along with a sense that it accommodated a moral center through which the comic plot could be recuperated and resolved. Fielding's definition is the basis for a comic realism that characterized the novel after Defoe. From Fielding to Dickens there is a moral center in fiction, often involving the estate (embodied by Fielding's Squire Allworthy) and men or women of good heart (embodied by Dickens's Joe Gargery and Esther Summerson). By the time the novel reaches Henry James, this moral center has become more ambivalent, and by the time we get to Zola, it is gone.

Fielding's *Tom Jones* (1749) makes use of three settings: the estate, the road, and the city. Under Squire Allworthy, the estate imposes moral imperatives. Once Tom leaves the estate for the road, he enters a realm where right and wrong mix. In the city, he confronts a world where deceit and pretense have cancelled out any reference to a moral center. *Tom Jones* addresses concerns of the middle class, especially that of courtship and marriage, which is the basis of the Tom Jones-Sophia Western plot. The novel makes use of the picaresque as Tom and Partridge set out like Don Quixote and Sancho Panza. The novel also makes use of coincidence: almost all of the major characters we find in the estate appear again on the road or in the city. And, finally, the novel revels in its play with pretense and disguise. In direct contrast to the estate stands the urban world of Lady Bellaston and her masquerade ball, in which pretense and concealment rule. This contrast between the built-in order of the estate and the institutional chaos of the city will characterize the novel for over one hundred years. Fielding had few models when he was writing *Tom Jones,* and in many ways he invented comic realism, a mode that extended Defoe's realism and dominated British realism from Fielding himself to Dickens.

In terms of the evolution of the novel, Dickens moved us even further away from Defoe's double frame of reference involving God and man, intensifying the pretense of Fielding's city, and creating a more secular novel. Dickens opened up the Victorian world and its institutions—offered insight into the new commercialism, with its grotesque embodiments emerging from the new world of banking and exchange, and institutions like Chancery, which held it all together at the expense of great human suffering. Dickens's city was both lure and trap—a lure to those who were called to it; and a trap in its workings, which led to human debasement.

In Dickens's later novels there is a sense of the uncanny. Between the country and the city is a strange, eerie, primitive world of the marshes—a world of water and mud, houses sinking into the earth, sluice gates, and mills. The narrative flash points in Dickens's fiction occur where water and land meet, or where the country and the city intersect, or where the past and the present verge. Here we find the return of the repressed: out of this world emerges primitive evil, the slink mutant outcast. In *Oliver Twist* (1839), Bill Sikes emerges from and goes to his death in such a region, as do Quilp in *The Old Curiosity Shop* (1841) and Bradley Headstone in *Our Mutual Friend* (1865). In *Great Expectations* (1861), Orlick slithers out from such a realm with a primitive, uncanny evil clinging to him. This evil exists prior to the city, is a natural condition to which humanity is subject, regardless of place. It is Dickens's version of original sin in Christian doctrine and what will become atavism in the naturalistic novel.

Such a condition is also connected with the cemetery: in *Great Expectations* both Magwitch and Compeyson emerge from the marshes, flee across its bogs, and take sanctuary in the cemetery. Compeyson is the final embodiment of evil, and he touches all the main characters of the novel—most directly Magwitch and Miss Havisham, and thus indirectly Pip and Estella. Dickens connects Satis House, the marshes, and the graveyard to the unweeded garden that surrounds Satis House, which reveals nature unreclaimed. This connection among various settings in the natural world has its social counterpart: the lawyer Jaggers, who bridges city and estate, has an information web that entangles and eventually controls all the main characters.

In *Great Expectations,* Dickens was beginning to show the limitations of both a feudal past and a materialistic present caught in the grip of death. Although he softened the difficulties that separated Pip and Estella in a revised ending of the novel (after many of his readers complained about the unhappy ending), it was still doubtful that they would ever be reconciled. As the urban world grew, the human world shrank, and by the time he reached *Our Mutual Friend,* his last complete novel, Dickens had serious doubts that the beneficent will could accomplish much against the forces of modern blight. In *Our Mutual Friend,* Dickens shows how London can no longer be redeemed in personal terms: he refers to it as a hopeless city. No longer is there anyone who can break through the uncanny maze, solve the mystery, and save the city. One wonders if this is why Dickens abandoned London in his next novel, the unfinished *The Mystery of Edwin Drood* (1870). There he centered the action in Cloisterham, his fictional name for Rochester, originally a medieval town, which was also being transformed into a modern, industrial city, but that was still intelligible in a way that separated it from the unredeemable London.

If narrative focus becomes darker in Dickens, in George Eliot it becomes more determined. George Eliot was a companion of Herbert Spencer and a close friend of T. H. Huxley and J. S. Mill. There is no doubt that these influential figures whetted her appetite for the new science. Coincidental with her interest was the publication of her *Adam Bede* in the same year as Darwin's *The Origin of Species* (1859) and that of her *Middlemarch* the same year as Darwin's *Descent of Man* (1871). Early in her career Eliot rejected her Methodist up-bringing for the new science. She translated David Strauss's controversial *Life of Jesus* (1846) and defied convention by living outside marriage with the critic George Henry Lewes. Her first three novels—*Adam Bede, The Mill on the Floss* (1860), and *Silas Marner* (1861), all stories of rural life—established her reputation. Her one political novel was *Felix Holt, the Radical* (1866). Her most important works were *Middlemarch* (1872)—a brilliant, realistic portrait of a whole community—and *Daniel Deronda* (1876).

Adam Bede deals with a master carpenter who lives in Hayslope, in the county of Warwickshire, a community in which class hierarchy demands moral and social responsibility. When Arthur Donnithorne impregnates Hetty Sorrel, he abandons that responsibility and sets in motion a process that plays itself out tragically. Adam Bede is the moral center of the novel, although he does not have the means to cope with the far-reaching effects of Donnithorne's behavior. The essence of Eliot's realism is found in this kind of predicament, where the man of good intentions (in this case Adam Bede) finds that the moral and social situation is more complex than his ability to resolve it. This sense of fated reality will become cosmic in the fiction of Thomas Hardy.

Middlemarch is a complicated story framed as a counter to the response of the town—from which the novel gets its title—to events that have occurred in it. The novel involves the romance and eventual marriage of four couples, and is especially concerned with Dorothea Brooke's realization that her marriage to Edward Casaubon was a dreadful mistake and that she is really in love with Will Ladislaw, Casaubon's second cousin. When the characters act against artificial forces—as, for example, when Dorothea forsakes Casaubon's legacy and marries Ladislaw—they triumph over what is false in the social codes and bring about a natural resolution. Eliot establishes a duality between a natural, human and an artificial, social realm and lets the natural realm eventually triumph. This dichotomy in her representation of the world was a by-product of the influence of Herbert Spencer's dualism on her thinking, and her novel is a realistic treatment of what would become a naturalistic theme.

3

Modern realism takes much of its meaning from the rise of the new
city, and this is true in American, English, and French fiction. Romantic realism involves the use of romantic themes and myths in an
urban context. Hawthorne used the method in *The Marble Faun*
(1860), Melville in *Pierre,* Hugo in *Les Misérables,* Eugène Sue in *Les
Mystères de Paris* (1843) and *The Wandering Jew* (1845), and Flaubert
in *Salammbô* (1862) and *La Tentation de Saint Antoine* (The Temptation of Saint Anthony [1874]). Flaubert's novels reveal an awareness
of the legend of the Wandering Jew and of Vico's theory of history,
narrative components that anticipate James Joyce.

As France moved from an agrarian to an urban base, the function
of Paris changed. In 1797 a far-sighted plan, known as the Artists
Plan, was drawn up under Napoleon and served in great part for the
city that Haussmann would later bring into being. By 1824 the Bourse
was as much a monument as Notre Dame or the Louvre. By the time
of the July Revolution of 1830 and the reign of Louis Philippe, the
seeds for a new Paris were already planted.

Paris was becoming a major subject for fiction, and what was
going on in the novel had its parallel in painting. The French impressionist painters, harbingers of the realistic novel, took the city as
their subject. From their perspective, there was as much beauty in the
city as there was in a pastoral landscape. Monet, Renoir, and Pissarro
felt that an urban setting was as worthy a subject for painting as a
biblical or classical subject or a waterfall or a flowered landscape.
They saw in what ways the city was transforming modern life.

Perhaps most instrumental in effecting the change in Paris's role
in the country was the invention of new sources of power, especially
the steam engine. This machine freed the factory from a rural source
of waterpower and allowed it to come into the city. It brought with it
the proletariat that would make up a major source of the new urban
population and become the major concern of writers like Sue and
Hugo, as well as of thinkers like Karl Marx and Frederic Engels. It
was also at this time that Louis Philippe drove the workers' movement underground and made little provision for absorbing their
rapidly expanding numbers.

It is exactly this world that Eugène Sue addresses in his monumental novel, *The Mysteries of Paris*. Sue's novel was published serially in the newspapers in 1842–43 and became a sensation in its time, attracting the attention of an unlikely reader, Karl Marx. His critique in *The Holy Family* (1845) is the most extended discussion of this novel that we have. Marx has two objects of attack: the overly idealist notion of reality held by Young Hegelians and Sue's idealized consciousness, Christian in content and embodied by Rodolph. Marx's point is that the social conditions of Paris under Louis Philippe have changed radically, but Sue not only holds on to the reality of medieval Paris, he holds on to the consciousness that keeps medieval Paris in place. As a result, instead of liberating Fleur-de-Marie, Sue only imprisons her more deeply within her subjectivity. By failing to see that a new consciousness is necessary to account for the economic evils that have kept the slums of Paris in place, Sue only intensifies the evil that he mistakenly thinks that he is opposing. What Marx is calling for is the new narrative mode that would replace romantic realism.

Hugo's *Les Misérables* brings us a step closer to the world that Marx advocated. This is not to say that Hugo is any less melodramatic than Sue. Hugo also invokes a multitude of coincidences to bring his principal characters together in the compressed space of a Paris slum. And good and evil are also represented in black-and-white terms in Hugo's world, although there are exceptions, such as Javert, whose move from a simple to a complex understanding of this world costs him his life.

The biggest difference between Hugo's and Sue's novels is that *Les Misérables* is compellingly told against the unfolding of history itself. Hugo completed the novel in 1862 after spending fourteen years revising an earlier draft. The novel covers the twenty years from 1815 to 1835—from the defeat of Napoleon at Waterloo until after the revolution of 1830 and the reign of Louis Philippe—ending almost at the point in time where Sue's begins. Hugo looked back on forty years of events—and from exile, after having been forced out of France in 1852 by Louis Napoleon, whom Hugo had accused of betraying the idea of the republic.

As in most novels informed by romantic realism, Hugo's superimposes a religious trope onto the city itself, and *Les Misérables* describes a climb out of hell toward secular redemption. Jean Valjean becomes a modern Christ: he is buried alive and then resurrected; he enters the gigantic Parisian sewer systems, a kind of Dantean nether world, carrying the wounded Marius like a cross; he crosses a River Styx, freed from hell by Thenardier, the gatekeeper. The descent into and the climb out of the secular hell of the city, the union of Cossette and Marius, their reconciliation with Valjean, and his death (like that of Javert's) all reinforce the concept of a Hegelian reality grounded in romantic history. The oppositions of life—such as represented in the conflict between Jean Valjean and Javert—find their synthesis in the person of a Marius, and history moves idealistically onward. The contradictions that would cancel out the lives of both Valjean and Javert were the contradictions of an age, and the spirit of a higher will works through Marius—a spirit that could redeem Paris, both as the capital of France and as the container of the poor. Hugo has taken us beyond Sue, but modern realism could not begin until a belief in Hegelian progression was tempered. That task awaited Balzac.

Honoré de Balzac did more to transform the romantic realism of Sue and Hugo than any other novelist, with perhaps the exception of Flaubert. Moreover, he connects the romantic realism of Hugo to the literary naturalism of Zola. Trained in law at the University of Paris, Balzac decided in 1819 to try his hand at writing. His early attempts were potboilers, formulistic thriller fiction that he later disowned. Like so many of the characters in his fiction, Balzac was driven by a desire to make large amounts of money. And again, like his fictional characters, his schemes usually failed. By 1824, for example, he had made enough money to invest in a printing business that then went bankrupt. Balzac's financial schemes left him heavily in debt, forcing him (like Dostoyevsky) to write simply to pay his creditors. Drinking quarts of strong, black coffee, and wearing a white monk's robe, he would work through the night, eventually turning out nearly one hundred novels and short stories. His own life—his pursuit of mistresses, his money schemes, his dandyish dress and jeweled cane, his attraction for and repulsion from high society—was as overwrought as his fiction. Balzac had Keats's gift of negative capability—the ability to empathize with others, even those he disliked, and to understand their personal motives.

A novel that exemplifies Balzac's narrative method is *Histoire des treize* (*History of the Thirteen* [1835]). The novel is made up of three shorter novels, each story involving a member of a secret society, a power cult, that allowed its members to cut through the red tape of the new bureaucratic society and work their will in both public and private matters. In his use of the thirteen as an organized power system for the outcast, Balzac anticipates Vautrin or the superman figure. Similarly, the first story involving Ferragus, an escaped convict, anticipates his creation of Père Goriot in his obsessive love of his daughter; the second story, "The Duchesse de Langeais," is a study of obsessive romantic love that turns violent when the duchess withholds sexual love from the Marquis de Montriveau; and the third story, "The Girl with the Golden Eyes," involves Henri de Marsay's sexual pursuit of Paquita Valdes. Each story treats paternal or sexual desire in a world encumbered by manners and regulations that prevent the satisfaction of such impulses and engender the machinations of the thirteen as a counterforce to this systematic frustration. Part of Balzac's method is to overlay his story with set pieces—long expository descriptions of Paris streets or the history of Parisian neighborhoods like the Faubourg Saint-Germain. These set pieces create a fixed reality against which the story is told—that is, they ground the story within a controlled environment that usually sets limits to human behavior. There is thus, as Leo Bersani has suggested, a center and a circumference to Balzac's world. The obsessive nature of his characters reveals the self drawn to a center; the destructiveness of such obsession opens the self to forms of disintegration. We have a tension between the centripetal and centrifugal pull in Balzac's novel or, slightly revising Bersani, between what the novel draws to its center and the limits that life sets by what it throws off.[4]

In 1829 Balzac published *Le Dernier Chouan* (*The Last Chouan*), which began *Comédie humaine* series (*The Human Comedy*, a down-to-earth version of Dante). Balzac's early novels *Eugénie Grandet* (1833) and *Père Goriot* (1835) advance the development of French realism along lines described above—expository passages anticipating the main narrative, the obsessive self competing with human limits, the compulsive antagonist caught in a tragic process. Balzac's depiction of the obsessional character—*Eugénie Grandet* is a study of miserliness, *La Cousine Bette* (1848) of unimpeded revenge—moves his novels away from the appeal to sentiment in the stories of Sue and Hugo toward the pathology of Zola's. And *Goriot*, as suggested, introduces us to the obsessed father and a totally new character—Vautrin, the strong man, whose desire for power undermines the working of sentiment that held both comic and romantic realism in place. *Illusions perdues* (*Lost Illusions* [1837]) and *Splendeurs et misères des courtisanes* (*Splendour and Miseries of Courtesans* [1846]) round out Vautrin's story, the essence of which is the belief that a Napoleon figure could confront the amoral city with a greater amorality. Balzac's handling of the urban theme took the young-man-from-the-provinces novel to a new level and gave the bildungsroman a new dimension, making failure the end product of the desire for success.

Père Goriot is deservedly the best known of Balzac's novels, and perhaps the novel that revised the whole idea of what realism is. A complex story, it sets the narrative agenda for his other novels. Eugène de Rastignac has come from the provinces to make his fortune in Paris. As a boarder at the Vauquer boarding house, he meets two others—the above-mentioned Vautrin, a famous criminal known as Trompe-la-Mort, who looks back to Milton's Satan and forward to Nietzsche, and Père Goriot whose story has a King Lear quality—and the three of them establish a circle. *Père Goriot* depicts the social world of Paris—its frauds, pretenses, and lack of moral authority. In the three principal characters Balzac introduces us to the ingénue, the young man who is overwhelmed by his circumstances, the master criminal, who tries to overpower the city, and the devoted father, the embodiment of a dying generation, whose devotion to family and love of his daughters are values that have lost their meaning in the new city. These three social types define the new urban reality. Balzac presents a world in which money and power render love and morality irrelevant. No one ever described this new reality more convincingly.

The novels that further this insight into the new city and which take us substantially beyond the political ideology of Sue and Hugo are Balzac's *Illusions perdues* and *Splendeurs et misères des courtisanes,* both a part of his famous *Comédie humaine,* a title that emphasizes that his concern is with human and not religious matters. Balzac is dealing roughly with the same narrative time span as Hugo; *Illusions perdues* begins after the defeat at Waterloo and ends around 1822, when the narrative is picked up in *Splendeurs et misères*. Like Hugo, Balzac sets his story against the history of the times, although his emphasis is far more on the way institutions work, especially when manipulated by a larger-than-life persona like Napoleon.

His central character in *Illusions perdues* is Lucien Chardon, who, like Eugène de Rastignac, finds Paris a battlefield. His story begins in 1824 and treats the last six years of the Restoration, concluding just before the July revolution in 1830. After having signed a kind of Faustian pact with Vautrin, the man of power, the two travel on to Paris, where Vautrin concocts a grand scheme to marry Lucien into royalty. This scheme eventually leads to Lucien's suicide, an event that moves Vautrin to genuine grief, perhaps for the first time. Vautrin's iron nature allows him to triumph over his enemies, but at a cost. The rest of the novel completes his story. Vautrin becomes a police collaborator and eventually a police magistrate. By the end of *Splendeurs et misères,* the archcriminal is running the police. Paris has been transformed: institutions have succumbed to the man of power.

In *Illusions perdues,* Balzac looked for inspiration to the historical life of Napoleon and the literary life of Stendhal's Julien Sorel. Illusion confronts reality. The illusion is Lucien's coming to Paris under the belief that it is a promised land, where the artist can nourish his imagination; the reality is a Paris as a lethal field of battle, where the poet no longer functions as prophet but is rootless and oversensitive, a walking bundle of nerves. Success involves recognizing that the values of Vautrin come with the new Paris, but repudiating the man; failure involves succumbing to Vautrin's power. Balzac contrasts two different urban prototypes in Vautrin and Daniel d'Arthez—one the man of power, the other of aesthetics. Unlike Lucien, Daniel triumphs over Vautrin. Both Vautrin and Daniel are men of strong character, but Daniel tempers ambition with imagination. Daniel is an anomaly in a society growing more and more materialistic, where the power to make money has become an end in itself.

Eugénie Grandet is Balzac's study of the effects of miserliness on a provincial French family. Under the Consulate that suppressed the Church after the Revolution, Grandet, a master cooper, buys up church property and then adds to his wealth the money his wife's mother and grandparents leave them. In *Eugénie Grandet,* Balzac shows the effect of miserliness on the human heart, depicts how wealth becomes destructive when pursued for itself, and shows the negative effects of money when it is separated from human benefits

Balzac's world turns on human emotions that are often out of control. His *La Cousine Bette,* for example, is a story of revenge and counterrevenge, in which characters are motivated by hatred so strong that it distorts their whole life. M. Crevel vows revenge against Baron Hulot for stealing his mistress. Balzac's novel—with its complicated plot—treats the effects of sustaining hate and the desire for revenge over a long period of time, showing the corrosive and destructive effects of such emotions and revealing the psychological source of compulsion that give his novels realistic depth.

Balzac moves us beyond premodern Paris to where good and evil are more entangled. Balzac attacks the Enlightenment legacy that elevates reason, science, and technology to positions of dominance and postulates instead human emotions working beyond the power of will to control them. Balzac's fiction takes us to the doorstep of the naturalistic novel, the completion of which will be left up to Zola, where men of power transform the city of Paris in the Second Empire. Balzac transformed the novel so that it would never be the same, and Emile Zola was the inheritor of that literary legacy.

What Balzac started, Gustave Flaubert helped finish. Like Balzac, Flaubert had serious reservations about the status of the middle class. He also had his doubts about the Enlightenment. His *Bouvard et Pécuchet* (1881) satirized bourgeois self-sufficiency, ridiculed the encyclopedic mentality, and suggested that man had minimized rather than enlarged the human self by defining it in such limited terms. Flaubert's realism anticipated some of the modernist's techniques. Heinrich Schliemann (1822–1890) discovered what he believed to be the historic city of Troy, and he thus fueled an interest in the old mythology as well as a belief in the relevance of the archaeological layering of time. The interest in archaeology found an important complement in the literary use of landscapes. In *Salammbô,* Flaubert superimposed Carthage on the specter of Paris in the Second Empire, an anticipation of Cubist technique that would influence James

Joyce, who superimposed the heroic world of Ulysses on modern-day Dublin. Flaubert also realized that the unfolding of artistic consciousness could be the basis for a new kind of novel. Such a novel would have an aesthetic hero for whom sensibility was more important than sentiment and who sought self-definition in the context of the beautiful rather than in the naturalistic context of a determining commercialized/industrial environment. Flaubert's *L'Education sentimentale* (1869) showed Frederic Moreau playing sentiment out to its final absurdity. Flaubert also showed in *Salammbô* and *La Tentationde Saint Antoine* the workings of an aesthetic consciousness.

But Flaubert's major narrative achievement was *Madame Bovary* (1857), which treated in realistic detail the compulsive nature of Emma Bovary and the theme of adultery. Flaubert's novel shocked its nineteenth-century audience by stripping away the sentiment that typically accompanied fictional descriptions of love (a sentiment that had made Emma vulnerable to love affairs that could only disillusion her). Flaubert's novel shocked even more in its straightforward treatment of adultery. In keeping with the realistic mode, Flaubert emphasized the cause and effect connection between illicit love and its consequences. Emma, of course, intuits such consequences, but she is unable to resist the temptations. In the tradition of Balzac—and later of the Goncourts's *Germinie Lacerteux* (1864)—Flaubert depicts behavior so compulsive that Emma is forced to play out a determined fate that allows no means of escape.

4

Once we examine literary works in historical contexts, we can begin to see parallel developments between the works in different countries and cultures. Writers in these countries shared experience, like the move from land to city, and it is from this shared experience that the commonality among realist works in large part stemmed. In nineteenth-century Russia, the move was from the countryside to St. Petersburg. That city represented the culmination of cultures: built on marshland in human defiance of the sea, it embodied the Western Enlightenment. And yet there was something inimical at work in the city itself. Peter the Great looked to Amsterdam for his model of the

city. Pushkin saw St. Petersburg as combining "West" and "East," in a
way that gave the city a homeless feeling and challenged national
identity, an impression shared by both Gogol and Dostoyevsky.

Feodor Dostoyevsky was born in Moscow, the son of an estate
owner who was murdered by his serfs. His early training was at the
College of Military Engineering in St. Petersburg. His interest in literature led to a successful first novel, *Poor Folk* (1846). Dostoyevsky's
career was interrupted, however, when he was arrested as a political
revolutionary and sentenced to death, the reprieve coming when he
was in front of the firing squad. He was imprisoned in Siberia for five
years and then forced back into the army. As a result, his writing career did not begin until 1859. He depicted his Siberian experience in
The House of the Dead (1862). Despite the way his father died, Dostoyevsky was sympathetic to the plight of the serfs, and despite the
cruel treatment he received from the czar, he was politically conservative; he supported the status quo and believed in the idea of redemption through suffering. His travels in Europe led to a dislike of
the West and a Slavophile belief in the Russian people and Orthodox
Christianity. His masterpiece is *Crime and Punishment* (1866) followed by *The Gambler* (1867), *The Idiot* (1869), and *The Possessed*
(1871). His last novel, *The Brothers Karamazov* (1880), ranks with
Crime and Punishment in its realistic achievement.

Dostoyevsky's realism stems in great part from his rejection of the
Enlightenment. He favored an idealized agrarian order, founded on
the Russian peasant. As Michael Harrington has aptly put it, "When
Dostoyevsky speaks of man without God, he really means man torn
from the land, and his condemnation of atheism is an indictment of
cities. . . . The Megalopolis which came after him is inhabited by a
rootless, confused people. The ancient God, the traditional wisdom,
the old institutions have either shattered or vanished."[5] Dostoyevsky
saw two aberrant character types emerging from the new urbanism:
the underground man and the grand inquisitor. The underground
man is alienated and isolated, the grand inquisitor is authoritarian
and totalitarian: the two are different sides of the same coin.

In *Notes from Underground* (1864), Dostoyevsky attacks the belief
in a society organized on a rationalistic basis, divorced from the values
of the Russian people, especially the values of the Russian peasants.
He bewails Enlightenment trust in reason and progress, insists that

imperfect human nature undercuts any hope for utopia. He believes that political change without prior change in the individual prevents the possibility of community. The underground man embodies the dead end of isolation. He represents the chaos of conflicting emotion that cuts him off from his own feelings. He drives away Liza, destroying his best chance of redemption, and demonstrates how removed he is from an ability to love or return love. Dostoyevsky's underground man is superfluous. The product of boredom, he has lost his place in the modern world and is unhappy and angry— self-exiled. He anticipates Raskolnikov and the uprooted characters of literary modernism. Nietzsche identified with *Notes from Underground,* as did Freud and Kafka. Freud saw his conflicted motives; Kafka a man of inverted nature, turning against himself, moving toward the transformation of the human into its opposite and thereby anticipating the grotesque. The underground man is in that middle state between human and bug.

In *Crime and Punishment,* Dostoyevsky drew directly on other nineteenth-century novels, especially Balzac's *Père Goriot.* Raskolnikov's desire to become Napoleon, the extraordinary man of genius, draws heavily on Vautrin, the individual who defies moral limits. His most radical change in the formula of the earlier novel manifests itself in the character of Porfiry Petrovitch, the police magistrate. Unlike Dickens's Inspector Bucket, who resolved the case by intimately knowing how to work the city, Petrovitch solves the case by psychological cunning, by knowing how Raskolnikov's mind works. He knows that Raskolnikov's guilt will eventually betray him—that a crossroads confession is inevitable. The crossroads as symbol combines the cross of Christ and the realm where people meet (the symbol of the city is a cross within a circle—roads meeting within the wall of the city). Raskolnikov kisses the earth at the crossroads to get back to the earth, to the people, the peasants. For Dostoyevsky, redemption is in the people and not the church. Raskolnikov sinned against mankind by glorifying radical individualism, in his belief that he was extraordinary and could kill with impunity, and it is to the community that Raskolnikov must return to expiate his murder.

Crime and Punishment makes use of the urban problems of Dostoyevsky's day—poverty, crime, prostitution, drunkenness, and child neglect. St. Petersburg is Baudelaire's unreal city—a place of extreme sensation and hallucinatory thought. It is a place of disease, fevers, accidents, fights, suicides, and murder: the outside turmoil finds correspondence within the mind. While an all-knowing narrator tells the story, it is also told from Raskolnikov's point of view. As Mikhail Bakhtin has pointed out, the novel has a polyphonic quality—it is a composite of many conflicting voices.

Two persons are instrumental in Raskolnikov's redemption. Porfiry Petrovich embodies the secular authority of the city, and Sonia embodies the religious spirit of the people. Petrovich brings him before the law, Sonia before the human community, concretized in Christ, where final redemption awaits. In *Crime and Punishment*, Dostoyevsky reconciled the grand inquisitor and the underground man, authority and isolation, the secular and the religious. Only a mystical community can redeem the fallen city.

Dostoyevsky treated these themes again in *The Possessed*, his answer to Turgenev's *Fathers and Sons* (1862). He depicted the destructive effects of nihilism in a rural Russian community. Stepan Verhovensky, a liberal university lecturer, and Pytor are the father and son of the novel. Pytor's nihilism finds its opposite in Nickolay Stavrogin, Dostoyevsky's strong man. Dostoyevsky uses the pair as doubles: he modeled both on a steel-willed radical named Nechayev. To move from Stavrogin to Pytor is to descend a moral ladder from the possibility of redemption to the inevitability of damnation. At the end of the novel, Stavrogin renounces his criminal self in the name of human limits. His disciple, Kirillov, moves in the opposite direction. He believes that man has invented God to give life purpose, and he takes his own life to mock the idea that it does have purpose, thereby supposedly freeing man from God. If Stavrogin turns his superman's hate toward others, Kirillov turns his hate of God toward himself.

While Nietzsche found something positive in a world without God, Dostoyevsky depicted the negative effects of such a world. The novel that speaks directly to this point is *The Brothers Karamazov*. The three brothers are seeking the new man: Dmitri's struggle is emotional, Ivan's intellectual, and Alyosha's religious as he tries to realize the God he carries within him. All three brothers suffer from the guilt of their father's murder. Dmitri lacks the means to expiate this guilt. Ivan, who believes he is guilty of his father's murder because he wished it and hinted at that wish to Smerdyakov, is also unable to expiate his guilt because his confession goes unbelieved. His pent up guilt drives him mad. Ivan is the first of the metaphysical rebels in insisting that if evil is essential to divine creation, then creation is unacceptable. Dostoyevsky rejects Ivan's repudiation of God by contrasting it with the belief of Alyosha, whose redemption stems from his sharing the guilt he feels with the community.

Once again Dostoyevsky takes us to a mystical community for purpose of redemption. His novels, a testing ground for complex religious questions, are saved from becoming tendentious because he had the ability to depict convincingly positions he did not himself accept, thus creating a compelling world of ideological doubles. A sense of the dual nature of reality runs throughout Dostoyevsky's works. In testing the natural against the supernatural, in seeing the temporal in the light of the eternal, Dostoyevsky connects the visible with the invisible, the ordinary with the extraordinary, the realistic with the fantastic. His realism, like that of Melville and Hugo, is a romantic realism. The fantastic is superimposed on everyday urban reality, turning the literal into the symbolic. The Russian critic Shklovsky has referred to this narrative quality as *defamiliarization,* making the familiar strange. In his ability to transform the ordinary, Dostoyevsky anticipates the realism of literary modernism.

As in France and America, Russian realism depicted among its subjects the corruption of the rural realm and the transformation of the land. In the city, the equivalent of peasantry was bureaucracy: the urbanized peasants became clerks and civil servants. Once a member of the bureaucracy, the urbanized serf took as his task the need to climb within the system, as we see in Gogol. The city, in other words, became a battleground, as it did in the novels of Balzac in France and Dreiser in America. Many of the new ideas, like the belief in anarchy, took hold in the city and were transported back to the provinces, corrupting that realm even further, as Turgenev showed. As the land lost its therapeutic grip on its inhabitants, the values of the province and the city merged, and an old, more vital Russia was transformed into something new, more diminished, as Tolstoy described it.

Nikolai Gogol (1809–1852) was among the first to take these themes as his subject. In *Dead Souls* (1842) he described rural Russia giving way to bureaucratic corruption. When Pavel Chichikov, a clerk, learns that the Trustee Committee will mortgage souls—that is, dead peasants still on the census lists—he goes through the provinces buying up the names of the serfs who have died since the last census. Gogol's novel depicts the corruption at the heart of Russian life, especially the sleaziness of provincial life. The city is no better in its display of human nature, as Gogol clearly shows in such stories as "The Nose" (1836) and "The Overcoat" (1842).

In "The Nose" Kovalev awakens one morning to find that he has no nose. His situation, meant to be taken as an absurdity, then becomes the basis for realistic treatment. Self-important to an extreme, Kovalev finds that without a nose he is seriously curtailed in his ambition to climb the bureaucratic ladder and to court the most eligible women in St. Petersburg society. The lost nose reveals the pretenses of this new society, embodies the grotesque intricacies at work in this new bureaucratic world. It becomes as big a handicap as not having the social skills or the proper credentials to operate in this intricate society. Kovalev not only contributes to the bureaucratic maze, but he becomes its victim when he runs into nothing but red tape trying to report his lost nose to the proper authorities.

Gogol gives us another version of this theme in "The Overcoat." Akaky Akakyevich, a copyist and civil servant, gains status when he begins wearing a new, expensive overcoat. Immediately his sense of self is bolstered, and he gains the respect of those who formerly looked down on him. All goes well until one night his overcoat is stolen. Akaky has as much trouble reporting his stolen overcoat as Kovalev does reporting his lost nose. Depressed and with no coat in the Russian winter, Akaky dies from a cold and fever. His story reveals a social truth to others and becomes a legend when it is reported that his ghost has appeared on the Kalinkin Bridge, stripping citizens of their overcoats. Like Kovalev's nose, Akaky's overcoat illuminates the nature of his reality, exposing the involuted values that now dominate.

Ivan Turgenev (1818–1883) also made use of these themes. Turgenev was the son of a prosperous landowner, who inherited an estate when his mother died in 1850. He showed little interest in running the estate, living mostly abroad, perhaps to be close to Pauline Viordot, a well-known opera singer whose marriage did not prevent

Turgenev from showing (Platonic?) affection for forty years, from their meeting in 1843 until his death from spinal cancer in 1883. Turgenev's realism was influenced by French fiction. He lived most of his life in Paris, where he was close friends with Henry James, George Sand, Flaubert, and Zola. He was very much the product of Western thought, which brought him into conflict with both Dostoyevsky and the authorities. Dostoyevsky in *The Possessed* rebutted Turgenev's defense of anarchy, parodying him as the inchoate writer Karmazinov. Turgenev's troubles with the authorities stemmed from a laudatory obituary he wrote on the death of Gogol, who was in disfavor for his attack on the establishment in his stories and in *Dead Souls.*

In *Fathers and Sons* Turgenev depicted the change in Russian culture by describing the difference between men of two generations. Bazaroff, an anarchist, embodied the younger generation. His friend's uncle, Pavel, embodied the older generation. Bazaroff's nihilism is more a kind of pragmatism than a rejection of meaning, a belief that there is no truth separate from the test of experience or scientific experiment. Pavel is a product of the landed estate and all the spiritual values that were connected to that life. Turgenev suggested, angering Dostoyevsky, that Bazaroff embodied the Russian future— the transformation from land to city and the amoral movement from the religious to the secular. Turgenev also angered the liberals, who thought his portrait of Bazaroff was a caricature of their position. He angered the liberals once again when he argued in *Smoke* (1867) that the young intelligentsia was ineffectual in bringing about needed social and political change. If rejection by both extremes does not reveal his balanced view, it clearly reveals how strong the ideological tug was from both sides.

Turgenev had voiced his disapproval of labor practices on the landed estate in his earlier *A Sportsman's Sketches* (1847). This series of short stories depicted peasant serfdom as a dying institution, a prophetic notion since the emancipation of the peasants was enacted in February 1861, although the promise was greater than the freedom delivered. His most extensive treatment of the land question is in *Virgin Soil* (1877), his last novel, which depicts young idealistic students moving back to the countryside in an effort to staunch the exodus from the land to the city. They hoped to incite the peasantry to oppose the landowners, but their plans for what would replace the lost order were at best vague. While Turgenev had ideological differences with this group, he did not approve of the government's retaliation against the revolutionaries or of the peasants' distrust of them, whom they often turned over to the police. Once again, Turgenev was attacked from the Right and the Left. Some critics claimed the failure of *Virgin Soil* stemmed from Turgenev's writing about Russia from Europe, but Joyce wrote brilliantly about Ireland from Trieste, Paris, and Zurich. A more likely reason the novel failed was that the Populist movement became more radical, and, in 1877, went far beyond Turgenev's description of events in it. While history went beyond Turgenev, he had intuited the direction modern Russia would go, perhaps because he had seen events in France moving it in the same direction.

Along with Dostoyevsky, Russian realism reached its height with Leo Tolstoy—especially with *War and Peace* (1869) and *Anna Karenina* (1877). *War and Peace* covers the years from 1810 to 1820. History is very much its subject: Tolstoy insisted that unfolding of history was complex, involving so many causal connections that its meaning went beyond human understanding. Thus what we get in *War and Peace* is a panoramic portrait of a decade in which a multitude of events are played off each other. Much of this involves counterpointing the estate and the city, war versus peace, Alexander I and Napoleon, the cold and aristocratic Balkonskys and the warm and indulgent Rostovs. The novel contrasts courage with cowardliness, altruism with selfishness, military brilliance embodied by General Kutuzov with military failure embodied by Napoleon. Pierre Bezukoy and Natasha move beyond this doubling and gain individuality as does Nicholas Rostov with his passion for the land, a sentiment that carries the novel's major theme: the superiority of rural life over that of the city.

In Tolstoy's fiction life unfolds on two levels: the individual, in which there is reckoning, and the historical, of which there is no true understanding. In *Anna Karenina*, Tolstoy makes use of this double vision by telling the individual story of tragic love as embodied by Anna and the more generalized story of Russia as embodied by Konstantine Levin. Anna's story shares many narrative elements with the

Goncourt brothers' story of Germinie Lacerteux and with Flaubert's *Madame Bovary*. The story of Levin reflects Tolstoy's desire to keep the landed estate in place, depicting Levin working alongside his peasants, revitalized by the land. The plot here owes much to the romantic trust in the redemptive power of the land.

Despite the intensity he brought to the idea of the soil, Tolstoy would end up on the losing side of history. Like Dostoyevsky, Tolstoy regretted the shift in cultural gravity from the land to the city. But in every major country in the world, the new commercial system, and the industrialization that would become a part of it, mandated such a shift. The Emancipation Act of 1861 transformed the landed gentry into a bourgeois reality; it resulted in the impoverishment of the estates and the rapid advance of a money system. The urban population doubled as the poorer peasants flocked to the cities to fill the demand for factory workers.

Anton Chekhov's career as a doctor was directly connected to this new world, but then he gave up medicine to write humorous stories and articles for the new urban magazines, and soon after took up playwriting. *The Cherry Orchard* (1904) explicitly takes as its theme the transformation of modern Russia in the face of the dying estate: Trofimov and Anya are pleased when the cherry orchard is cut down, believing it harbingers new possibilities. "All Russia is our orchard," Trofimov tells Anya, indifferent to what is being lost. Chekhov's play ends on a note of ambivalence: the cherry orchard must go, but with it goes a way of life that will never come again.

After 1917 the authority of the Communist state radically changed the nature of Russian realism. Socialist realism, as it was called, was really state propaganda. It modified the realists' sense of historical pattern into an historical determinism: history supposedly unfolded in keeping with the rise and evolution of communism. Socialist realism contradicts the major assumption of traditional realism by assuming that there is an ideological direction built into time, a quasi-religious teleology moving the world toward the communist state.

The last of the traditional realists in Russia was Mikhail Sholokhov. His *And Quiet Flows the Don* (1928–40) dealt with almost a decade of events (1912–20) from before the revolution and beyond, primarily from a Cossack and White Army point of view. His *Virgin*

Soil Upturned (1933, 1960) treated Stalin's 1928 reprisals against peasant opposition to collectivization as well as depicted the famine of 1932–33 and the purges that followed. Sholokhov, who had to wait until after Stalin's death to complete the second volume of his novel, was among the very last to treat the transformation of the land from a point of view that was more realist than socialist realist.

Throughout Western culture—including in Russia, at least until 1917—a fictional pattern was at work. Balzac and Zola in France, Defoe and Dickens in England, Norris and Dreiser in America, George Moore and the Joyce of *Dubliners* (1916) in Ireland, and Gogol and Chekhov in Russia—all described the cultural shift from land to city. And coincidental with this shift came the narrative variations we know as literary realism.

5

The realists in the United States—especially Twain, Howells, and James—took America, or the difference between America and Europe, as their major subject. The problem involved primarily how a new materialism could be reconciled to the ideals of democracy. Before the Civil War, there were two forms of agrarian life: in the South was the plantation system based on the use of slaves, and in the northwest (today the Midwest) and the plains were Jefferson's "yeoman" farmers who tilled their own land. After the Civil War, there was a natural rivalry between the yeoman farmers and the new industrialists. When Emerson spoke of American self-reliance, he did not have in mind the rapacity of Rockefeller, Carnegie, or Morgan. Even within the "idea" of America as expressed in the Constitution, there were contradictions that could not be easily reconciled. The early split was embodied in the difference between Thomas Jefferson and Alexander Hamilton, between the idea of an agrarian and industrial nation: one was based on yeoman farmers, the other on a factory system; one was subject to the workings of federal banks, a contractual basis of law, and a theory of property that involved commodities that could be sold, the other to a theory of property that reclaimed the wilderness by working it, by transforming the frontier into a democratic reality.

The problem of realism involved trying to find the ideals that could accommodate the new vision. The results were mostly failure: Howells never really came to terms with the rapaciousness of the robber barons; Twain saw the problem but was better able to address the origins of the problem (the transformation from a feudal to industrial world) than to resolve it; and James, in tune with his times as his *The American Scene* (1904) reveals, was better at stating than addressing the problem, as we can see by the fact that he abandoned writing *The Ivory Tower* (published in fragment form in 1917), his novel that most directly concerned the failures of the new commercialism. Over a hundred years after the drafting of the American Constitution, the hope of a Jefferson had turned into the despair of Henry Adams.

Industrial America was the product of technological success without the ideals that would have made it into a utopia. There were attempts to imagine such a utopia by Bellamy, Twain, London, and others—but they came to naught. American literary realism was thus an inchoate attempt to come to terms with a new world. American literary naturalism would go one step beyond and depict the problem both more objectively and more realistically, but still the representation of the social reality would want for the failure to find a redeeming ideal. The naturalists tended to move toward socialism and communism for the solution, the modernists toward forms of totalitarianism—that is, we had answers from the Right and the Left but little to nothing from the Center.

Mark Twain (the pseudonym of Samuel Langhorne Clemens) created his own brand of literary realism, much of it stemming from the conventions of frontier humor. Twain grew up in Hannibal, Missouri, on the Mississippi River, where he was a steamboat pilot. He also journeyed to the West, where he became a prospector and frontier journalist. Out of this experience came his frontier tale, *The Jumping Frog of Calaveras County* (1865). His next book was *The Innocents Abroad* (1869), a portrait of southern Europe and the Near East from a frontier perspective that intentionally failed to glorify civilization or the Holy Land. He depicted his days in the West in *Roughing It* (1872) and his steamboat days in *Life on the Mississippi* (1883). His novel about growing up in Hannibal, *The Adventures of Tom Sawyer* (1876), was followed by its famous sequel, *Adventures of*

Huckleberry Finn (1884). *A Connecticut Yankee in King Arthur's Court* (1889) contrasted modern America with feudal Europe and the industrial North with the antebellum South. The *Prince and the Pauper* (1882), another medieval fantasy, attacked the idea of royalty, depicting it as misplaced belief in the privileges of birthrights over natural rights, monarchy over democracy. Twain's novel argued that the difference between a princely and beggarly life was simply the difference between environment and rearing as expressed in social institutions. In his later years, Twain's realism, like Dickens's, became more bleak as illustrated by "The Man that Corrupted Hadleyburg" and "The Mysterious Stranger" (1916). His "What Is Man?" (1906)—arguing that man is an automaton, mechanistically determined—takes him to the doorstep of literary naturalism.

Twain's pseudonym was well chosen because it suggested the dualism that was embedded in his fiction. Huck and Tom, the prince and the pauper, and Tom and Valet de Chambers of *Pudd'nhead Wilson* (1880) all take us to the point where identities become confused, where one reality suddenly gives way to its opposite. In the case of Tom and Valet de Chambers, the difference between a Southern gentleman and a slave is (as we saw in *The Prince and the Pauper*) merely the difference of one's rearing. As with Carlyle, Twain believed clothes and learned manners determined the difference between being accepted or rejected.[6]

Critics such as Michael Davitt Bell question whether Twain deserves to be called a realist. Certainly his novels are different from those of such contemporaries as Howells and James, relying more on fantasy and more subject to variations in the mode. Any argument for Twain as a realist must turn on his attack of the romance, especially the romance of Cooper, and his invention of characters like Huck Finn whose sense of reality is based on observation and experience. The legacy of Twain's realistic writing is evident in authors from Stephen Crane to Ernest Hemingway. Twain's writing is also realistic in its taking up of the problems of the era, especially the political and social corruption that followed the Civil War. Twain's fantasy projections—*The Prince and the Pauper*, "The Mysterious Stranger," and *A Connecticut Yankee*—put a "frame" around his realism, which belies how these works are engaged with the immediate problems of his era—especially the fate of democracy in an industrial age.

Twain depicted an older world lost to a newer one. He lived in an era of transition, in an age that was fast foreclosing on the frontier during which people were moving from land to city. Twain attempted to come to terms with this era in works like *The Gilded Age* (1873), written with Charles Dudley Warner. He felt that the urban life was becoming more and more impersonal, that cities were repressing the inner life, corrupting an innocent state of mind. In 1882, he wrote in his notebook: "Human nature cannot be studied in cities except at a disadvantage—a village is the place. There you can know your man inside and out—in a city you but know the crust; and his crust is usually a lie."

Twain's world was the antebellum world of the frontier and provincial Missouri, which is to say that it precedes, even as it anticipates, the commercial/industrial world that followed the Civil War. There is thus a sense of American innocence about to be lost, a sense that becomes more emphatic when the stories are narrated by the adolescent Tom Sawyer or Huck Finn. One of the major disputes in the history of Twain criticism involves whether Twain was inhibited by his connection with genteel America (as argued by Van Wyck Brooks [1886–1963]) or whether he gave free expression to his idea of American lost innocence (the position of Bernard De Voto [1897–1955]). There are elements of truth in both positions. In creating a colloquial novel depicting a reality that is defined by wayward experience, he moved beyond the genteel tradition. But Twain set expandable limits to what he would represent in that reality. His fiction, for example, avoids the discussion of sex. But when Twain's later years were marked by the illness and the death of his wife and daughters, he was not reluctant to give us a more pessimistic picture of life such as in works like "What Is Man?" But even here his depiction is not of a piece. He suggests that the world is mechanistic but then has the Satan figure in "The Mysterious Stranger" tell us to create a better reality by dreaming better dreams; thus Twain abandons the idea of a mechanistic reality and consents to a form of idealism, to the notion of a reality dependent on mind.

Twain believed that human beings possessed a Rousseau-like innocence that was corrupted by institutions. Man acquired his "moral
sense," a conscience, through a training that was morally corrupting
and destructive. He briefly hoped that the industrial age might raise
men morally by creating a world of plenty. But he soon realized that
instead of decreasing man's greed, capitalism increased it. The new
technology engendered new forms of power that made the human
species more destructive than ever before. Man, capable of great
cruelty, now had the physical means to create evil, as Hank does at
the end of *A Connecticut Yankee*. Twain believed that it was more difficult to remain innocent in the face of the new industrial/urban
world. These themes emerge in works like "The Mysterious Stranger"
and "What Is Man?" The devil in "The Mysterious Stranger" tells the
boy that behind the illusion is a realm of causes, a set of circumstances already in play in the devil's mind, and that the boy is acting
out the devil's dream.

Innocents Abroad and *Roughing It* deal with the two poles of
nineteenth-century life: Europe, from which the immigrants came,
and the West toward which their descendants were moving. Twain's
views of Europe and America were never totally consistent. Twain
had a natural distrust of monarchy and hereditary aristocracy and
was suspicious of imperialism wherever he found it. England's
dealings in the Boer War, Russia's attempt to conquer Japanese land,
and America's snatching up of Cuba and the Philippines all equally
aroused his wrath. He also attacked Western missionaries because
they usually preceded the gunboats. He saw imperialism as the logical extension of capitalism, believed that urban America was becoming too centralized, and that democracy would fail in face of the mob
and other totalizing systems.

The possibilities of democracy competed with its limitations;
there was a conflict between the idea of freedom and the nature of
man. In "Notes for a Social History of the United States from 1850 to
1900," Twain maintained that America became money-mad after
1850. He believed that the California gold rush brought on the desire
for sudden wealth, an attitude of mind that was intensified by the
Civil War, which encouraged the Wall Street bankers and the railroad
promoters who financed the war. They were unscrupulous men who

wanted most to "Get rich; dishonestly if we can; honestly if we must." *The Gilded Age* depicted a corrupt America, a country that had betrayed its sense of promise.

The novel treats the connection between the frontier and the capital necessary to exploit it. Colonel Sellers, who wants to build the "city of Napoleon upon a prairie mud flat," says: "All we need is the capital to develop it. Slap down the rails and bring the land into market." Behind the capital, of course, are Wall Street and the Washington politicians—that is, behind the capital are the bank and legislature. By 1873, Congress had given away almost two hundred million acres of public land to the railroad corporations. Oakes Ames, brother of the president of the Union Pacific and a Massachusetts congressman, offered stock at inside prices to other congressmen. And in New York the Tweed ring robbed the city of almost two hundred million dollars with a series of fraudulent schemes. There is probably no novel that takes on the abuse of the age better than *The Gilded Age*.

In *Life on the Mississippi*, Twain contrasted the new and old river. Twain returned to the Mississippi twenty years after he had left it in order to get firsthand impressions for what was to be the setting of *Huckleberry Finn*. What he saw filled him with nostalgia, particularly for life on the river during the age of the old riverboats that had now been almost totally replaced by the railroad.[7] The story of Huck and Jim is the story of American innocence confronted with the evil of American slavery. In their trip down the Mississippi River on a raft, Huck comes to realize Jim's humanity and to transform him from slave to human being. No other work was as powerful in exposing a generation of readers to a human truth.

Twain, like Huck, tried desperately to hold on to his innocence in a world fast giving way to conformity and dull routine. He saw that a destructive state of mind had long been reworking the wilderness. Appropriately, he connected this state of mind with Daniel Defoe. In *A Connecticut Yankee in King Arthur's Court*, Twain's Yankee compares himself with Robinson Crusoe: "I saw that I was just another Robinson Crusoe cast away on an uninhabited island, with no society but some more or less tame animals, and if I wanted to make life bearable I must do as he did—invent, contrive, create, reorganize things—set brain and hand to work, and keep them busy. Well, that was in my line."[8] Ironically, like Locke, the Connecticut Yankee believes that the wilderness *is* waste, and is redeemed only when transformed into property. But Twain's writing taken as a whole proves the opposite—the wasteland is what is left when the wilderness is gone. Twain was among the first American writers to depict realistically the betrayed past, the selling of America. This is a legacy he shared with Howells and James, who treated the theme less successfully, and a legacy that he left to Willa Cather and F. Scott Fitzgerald, who made it a core subject of their realism.

William Dean Howells found himself caught between the new realism coming out of France and his affinity for such genteel writers as Longfellow, Lowell, and Whittier. While he encouraged the subscribers to the *Atlantic Monthly* to read Zola, Ibsen, and Tolstoy, he was himself only politely enthusiastic about the novels of Stephen Crane and displeased with Dreiser's *Sister Carrie*. And yet, after World War II and until about 1970, academic criticism in America used Howells as the benchmark for literary realism. While he wrote forty novels and novellas, his reputation as a realist depends on *A Modern Instance* (1881), *The Rise of Silas Lapham* (1885), and *A Hazard of New Fortunes* (1890).

As Howells's career proves, realism had to fight its way through the moral timidity of the genteel tradition. A lion in the path of realism was James Russell Lowell. He attacked Thoreau and Walt Whitman, had no sympathy for the Haymarket Square anarchists, and believed no author should write what he did not want his daughter to read, reducing the content of the novel to the sensibility of the innocent child. William Dean Howells shared a number of Lowell's literary values. Dreiser had little sympathy for either Lowell or Howells. In his essay "The Great American Novel," Dreiser accused Howells of being socially uninformed. Dreiser's assessment seems justified in the light of Howells's best fiction.

A Modern Instance, the first novelistic treatment of divorce in America, is the story of Bartley Hubbard, an amoral, ambitious young man, who leaves his wife Marcia in Boston and absconds to Chicago with twelve hundred dollars. In Cleveland, he has a change of heart and decides to return to Boston, only to discover that his wallet and the stolen money have in turn been stolen. As in many realist novels, an accident (here the stolen wallet) determines Bartley's fate. The conclusion of the novel is told from Marcia's point of view, and thus the story ends with Marcia morally triumphing and Bartley morally failing. After Bartley loses his wallet, Howells tells the reader "nothing remained for him but the ruin he had chosen."[9] But Bartley has not chosen at all, or if he has chosen, it was to return to Boston, just the opposite of what happens. Howells's desire to create a world of moral imperatives perhaps leads to unintentional ambiguity. If so, such ambiguity is a harbinger of the moral ambiguity that will run through realistic fiction.

Howells's moral confusion is also evident in *A Hazard of New Fortunes*, the story of Basil March, who takes on the job as editor of a literary magazine in New York that is controlled by a Mr. Dryfoos, whose natural gas holding has made him a newly rich millionaire. One of the main themes of the novel—Dryfoos's conversion from a right-wing capitalist to open-minded benefactor—is unconvincing. A Christian sense of fate runs through Howells's novels. Both old Dryfoos and Lindau, a socialist, men of extreme views, are punished in the end: the more humane values prosper, suggesting that the righteous walk a middle path.

As a political novel, *A Hazard of New Fortunes* does not come to terms with political reality, just as *The Rise of Silas Lapham* does not come to terms with the reality of post–Civil War business life in America. Howells's novel really depicts American commerce before the era of the robber barons. Silas rises morally as he falls economically—a possibility given the scale of the business in which he is engaged. As that scale expands, however, he becomes an anachronism. While Silas chooses poverty over dishonor, Rockefeller was ruining his competitors with deceitful deals and railroad rebates; Drew, Gould, and Fiske were bribing legislators; and Elkins, Widener, and Yerkes were deviously securing streetcar franchises. As Granville Hicks pointed out,[10] neither the great rewards nor the great achievements would have been possible if the robber barons had been distracted by the problems that worried Silas Lapham.

If Howells avoided coming to terms with the new commercialism, Henry James skirted the subject. James thought of the novel as an

advanced art form and endowed it with the same elevated status that
the French did. Influenced by Balzac and George Sand, he was also
among the first to see that the novel could reveal a state of mind. To
this end, he went beyond George Eliot and anticipated Flaubert and
the rise of the modern novel. His major contribution to the realist
novel was his ability to depict American innocence coming to terms
with European decadence and to reveal plot in installments (encouraged by serial publication), making the reader an active participant
in the narrative unfolding and a moral sense of right and wrong
more difficult to define.

His first important novel was *Roderick Hudson* (1874). A year in
Paris (1875) brought him in contact with Turgenev, Flaubert, Zola,
Daudet, and Maupassant. He was deeply influenced by Turgenev's
belief that character was more important than plot. The next year,
James was in London working to perfect his craft, the success of
which was displayed in *Daisy Miller* (1879). Between 1880 and his
death in 1916, he produced over one hundred volumes of fiction and
other writing (plays, autobiographies, travelogues, critical writings,
book reviews, and prefaces) that helped define the novel in a state of
transition. His fiction falls into three categories: those novels with an
international theme, which culminates with *The Portrait of a Lady*
(1881); those that address social issues including the *Bostonians* (1886),
The Princess Casamassima (1886), and *The Tragic Muse* (1890); and
those that revisit the international theme such as *The Wings of the
Dove* (1902), *The Ambassadors* (1903), and *The Golden Bowl* (1904).
These novels, complex in their use of character and plot, anticipated
the novels of Proust and what we mean by "high modernism." In his
fiction, James progressed from melodrama to the depiction of a
more complex reality.

Henry James created two orders of reality—an American and a
European. The American was characterized by residual innocence;
the European was defined by a hierarchical realm that was loosening
in manners as the aristocracy began losing its wealth and power.
With its financial sources curtailed, European aristocracy was becoming more desperate. The American, especially a wealthy American, was vulnerable in Europe, as we can see in characters from
Christopher Newman to Daisy Miller, from Isabel Archer to Lambert

Strether. The three novels of James's middle period—*The Bos-tonians, The Princess Casamassima,* and *The Tragic Muse*—address feminism, anarchism, and aestheticism. James saw masculinity giv-ing way to a militant feminism, viewed the realm of civilization as threatened by the violence of revolution, and believed the pursuit of the beautiful was compromised by the perpetuation of the material ugliness that came with the new order of commerce and industry. He longed for stability in an era of radical change, and he longed for so-cial decorum at a time when established manners were being tested. But the kind of desire for order he wished for was personal rather than social. It was the individual's sense of stability and manners that was being tested in his fiction, and he always depicted the response to disorder and the failure of decorum in terms of individual con-sciousness and temperament.

Along with Twain and Howells, James depicted the reality of a changing world. When in 1904 he returned to America from his long stay in England, he was greatly upset at the extent to which America had been commercialized. He voiced his discontent in *The American Scene* (1904) and in *The Ivory Tower,* a novel that significantly he was never able to finish perhaps because he could not come to grips with what America had become. James disliked the business world, ironi-cally so because his father's inherited fortune allowed him the means of leisure. James admired the aristocratic world of Europe. In his *Hawthorne* (1879), he listed the institutions that America lacked: "No sovereign, no court, no personal loyalty, no aristocracy, no church, no clergy, no army, no diplomatic service, no country gentlemen, no palaces, no castles, no manors, nor old country-houses, nor par-sonages, nor thatched cottages, nor ivied ruins; no cathedrals nor abbeys, nor little Norman churches; no great Universities nor public schools—no Oxfords, nor Eton, nor Harrow."[11]

But this was the world of the past, even in England. The aristoc-racy had been corrupted and was crumbling—and James knew it. In *The American* (1877) Christopher Newman gives up the seamy world of American business, tries to find himself among the dying French aristocracy, and becomes a victim of its machinations. Isabel Ar-cher's situation duplicates this plight. Caught between going back to America and Caspar Goodwood or returning to Italy and Gilbert

Osmond, she "chooses" Osmond, giving herself to a loveless marriage, sacrificing herself to keep the aristocracy alive, remaining faithful to her misguided decision to marry. Isabel is the product of James's own cultural dilemma.

Henry James empties out the realism based on a Christian sense of right and wrong that Howells gave voice to. James's moral ambiguity adds an important dimension to the rise of realism as a narrative mode. In Paris, Christopher Newman meets and falls in love with Claire de Cintre. It turns out that Madame de Bellegarde had killed her invalid husband when he opposed Claire's marriage to M. de Cintre. Newman cannot bring himself to bring charges against the Bellegardes and burns an incriminating document, an act the Bellegardes anticipated. James uses this story to emphasize the cultural differences between America and Europe—the bright innocence of the one, the dark intrigue of the other. Melodramatic to a fault, James, nevertheless, depicts a situation that is a model of the new realism, involving a plot that turns on an ambiguous moral choice that becomes an end in itself. Seemingly Newman triumphs morally when he burns the incriminating letter. But it is an empty triumph: Valentin is dead and Claire is in a convent. Newman's decision gives him an inner satisfaction, but there is otherwise nothing in the novel that would justify allowing the Bellegardes to go unpunished.

In *The Portrait of a Lady,* Isabel Archer finds herself facing this same plight with respect to right and wrong. Isabel goes to Europe in pursuit of experience and culture. In Florence she meets Gilbert Osmond, who persuades Isabel to marry him. As in many realist novels, romantic expectations are shattered, and Isabel is disillusioned with marriage. Despite Osmond's objections, Isabel leaves Italy to visit her cousin Ralph Touchett, who is seriously ill. There she is courted again by both Lord Warburton and Caspar Goodwood, giving her the opportunity to choose anew. Rejecting Warburton and Goodwood, Isabel intends to return to Osmond. *The Portrait of a Lady* is one of James's most complicated stories. Contrasting the cultural differences between American and Europe, Isabel has to choose between Warburton and Goodwood, finally settling on a composite of the two in the person of Gilbert Osmond. Although Isabel clearly knows that her future with Osmond has been compromised, she returns to him: she admits her mistake and accepts the consequences. There is probably no ending in fiction that is more troublesome to the average reader. In the absence of a higher authority to whom one can appeal as an arbiter of good and evil, the decision of how to act remains in the province of the individual. At the end of *The Portrait of a Lady*, Isabel has chosen. As mistaken as that choice may be, it is hers—and the idea that moral choice is personal seems to be the overriding principle of the novel.

In his later works James will undermine further the difference between good and evil, the innocent and the guilty. As Edmund Wilson has pointed out, *The Ambassadors* redoes the theme of *The American*, *The Wings of the Dove* the theme of *The Portrait of a Lady*.[12] The Bellegardes are stereotypical villains, while Mme de Vionnet is depicted sympathetically; Gilbert Osmond and his mistress are cunning and conniving, while Kate Croy and her lover, who exploit Milly Theale, have redeeming virtues.

3

Realism, Narrative Subforms, and Historical Process

It has been claimed by critics like Ian Watt that the novel was the product of historical change in culture. As Watt has shown, a new middle class created the demand for what it in turn received.[1] But the novel did not come to us fully formed; it evolved—and has continued to evolve—out of a number of subgenres. These subgenres include the diary, the travel adventure, the utopian novel, the comedy of manners, the gothic, the young man/woman-from-the-provinces novel, the bildungsroman, the detective story, the novel of imperial adventure, the spy novel, the western, the proletariat novel, the tough-guy novel, the regional novel (such as the Hollywood novel), the dystopian novel, science fiction, and a number of others. All of these narrative subforms came into being at different historical moments and served to codify social and cultural ideas that were themselves subject to the process of historical change.

The purpose of the following survey of subforms is to suggest how the radical change of an era was reflected in fiction. For example, the rise of anonymity in the city produced the fictional detective who could personalize this world; the extended conquests of a nation-state led to the fictional depiction of imperialism. It is important to see these subforms as sequential (the loss of the estate in the gothic novel anticipates the journey to the city, the rise of the urban detective, and the transformed self). They must also be seen as culturally equivalent (the British novel of imperial adventure found its equivalent in the American Western).

The historical elements described here become the narrative elements of realism and naturalism and create the common ground between and among what might initially appear to be diverse texts. The early diary, for example, cannot be divorced from the Puritan values that spawned it—it served as a kind of spiritual account book, and so was consistent with the Puritan belief that God revealed His beneficence through physical signs. The novel of travel adventure came into being coincidentally with the rise of the great trading fleet that literally undertook journeys around the world. The new social order of the post-Renaissance period was based on a new urban, merchant class and on a parliamentary form of government more interested in natural rights than birthrights. It was also built on a belief in progress through science and the new technology, which led to a fantasy projection of these ideas in the form of utopian thought. The rise of a new leisure class spawned the man-about-town and the social rogue whose adventuresome threats to domestic stability dominated Restoration drama and supplied in turn a comedy-of-manners plot for the novel.

A study of subgenre reveals that most novels are made up of several subforms through which they depict a special and distinct reality. *Robinson Crusoe* (1719), for example, is the composite of diary, travel adventure, and utopian vision. *Bleak House* (1852) is a gothic novel, a detective story, and a sentimental narrative. Many fundamental cultural ideas find expression, as might be expected, in the more popular subforms—for example, the novel of imperial adventure or the Western. It is then left to more serious writers to recast these formula plots—as E. M. Forster and Conrad did with the novel of imperial adventure or as F. Scott Fitzgerald did by inverting the Western in *The Great Gatsby* (1925).[2]

In this context, intertextuality becomes a deeply historical phenomenon. One text talks to another in contexts that are inseparable from the cultural/historical moment. Dostoyevsky's *The Possessed* (1872) is his answer to Turgenev's *Fathers and Sons* (1862). Twain answers Bellamy's utopian *Looking Backward* (1888) with his dystopian *A Connecticut Yankee in King Arthur's Court* (1889), as did Ignatius Donnelly in *Caesar's Column* (1890) and William Morris in *News*

from Nowhere (1891). James's *The Princess Casamassima* (1886) is his response to Ivan Turgenev's *Virgin Soil* (1877), and *The Bostonians* (1886) his answer to Hawthorne's *Blithedale Romance* (1852).

Novels record the historical moment and are then transformed by it, producing a correspondence between historical and fictional realms. Defoe and Dickens, for example, examine the new commercial society at different stages of its growth in England, as do Hugo and Balzac in France, and Twain and Dreiser in America. Once the critic sees these writers in the same historical context, it becomes clear that what appeared previously to be historical accident is not. Balzac read Dickens and Dostoyevsky read Balzac. Balzac, Hugo, and Twain had to come to terms with Scott and James Fenimore Cooper before they could go beyond them. Twain's *A Connecticut Yankee in King Arthur's Court* moved through both time and space. Twain superimposed the commercial/industrial world of the nineteenth century onto the aristocratic/feudal world of the sixth. Such a juxtaposition served to highlight the economic and cultural differences between the industrial American North and the agrarian American South, thus creating a parallel between a feudal and industrial Europe and a feuding America. William Faulkner looked directly back to Balzac's *Human Comedy* (1831–48) novels as well as to Twain's provincial novels when he was contemplating his Yoknapawtapha sequence. Further, it is not only writers reading other writers that produces a similarity in subject matter. Although many of these authors were writing in different countries and at different times, they paralleled each other in subject matter when the historical moment— especially the shared move from an agrarian to an urban society— created a similar historical situation.

1

The rise of realism took place simultaneously with the transformation from a feudal to urban culture, a transformation that was often depicted in the gothic novel. The gothic novel portrayed the decline of the feudal estate—that is, the decline of the aristocratic father—as this world became more mutant, and often cursed. Novels like Walpole's *The Castle of Otranto* (1764), Radcliffe's *The Mysteries of*

Udolpho (1794), and Godwin's *Caleb Williams* (1794) share a common plot: an "evil" comes into this world from the city, disrupts the agrarian order in a mysterious, often supernatural way. The victim is usually a young woman who is being used to acquire claim to the estate or to facilitate its growth. One can find elements of this plot at work in novels like Richardson's *Clarissa* (1748) and novels by Monk Lewis, and in nineteenth-century novels such as Bronte's *Wuthering Heights* (1847) and Dickens's *Bleak House*. Jane Austen celebrated the moral order of the estate and tried to suggest its vitality by parodying the gothic form in *Northanger Abbey* (1818).

With the exception of novels such as Brockden Brown's *Wieland* (1798), the gothic novel came to America about one hundred to one hundred-and-fifty years after its origins in England—and the same was true in Ireland. The historical process that marked the shift from the land to the city came later in Ireland and America and delayed the development in both countries of what was the counterpart to the British gothic novel. Hawthorne's *The House of the Seven Gables* (1851) and Poe's "The Fall of the House of Usher" (1840) are the American equivalents of the gothic novel, as is Faulkner's *Absalom, Absalom!* (1936), with its depiction of the breakdown of the southern estate after the Civil War. In *Sanctuary* (1931), Faulkner depicts the demise of the southern belle in a narrative that can be considered his rendering of the Clarissa story.

While they are technically not gothic novels, the historical process at work here is reflected in the novels of George Eliot and Thomas Hardy. Arthur Donnithorne fails to uphold the values of the estate, and Adam Bede eventually is forced off it to become another wage earner. Hardy's Jude is the fictional son of Adam Bede; driven from the estate, he moves from cathedral town to cathedral town repairing old medieval churches. He is a modern man misplaced in historical time, a human emblem of the completion of a historical process.

2

Where the gothic novel ends, the young-man-from-the-provinces novel begins. Whereas the gothic novel depicts the historical end of feudalism, the journey-to-the-city novel depicts the rise of urbanism.

The young are called to the city because only the new city is large enough to accommodate their heightened sense of self. Dickens's *Great Expectations* (1861) and Balzac's *Père Goriot* (1835)and *Illusions perdues* (1837) are the most famous nineteenth-century versions of this story. But the historical situation that gave it vitality persisted into the twentieth century in America, where we have counterparts to the European story in Dreiser's *Sister Carrie* (1900), Fitzgerald's *The Great Gatsby,* and Nathanael West's *The Day of the Locust* (1939).

In the tradition of Balzac, Dreiser saw the city as a magnet luring young men and women like Carrie Meeber from rural America. F. Scott Fitzgerald's *The Great Gatsby* also takes us from the provinces to the metropolis, telling a story against the panorama of American history. The loss of the frontier, the limiting nature of the provincial town, and the desire to fulfill oneself, which the megalopolis promised to offer, all played a role in the creation of a new America. Nathanael West incorporated both the meaning of the small town and the big city in his *Day of the Locust.* Homer Simpson is the product of the small town, while the novel itself is set in Los Angeles, more specifically the Hollywood of the thirties.

In Europe, the journey-to-the-city-novel was culturally important because it revealed new attitudes toward the land, the family, money, technology, and the city. The plots of these stories have a common structure. First, we have the lure of the city, which will later become a trap. We then have the rejection of the Old World of the estate or of the family, which no longer can satisfy the ambitious young. The young person journeying to the city often discovers a substitute family—as in Balzac's boarding houses—but these relationships are seldom substantial, based, as are most city connections, on a cash nexus. No subgenre better codified the full meaning of the commercial society or revealed so well the extent to which it was creating a new state of mind. Not only were family and personal relationships far more tenuous in the commercial/urban world, but also under the influence of the new technology, especially railroad building, the scale of the city was changed. The individual was more vulnerable; the dimensions of the world were not quite so human; and love and friendship were replaced by money, which hardened the heart, as Dickens showed in *Dombey and Son* (1848).

3

Even with the inception of the Enlightenment with its concern for individual rights, women were thought of as the property of their family, be it of father or husband. With the decline of the estate, it became less important to marry a daughter into another landed family in order to increase the size of the family holding. Marriage thus became less a property arrangement between families and more a matter of mutual attraction. As engagement now turned on love rather than property, the women insisted that their romantic feelings be taken into consideration. This became true inside as well as outside marriage, and a major theme of the realists was that of "fated love," the story of women who violate the codes of marriage. The theme of infidelity thereby took on new importance in the novel as well. Tony Tanner notes that adultery in the modern sense is an act a person engages in to satisfy his or her individual desires at the expense of the family. He speaks of an Old and New Testament version of adultery as the one involving the rigidity of law, the other engaging a more tolerant sympathy: he believes that the new bourgeois novel brought the two together, combining passion and property, in a narrative where marriage was the central subject. As the novel evolved, marriage vows lost their force: Goethe still insisted on them; Flaubert abrogated them; James found them problematic; and they disappear altogether by the time we reach Joyce and Lawrence.[3]

The Victorian woman, dutiful in respect to family and husband, gave way in the extreme to a kind of male counterpart, as in Norris's *Moran of the Lady Letty* (1898). But in novels where the deviancy was less radical, she became the obsessed woman for whom marriage was a barrier to self-realization. George Eliot's Dorothea Brooke never violates her marriage vows, although she is strongly attracted to Will Ladislaw. Hardy's Tess and Sue Frawley are wisps in the wind of love. Both Flaubert's Madame Bovary and Tolstoy's Anna Karenina commit adultery, for which they pay the supreme price. The French realists in particular—Balzac, Flaubert, Zola, Daudet, Maupassant, and others—treated the compulsive nature of love, a theme that, except in Flaubert's case, may owe its fictional origin to the Goncourt brothers' *Germinie Lacerteux* (1864). In drama, Ibsen's *A Doll's House*

(1879) and Strindberg's *Miss Julie* (1888) extend the theme of love-gone-wrong. Some of these works anticipated the doctrine of such decadents as Oscar Wilde and Aubrey Beardsley and their precursors: Swinburne, Pater, Wagner, and Baudelaire. It has been suggested that the story of the decadent and that of the new woman share the fin-de-siècle avant-garde desire to live in a world beyond Victorian culture. In the wake of realism/naturalism, Victorian moral codes were relaxed both in the realm of art and sexuality.

4

If sexual practices changed under the influence of a new commercial society, so also did the meaning of property and money. The idea of property is a modern phenomenon. Until Henry VIII, the king or the church owned all land. Henry confiscated much of the church's land and then sold it to the nobility in order to build an army. Later John Locke would argue a citizen's right to property once the land had been worked. If the peasant had no reason for owning land, he had even less need for money. The peasant worked the land for a lord. His reward was a share of the food he produced. What food he might sell in town gave him the little money he might need to buy salt or other luxuries. His world turned on work—not money.

But with the rise of a commercial society and the migration of the peasant from the land to the city, money came to play a major aspect in everyone's life. In the city the peasant became a wage slave: the value of his work was measured in money, and since there was an overabundance of workers, his individual work was sharply discounted. Money was connected to survival and had laws of its own. From Aristotle on, the assumption was that money was not a commodity; thus to sell it was "unnatural"—a policy adopted by the medieval church. Usury became a sin in the Catholic world and was practiced mainly by Jewish bankers, which perhaps explained the European disdain for Jews if not its anti-Semitism, as Shakespeare's *The Merchant of Venice* suggests.

Given its importance, it is not surprising that certain temperaments became obsessed with money as an end in itself, and Balzac in *Eugénie Grandet* (1833), George Eliot in *Silas Marner* (1861), and

Arnold Bennett in *Riceyman Steps* (1923) examined the mind of the miser. Realism/naturalism depicted the ways a character could become obsessed with love or money—depicted the neurotic compulsions built into the anxieties of modern life. Money is an important aspect of realism/naturalism because it is in keeping with the desire to quantify life. Naturalism was a philosophy of limits. Balzac's *La Peau de Chagrin* (*The Magic Skin* [1830]) is the story of an animal skin that shrinks a bit after each wish of its owner is fulfilled until finally it is all gone and the owner must die. Balzac's world involves a zero-sum game, a realm of physical limits, a fixed number to draw on, a win-lose situation.

George Gissing offers a slightly different version of the money theme. Gissing probably would have become a successful scholar of languages and the classics, except during his schooling he fell in love with a woman of the street, Nell Harrison (whom he later married), and was expelled when he was caught stealing to support her needs, including her alcoholism. Turning to fiction to make a living, Gissing wrote two early novels depicting the debilitating effects of poverty, albeit from a point of view that approaches social Darwinism. *Demos* (1886) portrays the failures that are an inevitable fact in the life of the working class, along with Gissing's fear of the mob. *The Nether World* (1888) depicts the dangers of socialism. Both novels reveal Gissing's perpetual desire for the good life and his disdain of the poor and the masses, especially when the masses are politically organized. While the subjects of Zola's fiction clearly influenced Gissing, he treated those subjects from a morally superior point of view that distanced his fiction from French naturalism.

Dreiser's view of money was closer to Balzac's: it was a giant force, stronger than familial love. Dreiser's world is controlled from beginning to end by money. Almost all relationships in his fiction are held together or broken by money and the influence that it can buy. In his story "Phantom Gold" (first published in 1921, later collected in *Chains* [1927]), he depicted the greed that beset the Queeder family when zinc deposits were discovered on what otherwise was their impoverished farm. Bursay Queeder—pitted against wife, son, and daughter—literally loses his mind in what becomes a free-fall play of avariciousness.

Like Balzac, Dreiser believed that there were material limits and saw the desire for ever more money as resulting necessarily in a zero-sum game. There are only so many slices to a pie, and if one person gets more, another gets less. Like so many of his contemporaries, Dreiser was aware of the growing gap between the rich and the poor. The Enlightenment may have promised the rise of a democratic society, but such a society was ultimately in the control of special interests. In a premarket economy, money follows power; in a market economy, power follows money.

5

As the city became more controlling, there was a tendency to idealize the meaning of the land. A number of writers felt that a life force emanated from the land and thus the soil was sacred. We find this theme in Knut Hamsun's *Growth of the Soil* (1917), O. E. Rölvaag's *Giants of the Earth* (1925), in both Dostoyevsky and Tolstoy, and in historians like Spengler, who carry over the romantic idea of the *Volk*, a sense of "blood" meaning stemming from a nationalized people. We can even find it in stories like Fitzgerald's "Absolution," where at the end we see vitalized farm girls ripening in the prairie sun.

The land was believed to be more fertile than the city and brought forth new life. And with this idea came the tendency to idealize rural people, to see them as separate and distinct from an urban population, and to characterize them as morally superior. One can find this tendency in both Europe and America. Thomas Jefferson gave us an American version of it in his desire for a yeoman aristocracy firmly rooted in the land. Rousseau's equivalent was his depiction of the noble savage.

Zola's belief that human nature was imperfect led to his realization that greed was not wholly an urban phenomenon. Yet, while he never idealized the peasant, he still believed in the redemptive power of the land, especially when the land was transformed by honest work. Work reclaimed the land in the name of self, created a basis for property separate from commercial and money values. The idealization of the land was in part a response to a growing industrial and urban process, in part the product of a belief that values had to be tempered through elemental experience, and in part due to nostalgia, a desire for a past time and a lost self.

6

The most radical change that took place in the late nineteenth century was with the concept of self. Under the influence of Darwin and his followers, the age had to reconcile itself to both the processes of evolution and devolution. While the Enlightenment had emphasized human rationality, evolution pointed to the animality on which it rested. As Freud (1856–1939) would later insist, human behavior stemmed as much from hidden as from rational motives, which accounted for obsessive and compulsive behavior as well as for both energized and inhibited libido.

Informed by a determined view of human nature, Freud's theories were consistent with elements of naturalism. Darwin early on impressed Freud, whose initial training was as a pathologist. Freud's theory of repression, of inhibition, of the affect of civilization on primitive instincts, of the animal basis of the crowd—these and his discussion of sexual taboos and the hidden meaning of dreams were of interest to the naturalists, especially Dreiser, who discussed these matters with A. A. Brill, the psychoanalyst who translated Freud in America. But at the center of Freud's theory is the idea of trauma, while a mechanistic notion that motives are the result of stimuli effecting an organism dominates much literary naturalism. For Freud, psychic injuries determine future behavior: motives come from within. For the naturalists, a given temperament responds to environmental stimuli: motives come from without.

Moreover, for the naturalists human development was subject to both the processes of decline and degeneration. Zola treated the comparative decline of the Rougon and Macquart families, while Norris and Dreiser depicted the fall of such individual characters as Vandover and Hurstwood, respectively, and Mann and Galsworthy treated the decline of a single family. Other novelists saw the process of decline in a social, historical, or cosmic context. Zola and Nathanael West depicted the crowd degenerating into the mob. As previously mentioned, Thomas Hardy's Jude picks up where George

Eliot's *Adam Bede* leaves off. Neither man ever comes to terms with the social forces working on him. Conrad's and Stephen Crane's stories gave voice to another idea, the belief that civilization concealed a cosmic force, one that typically worked destructively against human purpose, although sometimes a character, a Nietzschean overman like Balzac's Vautrin, was able to reconcile it to his enlarged pursuits. From *Tarzan* (1914) to *Lord of the Flies* (1954), these forces would be described variously.

The theory of evolution led to a belief in a divided self. The assumption was that an animality that created a force antagonistic to rational control and development complemented the human element. Robert Louis Stevenson's *Dr. Jekyll and Mr. Hyde* (1886) was one of the first novels to depict this divided self within one person. Earlier writers had used two separate characters in order to illustrate oppositional ideas. Dostoyevsky did it with Stavrogin and Pytor, Shatov and Kirillov; Twain with Huck and Tom, the prince and the pauper, Tom and Valet de Chamber; and Dickens with Magwitch and Compeyson, Joe Gargery and Orlick, Pip and Bentley Drummel. But after Stevenson's novel, more writers began portraying the oppositional aspects within the same character, leading to the divided self we find in Conrad's "Secret Sharer." Conrad's Mr. Kurtz embodies the civilized and the degenerative, as later will Tarzan, the product of both his aristocratic heritage and his ape-man rearing. Oscar Wilde depicted the divided self in *The Picture of Dorian Gray* (1890). Gray embodies two realities—a moral and an aesthetic, which in the novel become inverted. In an aesthetic bargain with the devil that calls to mind the Faust story, Dorian's portrait absorbs his moral lapses. His physical body (like a work of art) remains unaltered by time and moral transgressions—that is, until the novel's ending, when the reversal in physical-aesthetic being brings about Dorian's physical-moral transformation and his death.

In the more traditional naturalistic novels like Dreiser's *Sister Carrie* a second self is a residual part of the narrative. Dreiser postulated the existence of a second self within the individual. Hurstwood's decline stems from an inherent weakness that expresses itself under stress, especially once he no longer moves in the circles of conventional society. Carrie's rise springs from an element of self she discovers on the stage (indeed, on the stage, an actor or actress discovers another self within, projects another reality within the conventions of the drama). In *An American Tragedy* (1925), Clyde Griffiths is guided by his conventional rearing and by a second, demonic self that overpowers him.

As a sense of Western community gave way to a radical individualism, the novel began depicting transformations of character. The import of Napoleon's life, for example, took hold. Balzac depicted the rise of the "overman" in the character of Vautrin and Dostoyevsky in the character of Raskolnikov, both of whom would share the idea with Nietzsche. The feeling was that there were exceptional men—men of great force and genius—who were above the conventional laws of society, beyond good and evil, answerable only to themselves. The transformation of character into an overman parallels the transformation of the novel from comic realism to naturalism. The autonomous character was devoid of sentiment; beneficent human feelings no longer informed his or her motives; moral values stemmed from conventions, the false and contrived by-product of civilized society. Dostoyevsky showed the destructive nature of the overreacher. Just as the realistic/naturalistic novel depicted the extremes of society from its luxurious heights to its impoverished depths, the novel also depicted the extremes of individual life and consciousness. The overman believed that he could exploit the forces at work in nature, while the more ordinary person—often compulsively driven by a desire for love, sex, or money—tried to exert control over overpowering cosmic and social forces. The two extremes were simply the opposite side of the same coin.

7

Once writers made the city the locus of fiction, they began introducing a new subset of themes. The urban crowd itself becomes a major theme. There were three general ways of looking at the crowd. Gustave LeBon (1841–1931) showed how a crowd mentality transformed an individual state of mind and became the vehicle of a charismatic leader. Sigmund Freud showed how the crowd developed a consciousness and unconsciousness of its own, taking on an atavistic quality. And Elias Canetti (1905 –1994) argued that the crowd created a field of force that pulled a leader into its realm, the crowd creating the leader rather than vice versa.[4] By the late Victorian period, the crowd was being described as a faceless force. What these theories share is a changing concept of human nature in the aggregate, a different way of looking at mass humanity. One might think that the motivations of the crowd are a composite of those of the individuals who make it up, but recent studies reveal that the motivations arise out of the crowd itself and do not exist independently of it. In the feudal community, values—the product of hierarchal order— were embodied in the redemptive estate; in the post Darwinian community, such values—now the product of animal nature—were embodied in the destructive capacity of the crowd.

As early as George Eliot's *Middlemarch* (1871), the community has become a hostile force. In the stories of such American writers as Edgar Lee Masters and Sherwood Anderson, the small town has become even more antagonistic. In theory, the crowd was a force that mediated between the overman and the masses—a force one went beyond or which one was absorbed by. The crowd is also an important aspect of Zola's fiction. His crowd takes on an identity of its own, separate from the individuals that constitute it. It gives expression to an animality that defies human control, makes its behavior unpredictable. The crowd, only one step away from being a mob, could go in two possible directions—toward anarchy or toward a charismatic leader who could use the mob for his own political ends. Zola treated this theme in *Germinal* (1885), London in *The Iron Heel* (1908), Dreiser in his story "Nigger Jeff" (1899) and in the strike scene in *Sister Carrie,* and Nathanael West in *The Day of the Locust.*

8

Realism/naturalism came at a time of political violence in both Europe and America. Georges Sorel even wrote a book advocating the use of violence as a Syndicalist way of implementing a general strike. James, Conrad, Turgenev, Dostoyevsky, and Bely portrayed the anarchist threat to civilization. In novels like James's *The Princess Casamassima* (1886) and Bely's *St. Petersburg* (1913), the threat of political violence is deflected by aestheticism. Hyacinth Robinson refuses to carry out his anarchist mission once he realizes in St. Mark's Square that the heritage of the beautiful is more powerful than the destructive violence of the moment: that building a beautiful city is more important than destroying it. Thus, in a strange way, the violence of the anarchist movement is blunted by a revised notion of the romantic artist and by the rise of aestheticism.[5]

The romantic artist was a product of genius, inspired and privileged in almost godlike ways to bring the beautiful into being. The realist artist was more the product of his experience: he defied the transcendental explanations of the beautiful and went into the streets and public spaces to find the subject of his art, and then used his craft to render his observations. The impressionists painted railroad stations and clogged Parisian streets. In America, the Ashcan school went to the slums for their inspiration. Both Zola and Dreiser produced their version of these artists.

Eventually, aestheticism—the pursuit of the beautiful—would preempt the artistic theories of both the realists and the naturalists. *A Rebours* (*Against the Grain* [1844]) by Joris Karl Huysmans is perhaps the origin of this idea in literature. Des Esseintes wants life as artificial as art. But nature confounds him, tormenting him with a toothache, sickening him with rare perfumes, nauseating him with rich foods, forcing a return to society and nature. Despite Des Esseintes's failure, aesthetic ideas were quickly picked up by Walter Pater and Oscar Wilde and contributed to the idea of the artist in Mann's *Death in Venice* (1912) and Joyce's *A Portrait of the Artist* (1916).

The theme of the dandy was based on an aesthetic assumption—that the individual could be transformed into an art object. The idea of reinventing oneself ran through early modern literature from Mann's Tonio Kruger to Fitzgerald's Jay Gatsby. Dreiser's Carrie Meeber embodied the naturalistic expression of this theme. The recreated self was almost always an urban event, and the self who was recreated was often the urban detective.

9

As the city becomes more difficult to fathom, we get the detective who helps personalize it. It is not by chance that the detective novel is coincidental with the rise of the big city. From Dickens's Inspector

Bucket to Conrad's Inspector Heat, we have men who cut through the anonymity of the city, fathom its secrets, and help put it back on a human scale or protect its vital center. It is the vital center of the city that Arthur Conan Doyle's Sherlock Holmes seems to address. Holmes's world is set against the backdrop of the rise and the impending fall of the British Empire. London is not only the center of these novels; it is also the center of the world. And as Gibbon clearly showed, every empire weakens its center by giving its energies to the extremities. When the imperial city tries to control colonies all over the world, very seldom can the center hold. In a novel like *The Sign of Four* (1890), the evil comes into London from India—that is, from the far reaches of the empire. In *A Study in Scarlet* (1887), the evil comes from America, not literally part of the empire, but Doyle believed that the American Revolution was a historical accident and that the destinies of England and America were intertwined. Behind this, of course, was his belief in Anglo-Saxon and white supremacy and in Manifest Destiny. It is thus the function of the detective to protect the imperial center.

Sherlock Holmes embodies the system that he comes to protect. He is the man of reason, of science, of technology; he is from the upper class and was educated at Oxford; he eventually becomes rich; and he frequents the best city clubs and other haunts of the gentleman. *A Study in Scarlet* establishes a strange affinity between Jefferson Hope and Sherlock Holmes—the one, as his name suggests, the embodiment of the frontier dream; the other an urban sophisticate. The relationship between the two becomes symbiotic; Hope and Holmes, spawned by a historical moment, become cultural twins, preserving the spirit of the empire at both its extremity and its center, becoming the means by which the white man's destiny will be fulfilled. There is no better example of how narrative subforms are culturally encoded, the text itself inseparable from the historical meaning that informs it.

10

The popularity of the Sherlock Holmes stories in the late Victorian era was surpassed only by the popularity of Rider Haggard's novels.

Haggard's best-known novel is *She* (1887), which reflected the late Victorian interest in archaeology and anthropology that culminated with Frazer's monumental *The Golden Bough* (1890–1915). Perhaps at the extremities of the British Empire was an exotic realm like Kor that held ancient truths. Haggard brought together two narrative elements: a journey into the heart of central Africa with its mystery and intrigue, and a narrator who could interpret the significance of that realm. Haggard's novels tap a sense of the primitive and the mystery of faraway lands connected to imperial adventure. (Conrad in *Heart of Darkness* (1902) would make very different use of these elements.)

Another use of the primitive theme can be found in Kipling's *Captains Courageous* (1897), a story of imperial adventure written when Kipling was living in Vermont. When Harvey Cheyne, weak and sickly, falls overboard from an ocean liner on which he is traveling to Europe with his millionaire parents, he is picked up by Disko Troop, the fishing captain of *We're Here*. Harvey is transformed by the rigorous work and the discipline he must submit to aboard Troop's ship. (Jack London and Norris will make use of the same kind of plot device in *The Sea Wolf* [1904] and *Moran of the Lady Letty*). Harvey is initiated into a masculine realm distinct from that of his mother with her gentle, civilizing tendencies. When he is reunited with his parents, the boy has become a man. He can carry on in the spirit of his father, who came from poverty to conquer the West, helping to kill the Indians and to take control the land by running a railroad over it. In the novel, Kipling tells us that each generation of white men must rekindle a primitive kind of strength, must be challenged by the rudiments of nature if the white man is to fulfill his world-destiny.

11

A thin layer separates the primitive from the civilized, producing the racial bias that runs through fantasy literature. The Caucasian race is deemed superior to all others, and yet the white race has to be tempered by exposure to the elemental if it is to realize its superiority. Another fantasy version of this racial idea is Edgar Rice Burroughs's *Tarzan of the Apes*. One wonders whether in connecting man and the ape, Burroughs was building on Darwinian assumptions of evolution. One also wonders how deeply Rudyard Kipling's *The Jungle Book* (1894) might have influenced Burroughs. Set in an imperial context, *The Jungle Book* also depicts a jungle boy raised by animals who eventually demonstrates his superior powers of intellect and strength in the course of becoming civilized.

The difference between the jungle and the modern city is the code of behavior to which its inhabitants adhere and their state of mind. Both city and jungle involve a struggle for survival, albeit expressed differently. Like Kipling's jungle boy, once Tarzan lives for a time in the primitive animal world, he becomes wise in the ways of the jungle. His aristocratic origin, vitalized by the elemental realm, assures superiority in both the city and the jungle, as later versions of his story will reveal.

The idea here—that the primitive realm tempers the civilized soul—had wide application at this time. Burrough's Africa, Owen Wister's West, London's Far North, Kipling's India and high seas, and Hemingway's arena (from bullfight to big game hunt) became testing grounds for courage, where civilized values were transformed into something more noble, albeit primitive.

12

The connection between Kipling and Hemingway illuminates a spectrum of cultural meaning in realist writing. Kipling's early works celebrate British discipline and justify imperialism in the name of moral duty. Kipling was a product of his Victorian culture. He believed in the gospel of work, Progress through technology, Darwinian evolution, and regeneration through imperialistic conquest. In America he witnessed the closing of the frontier and the rise of the city, which he despised wherever he found it. With the city came immigration from Eastern Europe and intolerable ghettos, which, despite his tolerance for imperialism, led to his criticism of living and working conditions. Kipling became less rigid over time and softened his militaristic code in later works. As Edmund Wilson has pointed out, "Kipling [lost] his hatred. . . . His soldiers [were] no longer so cocky, so keen to kill inferior peoples, so intent on the purposes of Empire."[6]

Kipling portrays a change in the mind that confronts the imperialist world. There is now reciprocity between mind and reality—a willingness to concede limits. Hemingway begins where Kipling ends, albeit depicting a more hostile environment. As Wilson points out in a separate essay, the two worlds of Nick Adams—the world of the Michigan woods and the world of war—are really one and the same. Has not Nick "found in the butchery abroad the same world that he knew back in Michigan? Was not life in the Michigan woods equally destructive and cruel?"[7]

One can extrapolate from Wilson's point. Like Kipling who represents the way a state of mind can be brought to bear on reality, the way one can apply mental discipline to a task, Hemingway portrays an antagonist reality and takes as his subject the ability to engage it, to mentally confront it. In *A Farewell to Arms* (1929) the reality engaged is war, and Hemingway emphasizes the absurdity of combat; in *Death in the Afternoon* (1932) it is the bullfight—man against an animal force that embodies death; in *The Green Hills of Africa* (1935) the hostile reality is the big-game hunt; in *To Have and Have Not* (1937) the enemy is a decadent society; in *For Whom the Bell Tolls* (1940) decadence is replaced by fascism; in *The Old Man and the Sea* (1952) an engaged combat between man and the marlin is altered when the code of the sea is broken by the rapacious sharks. Each novel offers a different reality, albeit each a force that must be confronted by a state of mind. True to the assumptions of naturalism, Hemingway's nature does not change; but unlike in the naturalistic novel, the neo-stoical mind that confronts that reality is up to the occasion: mind overturns reality.

There is thus a synergy, a dynamic connection, between a hostile world and the mental capacity needed to confront it. The stories of Jack London mediate the difference between Kipling and Hemingway. By including a graphic dimension in his stories that is missing from Kipling's, London in effect brings Kipling into conjunction with Hemingway. Kipling's reality rests on romantic imperialism. London pictures nature as an ambivalent force that can transform humanity for better or worse. Hemingway's reality splits the difference. Nature, when not a harbinger of death, is a fundamental task that has to be faced; society, when not a decadent force, is a hostile challenge. The source of hostility in realism is varied; emanating from the elemental, social, and political realms. Whereas antagonism in the social and political world raises questions about civilization, that in the elemental world raises questions about evolution itself. Built into naturalism were the dichotomies of the age. On one side stood regeneration, the triumph within a primitive realm and the therapeutic effect of living close to nature; on the other was degeneration, an inability to restore oneself when caught in the process of physical decline.

13

What often goes unnoticed is that late Victorian writers like Kipling and Stevenson had latent fears about the effects of imperialism. Although the bulk of his writing celebrated imperialism, Kipling had residual doubts about its dynamics, seeing it as a tenuous extension of childhood fantasy. In his cryptic short story, "The Brushwood Boy" (1895), Kipling depicts George Cottar who comes from a privileged family and who, after attending the best public schools, becomes an officer in the army stationed in India, where he distinguishes himself in battle that preserves the imperial reach. Kipling treats at length George's childhood, especially his relationship with family and the influence of his schooling, because they speak to the value systems out of which come the romantic elements that underpin imperialism. George's responsibilities as an imperial officer separate him from his men, and an essential loneliness dominates his life, relieved only by his romantic expectations. When George returns to England, he finds that the girl of his dreams lives in reality on an adjoining estate; she also has independently shared the same dream. The dream suggests that there is a destiny behind both individual and national lives—and this destiny is grounded in fantasy. Put differently, a hidden self reduces the imperial dream to childish romance.

Kipling's doubts regarding the perpetuity of imperialism extended beyond his thinking that it might well be a fantasy. He also thought that there was a fundamental contradiction between what he believed were British and Indian cultural values. As a British citizen born and reared in India, he saw the impossibility of imposing

Anglicized values on an Indian culture. British culture was held together by conventions that subjected the individual to forces of social control. Conventions, the glue that held society in place, ultimately gave way to Law, based on the code of honor (loyalty, bravery, and generosity), which engendered civilization.

What Kipling depicted as fantasy, Robert Louis Stevenson depicted more realistically in *The Beach of Falesa* (1892), the story of two South Sea traders who come to a paradisal island, one to corrupt it, the other to save it from European exploitation. Case has murdered competing agents on the island and protects his copra mining interests (copra is dried coconut meat yielding coconut oil) by intimidating the natives with a feared shrine composed of luminously painted masks as frightening as the shrieks that come from the wind passing through an Aeolian harp, its power stemming from a religious mystique that holds a culture enthralled. Like Kipling, Stevenson suggests a childlike-form of play is at work in imperialism. Nevertheless, John Wiltshire exposes this fraudulent shrine and dynamites the mine before he kills Case. Wiltshire finds himself drawn in a direction opposite to what had brought him to the island in the first place. He had come to it in search of European company and in the hope of making enough money to return to England to buy a pub, but he ends up marrying a native woman and reconciling himself to spending the rest of his life on the island.

Whereas, in *Heart of Darkness*, Conrad shows what happens when the laws of civilization are relaxed, Stevenson in *The Beach of Falesa* shows what happens when the rapaciousness of colonization is intensified. Kurtz falls victim to the barbarism he finds in the jungle and in himself. His look into the abyss offers him a cosmic revelation into the mysteries of the universe. Wiltshire challenges neither the principles of civilization nor those of the primitive island. His anger is directed at the debasement of colonialism, where the copra trade is undertaken at the expense of the natives in an exchange that does not benefit but rather exploits them. Despite the initial difference between Wiltshire and Kurtz, the end results are the same: both Conrad and Stevenson bear witness to the process of corruption that is set in motion when civilized motives are undermined by being confronted with or superimposed on primitive reality.

14

The sequence of subjects realism addressed as it developed gave rise
to the subgenres of the novel. The realist novel paralleled and embodied the historical transformations of Western culture, and often
a subgenre in one country or culture would find an equivalent in
another country or culture undergoing similar historical transformations. For example, the British novel of imperial adventure had
its cultural counterpart in the American Western. Indeed, Kipling's
Captains Courageous supplies the connection between these two subgenres in its celebration of the imperial spirit of America, which
Kipling saw as the next mighty Western power. The fishing banks of
New England and Nova Scotia try men's strength and courage and
create a natural aristocracy. The Western, like the novel of imperial
adventure, grew out of the conflict between the city and the frontier
or the wilderness. There was the need for man to impose his will on
the land, to tame it, and thereby create wealth and power for himself
(the ur-story here is *Robinson Crusoe*).

The myth of the cowboy was primarily a literary matter. In reality
the cowboy's life was humdrum and ordinary: he herded cows, built
and repaired fences, and performed other daily chores. The subgenre
of the western introduced conflict—an element of the dramatic—
into this matter-of-fact existence and gave the cowboy an identity
that connected him with the romance of the frontier and the taming
of the West. Novels like Owen Wister's *The Virginian* (1902) and Jack
Schaefer's *Shane* (1949) codified this idea. They defined the cowboy
in semiheroic terms—depicted him as rugged individualist, independent of spirit, dedicated to the land and its physical and moral
transforming powers.

Both *The Virginian* and *Shane* are set against the same landscape,
and both involve the Johnson County wars in Wyoming between the
big ranch owners and the homesteaders. The novels depict this battle
from two different points of view, *The Virginian* from the point of
view of the ranch owners, *Shane* from the point of view of the
homesteaders. The same narrative formula is used to express two different social perspectives. What these two works share is the common belief that the land must be tamed. To conquer the land one has

to prove oneself in action by carrying the Virginian (that is, Jeffersonian) idea of aristocracy and honor across the country and creating in the West a new, natural aristocracy based on the test of courage and trial by ordeal (as in the works of Hemingway). After his ordeal, the Virginian remains on the land, marries, and becomes domesticated. After his ordeal, Shane, the loner, moves on—staying, like Cooper's Natty Bumppo, one step ahead of the frontier and the women who are trying to domesticate him.

The intersection between an idealized Western world and the more debased world of naturalism has been well studied by Mary Lawlor in *Recalling the Wild* (2000). Lawlor charts the rise of a mythic West in the "westernism" of Daniel Boone and James Fenimore Cooper. For a new generation of writers, including Frank Norris, Jack London, Stephen Crane, and Willa Cather, the Turner thesis that the frontier was gone served to undermine an idealized image of the West, which they replaced with a less romantic reality. The West of romance gave way to the West as a physical place, a product of material forces. One set of fictions competed with another.[8] There would next be an urban transformation of the idea of the West and its cowboy.

15

When this stereotype hits land's end on the West Coast, he becomes Raymond Chandler's Marlowe (as in Christopher Marlow and Thomas Malory, whose works invoke medieval chivalry). Chandler's loner, however, is not a chivalric cowboy, like the Virginian, but a hard-boiled detective, inseparable from the corrupted city that he engages in combat. Like the cowboy, he is an outsider—lonely, chaste, motivated by a desire to undo the corrupting of America—but the urban story he tells is a bit more cynical, his ideals a bit more tenuous, and his accomplishments a bit more morally dubious, which reflects the eroding of cultural values as they moved west, the collapse of a dream, the literary expression of which was the hard-boiled detective story.

Chandler's fiction has been connected with the *roman noir*. The principal characters in a noir story live on the edge of democratic society. The women are often femme fatales. They are usually out to destroy one man or another and have no desire to marry, settle down, or raise a family. The family, in fact, often serves as front for social respectability. The father in *The Big Sleep* (1939) will protect his daughter from the law or from blackmailers (the two are often the same) more because he wants to protect his own reputation than to preserve the integrity of the family. He hires the noir detective, a social outcast himself, because he believes that he can control him and use him as scapegoat. The noir novel with its antihero (now an inverted embodiment of the prototypical cowboy) takes us to the very margins of democratic society—to marginal men and women living by their wits. Once they are further socially alienated, they will become the drifters in James M. Cain, the seekers in Kerouac, the homeless derelicts in Nelson Algren and William Kennedy, and the family outcasts in Joyce Carol Oates.[9]

16

The idea of realism owes much to regional writing. "Local color" fiction—especially the local color fiction of the 1880s and 1890s by writers like Mary Wilkins Freeman and Sarah Orne Jewett—offered portraits of the small New England towns. As Michael Davitt Bell has suggested, this fiction is characterized by the absence of masculine activity because many young men had left the town for the city or the West. Bell argues that local color fiction deviated radically from Howells's realism and Norris's naturalism, and a novel like Jewett's *The Country of the Pointed Firs* (1896) resolves its own tradition of realism by divesting its heroine of the ambition that, when frustrated, leads to dissatisfaction. Thus transformed, the heroine can affirm a community of women.[10] The depiction of local color, however, went beyond New England: Dreiser provided a portrait of Indiana, Lewis of Minnesota, Masters of Illinois, Stribling of Tennessee, Suckow of Iowa, Cather of Nebraska, Glasgow of Virginia, Robinson of Maine, bringing us full circle. The image of America in these portraits is often bleakly realistic.[11]

Most of the commentators on local color see the realistic method as a given and regard the emphasis on "place" and "realism" as mutually reinforcing. Taken together, the uses of place in the American novel tell a coherent story about the loss of the frontier, the significance of the small town in America (those that survived after the frontier moved on), and the rise of the city that became the next order of human life. Novelists like Willa Cather analyzed the meaning of the (lost) frontier. Edgar Lee Masters, Sherwood Anderson, and Sinclair Lewis depicted the nature of life in the small town in psychological terms that distinguished their stories from Jewett's. And Theodore Dreiser, F. Scott Fitzgerald, and Nathanael West described the transition from one realm to another in novels like *Sister Carrie, The Great Gatsby,* and *The Day of the Locust.* These novels catch the spirit of why people were leaving the small town in the early part of the twentieth century. They also catch the urgency that the frontier dream still had, even if its reality was that of the mirage.

Willa Cather depicted the pioneer immigrants who were attracted to Nebraska after the Civil War by the free land that the Homestead Act of 1862 made available to people who would move out west. The Union Pacific Railroad had been completed by 1869. The Burlington route entered southern Nebraska. The decade from 1870 to 1880 brought thousands of settlers to the Nebraska prairie. *My Ántonia* (1918) describes their lives as a people both alone and part of a community. They were alone on the land, and yet more easily assimilated into a community than those immigrants in the city. Many were destroyed by the experience, such as Mr. Shimerda, whose homesickness for Bohemia led him to commit suicide. Many survived by simply enduring it—especially Ántonia, who not only perseveres but also sustains her husband (in a way her mother could not sustain her father) until a second generation is firmly in place.

Cather depicts the frontier as the true melting pot of America. People have to work together to survive. Whatever prejudices they bring from the Old World get resolved in the process of establishing a new community. As we move away from the frontier into the town, prejudices become more difficult to resolve. As he moves further and further away from the land, Jim Burden feels more diminished. Once again, there is the suggestion that the land is special. The road had taken him in a circle. Although he has moved far beyond Ántonia's world, he has been conditioned by both the land and the past that he shared with her and will always be different from other city dwellers and the better for it.

If the frontier is still a reality in the novels of Willa Cather, it has become a mirage in *The Grapes of Wrath* (1939) by John Steinbeck. Steinbeck believed America had been changed by the rise of a strong banking system and machine farming. His novel deals with the descendents of those who came to Oklahoma in search of free farmland. In the thirties, the drought dried up the overworked land and the Depression led to farm foreclosures, sending the farmers west to California. The Joad family—three generations strong—was among this group who pioneered to a second frontier. The California farm owners exploited this situation by advertising for farm workers, the abundance of which drove down farm wages. The Joads's trip is compared to the biblical search for the Promised Land, except now there is no Promised Land. The new frontier turns out to lack reality—long closed despite the false promise that it is still open.

17

What took the place of the frontier was the small town, Sherwood Anderson's subject. It found its best expression in *Winesburg, Ohio* (1919), which was influenced by Howe's *Story of a Country-Town* (1884) as well as by Twain, Masters, Turgenev, and Gertrude Stein. Anderson's work also owes much to both D. H. Lawrence's philosophy of the liberating nature of primitivism and unrepressed sex— ideas reinforced by Freudian theory. Anderson influenced both Hemingway and Faulkner, although Hemingway turned against him and satirized his fiction in *Torrents of Spring* (1926). *Poor White* (1920) and *Dark Laughter* (1925) were written after he lost his major talent.

Winesburg, Ohio is an exercise in psychological realism moving toward the grotesque. The grotesque involves the inversion of natural process, and what is inverted in these small, Midwestern town stories is sex. Puritanism has taken hold of the inhabitants, who have lost their natural instincts, and the stories are a catalogue of inhibited behavior. George Willard, the narrator, sees unhappy marriage (his parents'), repressed homosexuality, flight from sexual commitment, and voyeurism (the minister's). The town's young women, lacking instinct, make romantic mistake after mistake: they desire love but are afraid of sex, or they give themselves to someone they do not love. He sees no reason to stay in Winesburg after his mother dies, and so, like countless of his contemporaries, he leaves for the big city.

Dark Laughter is another attempt to address the matter of repression. John Stockton longs for a more instinctual life, as stereotypically embodied by the blacks and their "dark laughter." Anderson substitutes primal impulses for the God that both he and Stockton reject. The closest Stockton comes to this uninhibited freedom is an affair with Aline Grey, whose pregnancy necessitates that they leave Old Harbor. What lies ahead the novel never says, but Anderson's romantic belief that happiness waits beyond repression was in part the basis of Hemingway's ridicule of his work in *Torrents of Spring*.

Anderson was working the literary vein of D. H. Lawrence. A new industrial age and Christian restrictions created a population displaced emotionally and cut off from its natural instincts. Like Thomas Wolfe or Jack Kerouac after him, Anderson believed that sexual freedom could be found on the road, and, working the Freudian belief that modern humanity had lost contact with its sexuality, he thought that, once free of small-town restrictions, one would be able to discover the ineffable, which lay beyond. Today, Anderson's novel reads like a parody of itself, especially in its insistence that lost sexual freedom can be found in some ethnic realm.

Besides treating the sexual repression that characterizes Puritan America, Anderson also described the influence of the machine on man's natural feelings. In *Poor White* (1920) Hugh McVey invents an automatic sowing machine, builds a factory to produce it, and soon the small town of Bidwell, Ohio, has been transformed into an industrial city, a phenomenon that was occurring nation wide. Anderson depicts a radical transformation in American culture. Hugh's marriage to Clara reconciles her Puritanism and his Pioneerism, to use Van Wyck Brooks's terms, at the same time as the machine changes the very nature of what we mean by labor.[12] The machine now mediated contact with the land. Anderson's realism stemmed from romantic assumptions: he connected sexual energy with the land and saw it pitifully transformed by the rise of the machine.

Another anatomy of a Midwestern town is *Spoon River Anthology* (1915) by Edgar Lee Masters, a collection of poetic sketches, probably of Lewiston, Illinois, where Masters studied law in his father's office before moving to Chicago. From a cemetery on a hill, more than two hundred citizens return from the dead to record their memories of themselves, the town, and others. Their stories reveal corruption, adultery, abortion, suicide, and general town intrigue. Masters exposes a subterranean world, digging beneath the respectable surface of the small town, often thought of in ideal terms, to reveal its naturalistic reality—that is, to reveal the imperfections that abide in the human animal. Masters' work gives us the history of the town (anticipating William Carlos Williams's *Paterson* [1946–58]). The failure of the bank, stemming from the president and his son recklessly investing the bank's money in the wheat market, is a central concern and a carry-over theme from Norris's *The Pit* (1903). The sketches move from those of ostensibly reputable citizens to those who have been publicly shamed, even as the most respectable and most disrespectable citizens turn out to be morally on a par. Masters often uses one poem to silently comment on another, as when Elsa Wertman confesses her employer fathered her child, and then in the next poem the son honors his father and putative mother. Or the tale of Roscoe Purkapile, who is convinced his wife believes his story of why he disappeared for a year, but whose wife tells the reader in the next poem that she knows that he had run off with Mrs. Williams, the milliner. In moving from the depiction of individual self-righteousness to that of the town's collective awareness, Masters generates a new realism, undercutting the sentimentality that heretofore was a stock part of the way the small town was portrayed.

One of the most vivid portraits of the small town can be found in Sinclair Lewis's *Main Street* (1920), an American version of the Madame Bovary story. Flaubert took a provincial French woman, filled her with romantic passion gleaned from books, encouraged her to become disillusioned with her small-minded doctor-husband, and allowed her to destroy herself in the course of seeking romantic and material happiness. Lewis takes a Midwestern woman, endows her with idealist expectations, and turns her loose in small-town America, where she soon is unhappy with her conventional doctor-husband

and frustrated that she cannot change the values of her community. Just as Emma Bovary could not escape provincial France, Carol Kennicott cannot escape provincial America. After an unsuccessful retreat to Washington, D.C., she returns to Gopher Prairie, no longer in pursuit of some ephemeral ideal. She comes to realize that happiness is not something to be sought as an end in itself but as a by-product of experience—even the experience of the small town. Lewis's description of small-town America was both knowing and convincing: the small-town left a lot to be desired, but if one did not try to make it into what it was not, it could offer its own modest satisfactions. In the tradition of realism/naturalism, Lewis concludes that environment is stronger than personal character, and in the battle between the two, it is character, especially character informed by unrealistic ideals, which must give way.

18

The theme of the small town anticipates the theme of history as a force that interrupts the processes of nature in grotesque ways. The naturalistic novel moved beyond the conventional novel, depicted disruptive social entanglements, and engendered the subgenre of dystopia—novels of ideas that depicted a realm of political force, sometimes out of control. Thematically such novels looked back to those of Zola, Norris, and Dreiser. Zola had seen that the technological/industrial society depended on efficiency and that such efficiency demanded a control that anticipated totalitarianism. Dreiser's belief in political force—his distrust of capitalism and wariness of fascism—drew him toward communism (as he saw it, only one totalitarian force was strong enough to combat another and social justice better rested with the Left). Zola's mob, like Nathanael West's, reveals the potentiality for anarchy when undirected, and the capacity for fascism when controlled.

Edward Bellamy in *Looking Backward*, overlooking the political dangers of an engineer-dictator who could mislead the masses, saw the new technological society as the solution. Ignatius Donnelly in *Caesar's Column* expressed concern over industrial might and the new political power it brought into being. Jack London treated the same themes in *The Iron Heel*. Like Bellamy and Donnelly before him and Norman Mailer after him, London was concerned with how wealth generated by the industrial revolution could result in misdirected political power. The anxiety over where science and technology were going led to fantasy projections of naturalistic assumptions. H. G. Wells and George Orwell (as we shall see in chapter 6) advanced this aspect of the naturalistic narrative.

4

A Field of Force: The Biological Model

1

Industrial change was accompanied by a shift from a religious to a secular culture. Under the influence of Darwin and his followers like Herbert Spencer, T. H. Huxley, and John Tyndall, the old religious truths were being questioned. The authenticity of the Bible and the myth of creation competed with the science of geology and the new biology. The new science insisted on a universe that went back at least ten billion years in which modern man evolved out of the primate world as a different species, having existed according to recent fossil finds for 160,000 years, 230,000 at the most if Neanderthal man can be classified as *homo sapiens.*

Charles Darwin reinforced the plausibility of the preexistent biological idea that species have a mechanism enabling them to evolve, supplying the empirical evidence previously lacking in this theory. Darwin promulgated his views in two major books—*On the Origin of Species by Means of Natural Selection* (1859) and *The Descent of Man* (1871). These studies accompanied the rise of literary naturalism and explain the extraordinary emphasis writers like Zola, Norris, and Dreiser put on the idea of evolution, especially hereditary descent.

The Renaissance Chain of Being anticipated Darwinian thought: it presumed a gradation of life from the lowest to the highest. The difference—and it is an essential difference—is that the Chain of Being is static, while Darwin's theory rests on the idea of matter in motion, the notion that one form of life transforms into another. The tree can be used as a metaphor for conveying Darwin's thinking about natural selection. The tree is a part of nature as an organic whole; it takes its being from the soil (that is, adapts to its environment); and each tree is part of a larger species of trees that make up a forest.

Darwin came to believe that the human species evolved out of primate life. Today we know that there are small biological differences among primates. Just beneath humans on the evolutionary ladder are chimpanzees, gorillas, and orangutans. Darwin's suspicions anticipated modern conclusions: at least ninety-five percent of the genetic material of humans and chimpanzees is identical, they have similar blood types and brain structures, and they show similar behavior in the first three years of life.

Darwin's insight into the nature of evolution was advanced by his journey around the world as the unpaid naturalist aboard the *Beagle*. The general assumption at that time—disputed by such early theorists as Lamarck and Erasmus Darwin—was that God was the source of all creation and that each species was immutable or unchanging. But Darwin saw variations within the same species, which cast doubt on this conclusion. He noticed that the natives on oceanic islands resembled the inhabitants of the nearest continents. For example, those on the Cape Verde Islands resembled natives found in Africa, while those on the Galapagos Islands resembled those of South America. Moreover, he noticed that on the Galapagos Islands, ground finches with different kinds of beaks lived on different foods, suggesting that each breed within a species adapted differently to the conditions of an environment, independently of divine design. Darwin demonstrated how an organism's mechanism was directly connected to its capacity to adapt to its surroundings. The organisms that adapted survived and reproduced; those that did not either died or left fewer offspring. Since the environment continued to change, each species also continued to change in ways that best suited it.

Darwin was greatly influenced by two of his contemporaries. He read Sir Charles Lyell's *Principles of Geology*, in which Lyell (1797–1875) noted changes in fossil remains, thus suggesting a process of evolution or at least a change in life forms. And he was intrigued by Malthus's observations that more individuals of each species are born than can survive. Darwin put the two observations together:

each species must adapt to its environment to survive, and some within the species will do better than others. Life is an evolutionary process based on the necessity of adaptation.

Darwin's ideas involved the relationship between genotype and phenotype. Genotype is the sum total of inherited possibilities of the species; phenotype are individual traits expressed in the interplay between genotype and the environment. What the individual inherits is the capacity to develop certain traits within a specific environment. Genetically, some within the species will adapt; others will not. Literary naturalism involves the study of both possibilities, although the emphasis is usually on the latter.

The account just outlined provides the traditional interpretation of the way Darwin's ideas unfolded: Darwin put the emphasis on natural selection, Mendel supplied a theory of genetics that provided the missing piece, and then the two theories were synthesized. This explanation is the basis for the historical accounts found in books like Loren Eiseley's *Darwin's Century* (1958) and Ernst Mayr's *The Growth of Biological Thought* (1982).[1] A variation on this theory is that of Peter J. Bowler, who argues that Darwin's notebooks and letters suggest he was far more influenced than is believed today by the theories of non-Darwinian naturalists like Jean-Baptiste Lamarck. Bowler also maintains that Darwin, seeking to preserve a teleological view of nature, proposed a more progressive idea of evolution than we had previously thought. Consequently, Bowler argues, Mendel's thinking has to be seen as more revolutionary in relation to Darwin's ideas than it hitherto had been. As Bowler puts it, "the advent of genetics has to be seen, not as filling a gap in Darwin's thinking, but as a significant break with the developmental view of evolution that prevailed up to that point."[2]

However this dispute may be resolved, later thinkers did not undergo a radical change in Darwinian belief; rather the differences among early and later thinkers was a matter of emphasis. Clearly Darwin's ideas were revolutionary and much evidence had been adduced to support them long before the importance of Mendel's theories was recognized. Darwin's ideas and their progeny were both a continuation of and a challenge to Enlightenment assumptions. On the one hand, Darwin reinforced a belief in the material—that is, physical—nature of reality. On the other hand, his ideas gave rise to a theory of nature and society as realms of force affecting the general population and limiting the individual. Thus the Enlightenment idea of the individual as free to create him- or herself was seriously diminished. As a theory of evolution, Darwinism put emphasis on the physical processes of the universe, reinforcing the mechanistic belief that matter unfolds in time. But as a theory of natural selection—that is, the theory that species change by adapting to their immediate environment—Darwinism suggested that the unfolding of matter in time was accidental rather than necessary, seriously challenging the notion of design. Even as qualified by Bowler, a theory of adaptation goes a long way in challenging the assumption that evolution is always a form of progress. That species adapt to their environment is connected to a process of survival, but the change in the species may not, in absolute terms, be for the better. But Bowler is correct in insisting that at the time there were theorists who argued that such change resulted in a species moving onward and upward. Among the most important advocates of this belief was Herbert Spencer.

2

Herbert Spencer was an English sociologist and philosopher, who early supported the theory of evolution. He became a close friend of Marianne Evans (the novelist George Eliot) as well as of T. H. Huxley and J. S. Mill. Spencer wanted a scientific summa to replace the theological summa of the Middle Ages. His *First Principles* (1855) maintained that there was a fundamental law of matter, which he called the law of the persistence of force. In his early works, he argued evolution was limited to inherited traits. When Charles Darwin and Alfred Russel Wallace (1823–1913) introduced their theory of natural selection, Spencer abandoned his inheritance theory and accepted their explanation, coining the phrase the "survival of the fittest." Spencer believed that the second law of thermodynamics applied to biological and social systems as well as to physical systems. Evolution affected energy as well as matter: correspondences existed through all levels of reality.

His main work was *The Synthetic Philosophy* (1862), dealing with biology, psychology, morality, and sociology. Spencer saw human society evolving by means of an increasing division of labor from the communal organization of hordes, characteristic of primitive life, to the increasing individuation found in sedentary societies, characteristic of civilization. Social evolution involved moving from an authoritarian society, needed to maintain harmony and public defense, toward a more liberal society, in which industrial prosperity freed the individual from the authority of the state. A major concern of Spencer throughout his career was how a balance could be struck between individualism and altruism, between self-preservation and community welfare. He eventually concluded that in the course of civilized progression, humanity would postpone immediate gratification and develop altruistic responses that would benefit the general good. Spencer thus differentiated two forces at work in modern society: the military, in which cooperation was secured by force, and the industrial, in which cooperation was voluntary. He argued that society must guarantee the individual-communal balance. Liberalism limited the power of monarchy and other forms of authoritarian government, but he saw that it in turn could be threatened by new forms of modern power such as the "coming slavery" of totalitarianism. He compared animal organisms to human society, seeing parallels between the human body and centralized government—for example, between arteries and roads and nerve endings and telegraph and telephone connections. Many of his ideas became the basis for social anthropology.

A beneficiary of Spencer's philosophy was Theodore Dreiser. His story "McEwan of the Shining Slave Makers" is a fantasy in which a human who has been transformed into an ant participates in the jungle struggle between colonies of black and red ants and comes to the realization that communal effort must take precedence over rugged individualism. The conflict between the needs of the community and the desires of the individual was a social problem the resolution of which was one of Spencer's major concerns. Despite his thinking on altruism, Spencer's notion of the survival of the fittest led to the philosophy of social Darwinism, a radical individualism. Dreiser's

Carrie Meeber embodies such self-interest and desire for individual survival, an attitude that Robert Ames persuades her to modify by novel's end and that Dreiser repudiated in his later years.

Spencer's philosophy is a combination of nineteenth-century mechanistic and romantic assumptions. Like the mechanists, Spencer believed that we live in a world composed of matter in motion, the natural process of which is both repeatable and hence describable in scientific terms. Like the romantics, Spencer also believed that nature symbolically reflected its inner meaning, so to read the universe was to read the unfolding of nature and to understand the correspondences that existed between the human and, say, the animal world.

The key to Spencer's philosophy was his belief in force, not a life force as in Bergson (1859–1941), where the impetus comes from within, but a force that emanated from without. Spencer believed that life was a moving equilibrium, a balance between external and internal forces. This theory of equilibrium or balance was central to the ideas of Dreiser, who saw life as combat between order and chaos, wealth and poverty, the beautiful and the ugly, regeneration and degeneration. Physical forces limit ability for unrestrained action, but as one becomes more powerful one can go beyond those limits, at least to a point. The moment of stasis creates a reversal in the flow of matter, and a process of dissolution occurs. Dissolution is evolution in reverse. After equilibrium has been reached, reverse motion occurs, and organization gives way to disorganization, definiteness into indefiniteness.

Thus, while the fate of the individual is cyclical (a process of birth and growth leading toward maturity, followed by physical and mental decline leading toward death), the fate of the race is progressive. The idea of cycles within the march of time was central to Spencer's belief in evolution: mankind was advancing even as the individual was circumscribed by physical limits. Spencer believed that all matter was passing from homogeneity to heterogeneity—from the more simple toward the more complex, at which point stasis would occur, followed by dissolution and the creation of new homogeneous forms, as the cycle repeated itself.[3]

Society is a mechanistic unit subject to undirected physical or man-made force. As barometric high and low pressure determine the weather, institutional forces determine social conditions, and these forces are inseparable from the workings of nature. Not even gigantic cities can escape this elemental relationship. We are all affected by harvests and droughts: a bad wheat crop affects every member of a society. As in nature, the fittest will survive and creatures insufficiently adaptable will be eliminated.

In America, the idea of the survival of the fittest was opposed by Lester Ward (1841–1913), whose *Dynamic Sociology* (1883) proposed a social evolution that would stem from the mind—that is, from a planned society that would move history in beneficent ways. His ideas helped modify those of William Graham Sumner (1840–1910), an American advocate of Spencer's belief in the survival of the fittest and laissez-faire. Sumner's response to Ward was *Folkways* (1907), which argued that the irrational nature of folk customs negated planned social reform.

A close friend of Spencer and another important interpreter of Darwin was Thomas Henry Huxley (1825–1895). At the age of twenty-one, Huxley voyaged, much like Darwin, to the South Seas on the *H. M. S. Rattlesnake,* and collected biological specimens. Darwin sought out Huxley's opinion before he published *The Origin of Species* (1859), and for the next decade Huxley became his stalwart defender, earning the title "Darwin's bulldog." His major works helped create the intellectual environment that led to literary naturalism. They are *Evidence as to Man's Place in Nature* (1863), *Protoplasms: The Physical Basis of Life* (1869), *Science and Culture* (1881), *Evolution and Ethics* (1893), and *Collected Essays* (1894–1908). Dreiser supposedly read his *Science and the Hebrew Tradition* (1894) and *Science and the Christian Tradition* (1909), along with Tyndall's *Fragments of Science* (1897).

With the new science came the scientific method for testing reality: truth became that which could be experimentally verified, and conclusions were constantly being retested to see if they would hold up under changed circumstances. This wholly new way of looking at reality influenced the literary imagination as well as the scientific mind. Along with the rise of individualism and the materialism that accompanied a commercial-industrial society, the new science helped supply the tenets that grounded literary realism and later literary naturalism.

In America William James early in his career fell under the influence of Herbert Spencer's *First Principles* before he repudiated the
idea of force with the help of C. S. Peirce. John Fiske (1842–1910),
who became the American spokesman for Spencer from 1870 to
the end of the century, better carried Spencer's ideas. Fiske's major
work was the encyclopedic two-volume *Outline of Cosmic Philosophy*
(1874). Fiske believed human progress stemmed from evolution, and
evolution from the persistence of a cosmic force. Like Spencer, Fiske
spoke of matter in motion. Society developed away from militarism
and toward industrialism, paralleled by authority giving way to individualism, selfishness to altruism and forms of sympathy. Both
Spencer and Fiske diverged from strict Darwinian theory in their belief that nature was working toward the perfection of humanity. And
Fiske went beyond both Spencer and Darwin when he claimed that
evolution didn't merely account for the genesis of the species but
also guaranteed the progress of civilization. Along with Spencer,
Fiske would have a strong impact on American literary naturalism,
especially on the works of Jack London.

3

At the same time that the influence of Darwin was being felt in Europe and America, an anti-Darwinian movement was also at work.
The effect of anti-Darwinism in the literary realm was to undermine
the emphasis on scientific observation and promote an interest in
narrative subjectivity and impressionism. One of the early spokes-
men of this movement was Samuel Butler (1835–1902), whose ideas
anticipated those of Henri Bergson. Butler directly challenged Darwin's theory of evolution and helped formulate a theory of mind-
directed evolution that, except perhaps for some of its terminology,
is at times startlingly close to Bergson's theories.

Butler began by challenging the world of his fathers (both his
father and grandfather were ordained ministers). He once told J. B.
Yeats that *The Origin of Species* had destroyed his belief in a personal
God.[4] But when Butler examined Darwin closely, he found his teach-
ings as unconvincing as those of the fathers. In two early essays,
"Darwin among the Machines" (1863) and "*Lucubration Ebria*"
(1865), which he wrote while sheep farming in New Zealand, Butler

maintained that Darwin's account of evolution eliminated the idea of mind and purpose and turned nature into a machine. He believed that man and the machine were both part of an evolutionary process, and maintained that man would eventually incorporate the machine into his being so as to better reconcile himself with it and to control his immediate environment.[5]

In 1872, Butler revised these essays and published them as chapters 23 and 24, entitled "The Book of the Machines," in his satire *Erewhon*. Butler was afraid that these chapters had offended Darwin, since they were so directly connected to his earlier attack on the idea of natural selection, and he later became convinced that Darwin had found the means to gain revenge. In November 1879, Darwin published *Erasmus Darwin*, a memoir of his grandfather to which he appended a translated essay by a German scholar, Dr. Krause, which had appeared in the February issue of the journal *Kosmos*. Darwin gave the impression that the translation did not vary from the original essay, but when Butler read the essay he found evidence that it had been revised (for example, it included a new paragraph that he took as a personal attack) and that it borrowed material from his *Evolution, Old and New* (1879). When Darwin's explanation failed to satisfy him, Butler broke with him, convinced that Darwin was capable of fraudulence, and that he could be trusted neither in this project nor in his previous work.

What Butler felt was lacking from Darwin's theory of evolution was a convincing account of mind—especially the way mind works in the matter of memory. Butler felt the key question here involved identity or what he called "sameness." We believe that there is continuity between the past and present self, but every cell in the human body of a fifty-year-old is different from the cells that were there when he or she was born. What holds the self together, Butler insisted, was mind—or, more specifically, memory. Instinct, he claimed, is only inherited memory—that is, memories of actions done repeatedly (he would call them habits) in innumerable past generations. If this were true, then unconscious memory—and not natural selection—was the real clue to heredity.

Butler thus questioned Zola's belief that art originated with a scientific observer, arguing instead that its source was in the unconscious. He initiated, in other words, the upending of the dictates of naturalism and the birth of modernism. Butler insisted that memory went beyond the physical self, that it was inherent in the embryo and reached back to one's parents and foreparents, existing unconsciously within us, supplying motives and structuring heredity, but in ways too remote for us to be aware of. The notion of such carry-over memory may seem far-fetched today. But if we substitute the idea of DNA for personal memory, we can see that Butler's idea was not that different from the modern belief that bonded to the genes is in fact a memory system passed on from generation to generation.

Butler at first believed that his theory of memory was not inconsistent with Darwinian thinking, and he offered it as a correction to the theory of natural selection. But when he read St. George Mivart's book, *The Genesis of the Species* (1871), his thinking was turned around. Attempting to reconcile his evolutionary beliefs with his Roman Catholic faith, Mivart, a distinguished biologist, attacked natural selection in a way that made it clear to Butler that one did not have to believe in natural selection to believe in evolution. When Butler began retracing the history of evolutionary theory, he concluded that Lamarck was more convincing than Darwin. From this point on, Butler believed that evolution could not be divorced from teleology.

Butler was so obsessed with these theories of evolution that he gave the better part of his life and his writing to this topic. He rehearsed his initial skepticism about Darwin in *Life and Habit* (1878). Here Butler claimed that the most serious weakness in Darwin's theory was that it explained variations that already existed but that it had no satisfactory way of anticipating intelligent change: "The weak point in Mr. Darwin's theory would seem to be the deficiency, so to speak, of motive power to originate and direct the variations which time is to accumulate. It deals admirably with the accumulation of variations in creatures already varying, but it does not provide a sufficient number of sufficiently important variations to be accumulated."[6] Butler was not convinced that evolutionary design was a matter of "unintelligent variations." He felt the need for an explanation that would go beyond the accidents of natural selection: "I cannot think that 'natural selection,' working upon small, fortuitous, indefinite, unintelligent variations, would produce the result we see around us. One wants something that will give a more definite aim to variations, and hence, at times, cause bolder leaps in advance" (261).

Butler's skepticism stemmed from his vast distrust of the idea that all reality was limited to the physical realm. The self, he insisted, has a dimension that is not adequately accounted for by a material definition of man. He tells us that "we can apprehend neither the beginning nor the end of our personality, which comes out of infinity as an island out of the sea. . . . Not only are we infinite as regards time, but we are so also as regards extension, being so linked on to the external world that we cannot say where we either begin or end" (104). Butler came to believe that the more we know and the stronger our will power, the more unconscious we become of our knowledge and our desire (43). The mind, he insisted, cannot be limited to the physical realm of the brain. Begging the question of at least the human brain, he referred to experiments that had been carried on with frogs. When the frog's head had been cut off, the frog's limbs could still respond. He concluded: "the headless body can still, to some extent, feel, think, and act, and if so, . . . it must have a living soul" (115).

The faculty that most established a kind of spiritual dimension for Butler, as it would later for Bergson, was, as we have seen, that of memory, which Butler insisted functioned on the level of the unconscious, independently of the material realm of brain and nervous system. Like knowledge and desire, he claimed, "Memory is no less capable of unconscious exercise, and on becoming intense through frequent repetition, vanishes no less completely as a conscious action of the mind than knowledge and volition" (131). Like Bergson, Butler believed that this unconscious power of memory gave a kind of being to the past and helped direct what Darwin saw as the accidental variations of natural selection. At one point, Butler quotes directly from Darwin: "In every living being we may rest assured that a host of long-lost characters lie ready to be evolved under the proper conditions." And then Butler comments: "[D]oes not one almost long to substitute the word 'memories' for the word 'characters?'" (196). Here Butler has gone to the heart of the matter. By "characters," Darwin had meant that natural selection is the determining factor in evolution; by "memories," Butler substituted the mind as the determining factor. The two words encapsulate the difference between Darwin and Bergson, and Butler had clearly conceptualized that difference before Bergson himself.

Mind then was inseparable from the forms that came and went in the flow of time. While Butler did not actually see intuition as the means by which that flow is accessed, he arrived at a parallel idea with his theory of instinct. While Bergson believed that instinct absorbed into intelligence led to intuition, Butler believed that instinct absorbed intelligence; instinct thus becomes for Butler the highest form of intelligence, and he maintained that the mechanical world around us would eventually be absorbed into its realm—that mind would transform the mechanical. Butler thus believed that change (what he called "transmission") took place when mind (what he called "instinct") altered form (which he connected with the mechanical) in the realm of time. Except for the notion of the mechanical, this is a totally Bergsonian idea.

In *Evolution, Old and New* (1879), Butler goes on to place Darwin's theories in the context of the history of evolution. After long discussions of Dr. Paley, Buffon, Erasmus Darwin, and Lamarck, Butler once again treats Darwin's theory of natural selection. Butler questions how the selection process actually takes place. Darwin tells us through variation, but "the variations must make their appearance before they can be selected."[7] Thus Butler believed that Darwin's reasoning was circular: Darwin tells us that natural selection is " 'a means' of modification," and treats it as an efficient cause, but at the same time protests "again and again that it is not a cause" (347). When writing about the eye, Darwin says: "Variations will cause the slight alterations"—but the " 'slight alterations' *are* the variations," so, concluded Butler, "Darwin's words come to this—that 'variation will cause the variations' " (347). While Darwin explained the variations as a matter of chance, Butler insisted that they were willed into being through inherited memory—that adaptation was a matter of intelligence and not mere accident.

Butler carried these ideas to his literary works. He was so much taken by his theory of hereditary memory that when it came to creating the character of Ernest Pontifex in *The Way of All Flesh* (1903), he described four generations of the family to suggest their mental/emotional continuity. Each generation has the same reservations about a religious commitment until Ernest, acting in a way that his father could not, finally makes a break with the past. Throughout the novel, it is Ernest's "unconscious self" that often speaks truths "to which his conscious self was unequal."[8] And because memory has been so internalized in the flow of life, we cannot separate the inner and outer realms of being. This truth is one of the major conclusions the narrator of the novel comes to: "The trouble is that in the end we shall be driven to admit the unity of the universe so completely as to be compelled to deny that there is either an external or an internal, but must see everything both as external and internal at one and the same time, subject and object—external and internal—being unified as much as everything else" (327).

In his only other significant artistic work, *Erewhon,* Butler once again inserted his major ideas concerning evolution. As satire *Erewhon* finds its center of gravity by reversing dominant social and moral consciousness and turning things upside down (the citizens of *Erewhon* are rebuked, for example, for becoming sick but excused for moral failings). But when the text does speak in a straightforward way, it stresses ideas that bind Butler and Bergson together. Like Bergson, Butler insisted on the unity of creation. He maintained, for example, that vegetative and animal life could not be separated from the evolutionary process that brought forth man. Such forms did not undergo separate evolutionary developments; rather they were two stages in the same process: "both animals and plants have had a common ancestry," he tells us, "and animals and plants [are] cousins."[9] And there is an intelligence working through such creation—an intelligence that we could better recognize if only the individual human mind were not limited in its temporal cycle (246). Furthermore, this intelligence both informs and directs the flux of life, and while the rise of the machine may seem to threaten its integrity, the mind is capable of reconciling the opposition between the mechanical and the natural (see 222–60). In challenging the mechanistic nature of Darwinian evolution, in insisting that mind (memory) works through the unfolding of time, and in seeing evolution directed by forms of such intelligence, Butler anticipated many of Bergson's major ideas. In fact, only Butler's theory of teleology and his belief that man could absorb the machine separated him from Bergson's final position.

4

Terms like "realism" and "naturalism" had specific meaning in the nineteenth and early twentieth century—an historical meaning that, when reclaimed, allows critical revision of recent studies that have abandoned originary thinking. These terms took much of their meaning from the French novel. Balzac pushed the novel beyond the romantic sentiment of Sue and Hugo, allowing Henry James to write a new kind of realist story—and Zola and Dreiser among others transformed that realism into literary naturalism. An important but often overlooked link in this chain of writers is the Goncourt brothers, whose study of compulsive love, *Germinie Lacerteux* (1864), created a subgenre of fiction that reached from Zola and Flaubert to Tolstoy and Hardy.

Spencer's concern with forms of slavery and compulsive behavior is foreshadowed by the Goncourts's novel, which tells the story of a servant girl who has come from the provinces to Paris. There she falls in love with an adolescent boy whom she has been hired to help through an illness. *Germinie Lacerteux* is a study of obsessional desire so strong that it produces what the novel calls a "physiological phenomenon." Germinie loses her free will; no matter how cruelly Jupillon or his mother treat her, she cannot free herself from the compulsion of loving him—a compulsion that becomes self-destructive. The force that works against her comes from within; it is not a cosmic force but a part of her nature, a second self, over which she has no control. Her very being, her temperament, is thus the antagonist in this story. Zola was much moved by this novel, wrote a complimentary review of it, and began his *Thérèse Raquin* (1867) in imitation of it. The Goncourt brothers added a now famous preface, and their novel became the bridge between Flaubert's *Madame Bovary* (1857) and Zola's *Rougon-Macquart* (1871–93) series and beyond.

Emile Zola served his apprenticeship by writing a *roman feuilleton* entitled *Les Mystères de Marseilles,* an attempt to apply the formula of Sue's *Mystères de Paris* to a novel set in Marseilles, to be published by a Marseilles newspaper. He began work on this project in January of 1867 with the intention of superimposing Balzac's realism onto Sue's romantic narrative, but the result was a potboiler, even by Zola's own admission.[10] But the exercise served him well as a preparation for his later work, including the contemporaneous *Thérèse Raquin:* the story of a woman's attraction to a young laborer, Laurent, with whom she plots the murder of her husband, Camille. In this story Zola reveals the underworld of Paris as well as the depths of the psyche. After the murder, guilt replaces passion, and the lovers sink deeper and deeper into remorse, haunted by the accusatory eyes of the dead man's mother, who has been silenced by a stroke, and worried by the festering sore from Camille's bite on Laurent's neck, which will not heal. Unable to find any way back to the community from which their crime has isolated them, they commit suicide by swallowing poison.

Thérèse Raquin is at least in part the product of her heredity and temperament. Once into this story, Zola got the idea of writing a sequence of twenty novels treating the various temperaments that made up French life in the Second Empire. Zola went to life for his narrative material; interested more in the psychological type than in the individual, he sometimes superimposed the traits of several persons onto one character. In this context, most studies of Zola's literary naturalism begin with his *Le Roman expérimental* ("The Experimental Novel" [1880]). Zola in turn based his theories of heredity and environment on Prosper Lucas's *Traité . . . de l'hérédité naturelle* (1850) and especially Claude Bernard's *Introduction à l'étude de la medécine expérimentale* (*An Introduction to the Study of Experimental Medicine* [1865]).

Zola's theory of fiction is presented in his essay "The Experimental Novel." The novelist is like the scientist: he is both observer and experimenter. As observer, he presents data; as experimenter, he sets the characters of a particular story in motion, portraying events consistent with—that is, determined by—the data.[11] Zola's theory, adapted from the writing of Lucas and Bernard, is clearly contrived, since the novelist, unlike the scientist, has to know how his characters will respond to a given situation before he can depict that situation—that is, Zola's procedure is not an experiment at all because the conclusion is built into his starting assumptions and events do not freely unfold.

Despite the contradiction, Zola's theory led to a powerful narrative mode, and within a period of fifteen years he produced at least three classics—*L'Assommoir* (1877), *Germinal* (1885), and *La Débâcle* (1892). Following his own dictate that the novelist must function like a scientist, Zola closely observed nature and social data, rejected supernatural and transhistorical explanations of the physical world, renounced free will and absolute standards of morality, depicted nature as a mechanistic process and human experience as determined. All reality could be reduced to a biological understanding of matter, matter regulated by natural laws and subject to the scrutiny of scientific methodology. Controlled by heredity and environment, man was the product of his temperament in a social context. "I wanted to study temperaments and not character . . . ," Zola wrote. "I chose beings powerfully dominated by their nerves and their blood," he went on, "devoid of free will, carried away by the fatalities of their flesh."[12] Zola repudiated the idea of miracles and distrusted the imagination: there were no miracles in nature, and the proper novelist was an empirical observer rather than imaginative creator. Influenced by Lucas's and Bernard's theories, Zola believed that his characters were products of heredity and environment, situated temperaments subject to human observation, their behavior a matter of predictable unfolding.

5

Zola captures the sweep of historical events in his *Rougon-Macquart* novels, which cover the years from the eve of the second Empire (1851) to the French defeat at Sedan during the Franco-Prussian War (1870), or as Zola put it in his introduction, "from the perfidy of the coup d'état to the treason of the Sedan."[13] Zola sets his story of these years both in the countryside, where a greedy peasant class begins to consolidate power, and in the city, where a new middle class rises to power under the auspices of Napoleon III.

Zola's sequence begins with *La Fortune des Rougon* (1871), which describes the origins of the two families, the Rougons and the Macquarts. Both spring from the defective blood of Adelaide Fouque (Aunt Dide), who marries the respectable Rougon, by whom she has a son, Pierre. After her husband's death, she takes the drunkard Macquart as her lover, by whom she has a son and a daughter, Antoine and Usule.

Until 1830 the inhabitants of Plassans (based on Zola's own Aix-en-Provence) were fervent Catholics and Royalists. But when it became evident that Louis Philippe would triumph, they gave up the cause of legitimacy and espoused the democratic movement and the revolution of 1848. When, in turn, the republic falls, the Rougons prey off the ruins and become rich. (In their unscrupulous and greedy behavior, the Rougons have much in common with William Faulkner's Snopes family.) In portraying the Rougons and others, Zola describes the political shifts among the peasants as they jockey for power in the Second Empire. But the center of the Rougon-Macquart novels is the center of France, Paris, to which many of the townspeople come in search of greater self-fulfillment. Over half the novels in the series deal with the world of Paris, and life as depicted in the rest is inextricably tied to it.[14]

La Curée (1872) is the first novel to establish Paris as both the center of France and the center of Zola's narrative world. Aristide Rougon comes to Paris from the provincial town of Plassans to hunt *la curée* (the quarry). In Paris he joins his brother Eugene, a minister in the emperor's government, and goes about making a fortune out of Haussmann's rebuilding of Paris. Like Balzac, Zola depicts a city that creates its own reality, instilling a greed in the ambitious that separates them from family and causes them to prefer commodities to human relationships. In the modern world, the forces of nature have been replaced by the force of money.

Zola continues the story of avarice in the more ambitious novel *L'Argent* (*Money* [1891]). Zola saw how in the modern city the new temple was the bank, bridging political and religious worlds and financing investments (a silver mine in Palestine, for example). Power works through money, money that invisibly controls all it can reach. In *Le Ventre de Paris* (*The Belly of Paris* [1873]) and *Au bonheur des Dames* (*The Ladies' Delight* [1883]), Zola analyzes the connection between money and nature in some detail, describing two kinds of marketplace—les Halles Centrales, supplying food, and the modern department store, supplying material goods. These markets turn self-destructively on money and on a modern combativeness that suggests an atavistic connection with the jungle.

In *L'Assommoir* (1877) the desire to survive rather than the desire for money dominates. Zola's method was to create large, set scenes and then move in sequence from one to the other. We have a fight scene in the washing room between Gervaise and Virginie; the scene in the museum that magnifies the difference in state of mind between those of the genteel world and those of the slums; the birthday dinner, a sumptuous moment in an otherwise dreary life; Coupeau's fall from the roof and into alcoholism that leads also to Gervaise's decline. Despite her lack of discipline, Gervaise holds this world together. Her men—Lantier, Coupeau, Goujet—all take their being from her, as do Coupeau's mother and sisters. And yet her presence is not enough, and Gervaise is in turn worn down by alcohol and poverty.

L'Assommoir not only was the first working-class novel—the main subject of which was the poverty that went with that class—but also became its model. "I wanted," says Zola in his preface, "to depict the inevitable downfall of a working-class family in the polluted atmosphere of our urban area."[15] As in so many naturalistic novels, money sets life's limits. Gervaise keeps her bankbook in the back of a grandfather clock—and time and money are equated in the novel. Time becomes a burden, often relieved by money. Over time Gervaise and Coupeau are worn down by accidents and disappointments; they end up surrendering themselves to the self-abandonment of drink and exhausting the little money they have saved. Zola does not morally condemn Gervaise for her plight: the system within which she is trapped is more to blame, reducing her life to the bare essentials—food, sex, and drink—and leading to the debauchery that follows. Here we have the beginning of one of the key themes of literary naturalism: the force of social circumstance is such that the individual cannot be held responsible for his or her actions. It is this loss of personal freedom that will become one of the more controversial aspects of naturalism.

It is in the squalor of this world that Nana, the daughter of Gervaise and Coupeau, is born—and before *L'Assommoir* is over she has already been given to prostitution. Zola depicts in *Nana* (1884) a public world—the theater, restaurants, hotels—a world in which Nana can come from nowhere and become the center of attention through the power of her beauty and sensual charms. Zola also takes us in this novel into the world of the aristocracy, where we see the emptiness of people whose money and power come from the work of others. The more they have, the more they want. Fauchery, the journalist, gives us an insight into the determined nature of Nana's character. His article describes "The life of a harlot [Nana], descended from four or five generations of drunkards, and tainted in her blood by a cumulative inheritance of misery and drink, which in her case has taken the form of a nervous exaggeration of the sexual instinct. She has shot up to womanhood in the slums and on the pavements of Paris and tall, handsome, and as superbly grown as a dunghill plant, she avenges the beggars and outcasts of whom she is the ultimate product."[16]

Fauchery's metaphor is apt. Nana, like a plant, is the product of her environment; her beauty is destructively compelling, and her smallpox a final, visible sign of an abiding physical, moral, and social decay: "Venus was rotting. It seemed as though the poisons she had assimilated in the gutters, had but now remounted to her face and turned it to corruption" (544–45). Nana dies of smallpox, her suppurating and purulent body inseparable from the corruption of the aristocracy, whose end is harbingered by the call of the mob— "A Berlin! A Berlin! A Berlin!"—that signals the disastrous Franco-Prussian War and the end of the Second Empire.

The city in which Nana so compellingly moved depended on both an agrarian and industrial source of food and minerals. Zola saw the symbiotic connection between the city and its extremities, and in *Germinal* (1885) depicts the northern coalfields, where the miners are on strike. The workers embody a force, like the force of nature, which in some vague Darwinian way will redeem the system from within. The worlds of *Nana* and *Germinal* are one: the workers produce the wealth that creates the life of luxury of a Nana at the same time as they embody the hope of redeeming the system. Almost everything in Zola's world comes back to the nobility of work. But Zola never addressed the equally important question of who would lead the new workers, who would set the limits on this new source of power. In *Germinal* Zola took us to the doorstep of totalitarianism. It is not that he was unaware that he was dealing with the forces of power—*La Bête humaine* (1890) revealed his absorption with this theme. Still, like other naturalists, Zola never asked who was to be trusted with the power vacuum that would exist after the fall of a decadent ruling class.

If *Germinal* looks toward industrial France, *La Terre* (1887) looks toward agrarian France and shows how the new commercial process reached a peasant world. But as the peasants try unsuccessfully to hold on to their condemned way of life, the institutions of the city continue to absorb the land. The bread that comes from the land is taken to Paris to feed the city. The connection between the city and the land is the railroad, the subject of Zola's next novel, *La Bête humaine*, in which the power of the train (the machine) and sexuality is equated. In this novel, Zola introduced Jacques Lantier, whom he created in order to accommodate his plot. In Zola's revised chronology, Jacques becomes Gervaise's middle son, born between Claude and Etienne. He suffers from the same hereditary defects as do his brothers. Troubled by the idea of sex (he thinks of it as some ancient curse thrust on the human race), he can be brought to a psychotic rage that induces in him a desire to murder when he is sexually aroused. Zola depicts this urge as a wild beast within him, just waiting to express itself: it exemplifies the second self that runs through naturalistic fiction. As a substitute for sex, Jacques gives his affection to the steam engine of the train he drives on the Paris-Rouen-Le Havre route. Jacques embodies the modern man who has become alienated from natural human instincts and now connects his sexual energy with the machine. Zola then goes on to assert a connection between the machine and the crowd—the masses that take on an animality in themselves. There are thus forces at work on several levels, and we have an equation between and among human sexuality (often beyond individual control), the machine (embodied by the steam engine of the train), and the crowd (with its own unique expression of mechanistic power and animal force). Zola once again ends a novel in a way that reveals blind power working in an undirected way. The train—without engineer or fireman, its cattle-cars filled with troops—hurtles through the night, blind energy running loose, Zola's image of France on its way to the disaster of the Franco-Prussian War. Jacques Ellul would point out how such undirected power was waiting to be exploited, how this was technology preparing the way for totalitarianism.[17]

La Débâcle (1892) picks up where *La Bête humaine* ends with the soldiers going off to fight. The novel treats in detail the defeat of France at the hands of the Germans at Sedan in 1870. The action is presented from an omniscient point of view that encompasses the experiences of Jean Macquart and Maurice Levasseur—one a peasant, the other an educated intellectual. Both fight the Germans and then end up fighting each other in the Communard revolution that follows. Zola depicts the French army losing discipline and simply becoming a crowd, a leaderless mob. Jean is badly wounded in the conflagration and nursed back to health by Henrietta, Maurice's twin sister, who supplies that double that Zola's plots seem to need. By novel's end Maurice is dead and Jean, Zola's embodiment of hope for the New France, takes the burning Paris as his task. The military defeat had broken the hold of Napoleon III. The corruption of his empire had radiated beyond Paris throughout the whole country. The hope of a new Paris resides in the land. Zola was voicing the romantic belief that the land was more vital than the city. Hope stemmed from simple people like Jean Macquart—with their love of the earth and their capacity for work. A New France would rise from the redeeming vitality of the land reworked.

6

New ways of seeing the world are often greeted with suspicion and hostility. Realism—and especially naturalism—were met with such a reception. The new fiction had to do battle with the censorship of middle-class vigilantes, as the experience of Henry Vizetelly (1820–1894) illustrates. Vizetelly issued English translations of Zola's major novels. He began with *Nana* and *L'Assommoir*, and by 1888 he had issued sixteen more translations. Vizetelly was from an Italian family that had settled in Elizabethan London as glass merchants and later became printers. He had already published without event translations of novels by Daudet, George Sand, Flaubert, Dostoyevsky, and Tolstoy. But the Zola translations he published caught the attention of the National Vigilance Association. They encouraged a member of Parliament, Samuel Smith, to attack Vizetelly's publication from the House, where his motion to censure won a unanimous vote.

But the suppression of Zola's work was left to private means. Thus, in August 1888, a firm of solicitors retained by the National Vigilance Association brought charges of obscenity against Henry Vizetelly for issuing translations of *Nana, La Terre,* and *Pot-Bouille* (1882). At the trial, on October 31, 1888, the prosecutor read twenty-five isolated passages to the jury, which asked him to stop. Given this sign from the jury, Vizetelly withdrew his plea of not guilty for one of guilty. He was fined one hundred pounds and placed on one year's probation. In 1889 the same association brought additional charges against Vizetelly for selling new translations of Zola's work as well as of Flaubert's *Madame Bovary* and Maupassant's *A Woman's Life* (1883). This time Vizetelly was sentenced to three months in Holloway Prison. This led to a petition signed by over one hundred writers and artists demanding Vizetelly's release. Thomas Hardy, whose own *Tess* (1891) would also be suppressed, signed the petition, despite Hardy's ambivalence about Zola's work. The attack on Zola, however, did more to establish than to destroy his reputation in England.[18]

Zola's influence on his contemporaries was pronounced. His work directly influenced Alphonse Daudet and Guy de Maupassant in France; Theodor Fontane and Gerhart Hauptmann in Germany; Giovani Verga in Italy; and George Moore and George Gissing in Ireland and England. But, directly or indirectly, the real inheritors of the method were American writers like Frank Norris, Theodore Dreiser, Jack London, and Upton Sinclair.

7

The streams of literary naturalism in America branched from the rivers of naturalism and literary realism that originated in France. The influence of Zola on Frank Norris was direct, on Jack London and Upton Sinclair real but less direct, and on Dreiser the Zolaesque effect came through Balzac. French literary naturalism initiated an international movement, but it was brought to distinction in America.

Frank Norris was born into comfortable circumstances in Chicago on March 5, 1870. His father owned a successful wholesale jewelry business and his mother was an ex-actress who pursued the arts. In 1884 the family moved to California, first to Oakland and then to San Francisco, where they settled. His mother encouraged her son's interest in art, eventually enrolling him in art schools in both England (the National Arts Training School) and in France (the famous Academie Julian). Norris's training as a painter led him to believe that observation negated imagination. While in Paris, he fell under the influence of Taine's (1828 –1893) theory of forces: race, environment, and historical moment.

When Norris returned to America, his interest shifted to literature, especially the genre of the epic. He wrote a long medieval poem, *Yvernelle* (1892), published thanks to a subvention from his mother. He attended the University of California at Berkeley, where he was introduced to the ideas of the biologist Joseph Le Conte, and later he attended Harvard, where he was influenced by the literary critic Lewis E. Gates. At Harvard, he began versions of *Vandover and the Brute* (1914) and *McTeague* (1899). After Harvard, a number of adventures misfired, including a planned trip to Africa. Settling down for the moment, he worked as assistant editor for the weekly San Francisco *Wave*.

Based on his first novel, *Moran of the Lady Letty* (1898), published weekly in the *Wave*, Norris was offered a position by S. S. McClure with Doubleday and McClure in New York. He was sent by *McClures* to Cuba to cover the Spanish-American War, where he met Stephen Crane and Richard Harding Davis. Although he returned from Cuba ill (partly a result of mental depression), he recovered enough energy to finish *McTeague*. His next major effort, *The Octopus* (1901), was the first volume of a trilogy involving the production, distribution, and consumption of wheat.

Norris believed that wheat was a natural force, like the sexual drive, moving life ahead of it. This force existed within humanity as an atavistic drive, as what one critic has called "instinct,"[19] inseparable from man's animal origins and more constant than the forces driving civilization. The heroic as well as the degenerate lay buried as instinct in the human species, embodied as both giants of industry and as the profligate. Norris's sense of the heroic stemmed in great part from his reading of Spencer. His sense of the degenerate emanated from his reading of Cesare Lombroso (1836 –1909) and Max Nordau. These men were in turn influenced by B. A. Morel's *Traité des Dégénérescences Physiques, Intellectuelles et Morales de L'Espèce Humaine* (1857).

The causes of degeneracy were numerous. Norris held fast to his racial beliefs, especially his belief that Spanish and Jewish blood was inferior to Aryan blood, and to other ersatz theories promulgated in books like Charles Morris's *The Aryan Race* (1888) and repeated in others like Madison Grant's *The Passing of the Great Race* (1916). Another cause of degeneracy was alcoholism, which perpetuated chemically destructive instincts. Norris brought both of these causes of degeneracy to bear in *Vandover and the Brute*. Chance also worked as a catalyst: the gambler, seldom winning, tempted fate.

As modern man became more civilized, more cut off from his instincts, he lost his manliness, lost a sense of the heroic that had allowed him to engage the life force. Norris admired masculine women, so long as their masculinity had limits. But he distrusted women in general, seeing them as possessive and selfish, as engaging destructive impulses. He had even greater disdain for the emasculated male (such inhibited creatures present or to come in American literature as Henry James's John Marcher, Edith Wharton's Newland Archer, and T. S. Eliot's Prufrock—men to whom nothing happened, whose timidity had tamed the beast in the jungle). Like Jack London and Ernest Hemingway after him, Norris's belief in a universe of force demanded strong, virile, committed men—and masculine women—who could accommodate the life force.

Norris's *McTeague* was based loosely on a San Francisco murder in 1893. A laborer named Collins, separated from his wife, stabbed her to death in the cloakroom of a kindergarten where she was a charwoman after she had refused to give him money. McTeague carries on the Irish heritage of Collins. Consistent with the belief of the time with respect to Irish degeneracy, McTeague's degeneracy seems to be an inherited matter: his father died of alcoholism, and McTeague's condition can seemingly be traced back for many generations. Norris probably took such ideas from the works of Caesar Lombrosa, whom he knew through his reading of Max Nordau. McTeague's protruding jaw and square head seem to match the facial characteristics of Lombrosa's criminal type.

McTeague functions on two levels—the ordinary and the pathological. As a self-taught dentist practicing on Polk Street in San Francisco, a working-class district, McTeague's life is both routine and predictable. The same is true of his wife's life. But when aroused by anger or alcohol, McTeague becomes another person, bestial to the point of violence. And when his wife Trina wins five thousand dollars in the lottery, she begins to covet money in a miserly way so obsessive that it changes her very being. Both McTeague and Trina are the products of their compulsive temperaments.

The plot of Norris's novel turns on McTeague's infatuation with Trina, whom he takes away from Marcus Schouler. After Marcus "gives up" Trina to McTeague, he develops a subconscious hatred of McTeague so intense that it eventually results in the destruction of all of the principal characters. The sequence of events leading up to this finale is set in motion when Marcus uses his influence to close McTeague's dental office. The resulting loss of income leads to McTeague's degeneracy and Trina's miserliness, which in turn leads to murderous hate. Pursued as an outlaw into gold-mining territory, McTeague is confronted by Marcus in a Death Valley scene that culminates in mutual destruction.

A subplot involving the marriage of Maria and Zerkow anticipates the details of the McTeague-Trina plot. In both plots, the obsession with money displaces a more fundamental anxiety—the anxiety of survival. Strangely, Trina's winning the lottery deepens her insecurity. The major characters are all living from hand-to-mouth on the edge of society. They treat money or gold as prized possessions, so much so that they lose their utility value; the physical possession of money becomes for Trina a symbol of her ability to go on, and gold for Zerkow becomes an end in itself, a mirage of the good life. The anxiety generated by gold and money spirals out beyond their control.

What begins as chance in the novel (for example, Trina coming to McTeague to have her tooth fixed) produces a determined chain of events. Character becomes fate: Maria and Zerkow are overcome by greed, McTeague by his animality, Trina by her miserliness. Throughout the novel, animality parallels humanity. Dogs take a bitter dislike to each other, as do Marcus and McTeague. Another subplot involves the sentimental love story of Miss Baker and Old Grannis, which in its gentleness underscores the violence of the other plots, just as McTeague's loving care of his canary contrasts with his brutality toward Trina. The transition from the commonplace to the extraordinary in the novel is so rapid that it taxes credulity, despite the abundance of realistic detail. What restores realism is a sense of inevitability in the progression of events.

As in Dreiser's *Sister Carrie* (1900), once McTeague can no longer support Trina, the male-female, superior-inferior roles are reversed. Trina becomes the breadwinner. Once McTeague steals her money and abandons her, she strikes out on her own, but unlike Carrie, who will ultimately succeed, she is headed toward her death. There are other similarities: in *Sister Carrie,* when the safe clicks, Hurstwood's fate is sealed; in Death Valley, when the handcuffs click, McTeague's fate is sealed. Both novels move inexorably toward a fatal moment; each "click" suggests the existence of a host of hidden impulses. The line separating the lawful from the unlawful is a thin one in the novels of Dreiser and Norris. Like Hurstwood and Clyde Griffith, McTeague moves from functionary citizen to outlaw—from the security of being a part of the citizenry to the anxiety of being hunted criminal. Beneath the calm of civilized life is a disruptive element—buried motives—as long-lived as human reality itself.

The Octopus (1901) is another major achievement of Frank Norris, despite the fact that it is grossly overwritten and thematically confused. This novel, perhaps more than any other, gives critical support to those who argue that there was a confluence of naturalism and transcendentalism, naturalism and the romance. Norris's story is told against the backdrop of the workings of a life force, an energy that results in the germination of powers like the wheat and that pushes life ahead of it. *The Octopus* is Norris's novel of resurgent continuity in which life emerges from seeds and overpowers forms of death.

The novel functions in an almost formulistic way with the principal characters embodying stereotypes. Vanamee is cast in the role of the Hebraic shepherd; he is a mystic, prophet, visionary, and dweller in the wilderness. He can hold his flock of sheep in place or call to others by an inexplicable power of mind. He mourns the rape that led to the death of Angele in childbirth, even as he believes her spirit lives on in nature, as alive as the wheat and the flowers that burst from the land in the spring.

Annixter is Venamee's opposite. A wealthy wheat grower, he fights the railroad on its own terms through legal action and by bribing the railroad commission. His courtship of Hilma is as clumsy as Vanamee's love for Angele is tender. He is deeply suspicious of women, whom he regards as grasping, until he is transformed by his marriage to Hilma, his self-concern giving way to a redeeming altruism. Magnus Derrick and his son Harran complement Annixter in his fight against the railroad, although Magnus is more politically ambitious than Annixter and more reluctant to bribe state officials.

The main concern of the novel is with how vulnerable these men are to the power of the railroad: their land, the quality of which they have improved by working it, is subject to reclamation by the railroad, and their crops and the machinery needed for planting and harvesting are carried at rates and on routes determined by the railroad. The most pure victim of the railroad's machinations is Dyke, fired as an engineer by the railroad for protesting wages, and then ruined as a hop farmer when the railroad raises the rates for bringing his crop to market. In revenge, he robs the mail train and kills a brakeman, turning himself into a criminal outcast, who is hunted down, caught, and then sentenced to life imprisonment.

The connecting link in this chain of characters is Presely, the poet, whose understanding of the situation leads to an epic vision out of which comes a socialist poem that marshals sympathy for the victims of the railroad's greed, embodied by S. Behrman. Presley moves throughout the novel as a kind of choric presence, bearing witness to the major narrative events and becoming an active agent himself when he resorts to bomb throwing.

The feud between the ranchers and the railroad grows more heated, exploding into a shootout at Hoven's irrigation ditch, where men from both sides die, including Annixter. In the wake of this event, Derrick Magnus is ruined when his bribery deal is exposed, and he loses both his sons—Harran is killed in the shootout and Lyman betrays the farmers to gain political support from the railroad. Magnus also loses his rich wheat farm when the railroad breaks its lease with him. Like Dyke, he is an emblem of the power of the railroad to break its opposition. At this point, the novel looks more like a melodrama of good versus evil than a naturalistic tale in which the source of evil is usually human limitation. The novel becomes even more melodramatic when Mrs. Hoven dies of starvation in San Francisco, and her daughter becomes a prostitute, these events being counterpointed to a sumptuous dinner given by one of the railroad executives.

But the novel does not end on this negative note. Presely returns for a last visit to the ranch where Vanamee tells him that evil is only a transitory phenomenon in the world force. Forms of evil are "short lived" as "the race goes on." Truth in the end will prevail as all things "work together for the good."[20] While Norris ends his novel with these words, there is nothing in the text that justifies them. To be sure, S. Behrman is dead, having been suffocated by wheat when he falls into the ship's storage hold, and Vanamee has visions of a returned Angele. But the railroad still remains a prevailing force, and Angele is still dead. Vanamee's vitalism reflects the influence on Norris of Herbert Spencer, whose ideas he modified, as well as that of Joseph Le Conte and Asa Gray, both of whom strengthened Norris's appreciation of Spencer. Norris's views are the basis of Charles Walcutt's idea of the "divided stream," the belief that transcendentalism is a vital aspect of literary naturalism. But transcendentalism contradicted the mechanistic aspects of naturalistic philosophy, and most naturalistic novels rejected such romantic endings. Even within the Norris canon, Vanamee's is an anomalous philosophical position.

In addition to holding with a modified form of vitalism, Norris had a theory of the West. He believed that modern civilization, with some starts and stops, had been moving along a western frontier, jumping the Atlantic after the Crusades, progressing across the American continent, and then jumping to the Pacific once the American West had been settled. Dewey's exploits at Manila and the landing of United States marines in China during the Boxer Rebellion in 1900 were significant events in the documentation of this thesis.[21]

His trilogy would begin at what was at the time the cutting edge of the frontier (California), move eastward to the commodity markets where wheat was bought and sold speculatively (Chicago), and end where the movement began (Europe). What Norris wanted to show was how modern capitalism had created an economic network that spread over thousands of miles and that had life-threatening consequences for markets all over the world. In *The Octopus*, for example, he describes the telegraph lines that connect the ranchers, "by wire with San Francisco, and through that city with Minneapolis, Duluth, Chicago, New York, and at last the most important of all, with Liverpool. . . . The ranch became merely the part of an enormous whole, a unit in the vast agglomeration of wheat land the whole world round, feeling the effects of causes thousands of miles distant—a drought on the prairies of Dakota, a rain on the plains of India, a frost on the Russian steppes, a hot wind on the llanos of the Argentine."

While Norris's sympathy in *The Octopus* was clearly with the ranchers, he showed how the ranchers were also corrupted by money. There were no innocents in this economic process except for the wheat, embodying the great force of nature itself. What used to be a symbiotic relationship between city and countryside had broken down; the city fed off the land, depleting it without restoring it. In *The Pit* (1903), Norris indicted a speculative market economy because it substituted stock-market for natural values. Instead of measuring the value of wheat by the process, including the work, that brought it into being, the men on the exchange, who have nothing to do with its natural production, are concerned only with whether its price will rise or fall.

A market system—that is, an artificial process—has been substituted for a natural one. The value of the wheat is now measured by a set of concerns—such as the gamble on future supply and demand—which has nothing to do with wheat as an end product of natural forces. In fact, the speculators could actually control the workings of the market by buying future wheat in abundance, depressing the market, and then holding the nonexistent wheat until they depleted the supposed supply and were ready to sell at an inflated price.[22] Such manipulation became even more rampant with the rise of the trusts and monopolistic control of the market. Like Zola, Norris depicted the movement away from the land to urban markets: the wheat, now merely an abstraction, was funneled through stock exchanges to markets all over the world.

Chicago is the center into and out of which that energy flows. Chicago was a "force" that "turned the wheels of a harvester and seeder a thousand miles distant in Iowa and Kansas," the "heart of America." It was a force of empire that determined "how much the peasant [in Europe] shall pay for his loaf of bread."[23] But as central as Chicago and wheat speculations are to Norris's story, the wheat is an even greater force, larger than both. In *The Pit* Norris depicts the limits of human power: when Jadwin tries to raise the price of wheat beyond its limit, the market breaks and he is a ruined man. Every man and every social institution has its limit, and even abstract matters like wheat speculation are governed by laws that ultimately come back to nature—back to the land, back to wheat, and to the forces out of which life germinates—which is another theme Norris shared with Zola. Norris never began the third volume of his story about the wheat, never got to Europe where the consumption of wheat would be the final step in the cycle of life. But thematically Norris had already shown how the growing and selling of wheat touches the lives of everyone, and he had clearly documented the biological basis of economics and the process of degeneration that can occur when civilization loses touch with the rhythms of the land.

Norris's use of extreme pathology can be found again in *Vandover and the Brute* (1914). Vandover's decline involves physical and mental sickness, which Donald Pizer reads as general paresis, depicted in the novel as a form of lycanthropy, in which Vandover feels that he is becoming a wolf. As in Zola's novels, animality is a latent state in human beings that is aroused at moments of physical crisis and emotional stress, and a process of degeneration always follows the emergence of this animality. Society is continuously breaking down, throwing off its waste and debris, including the human jetsam that makes up this world. There is always a process of death and renewal going on, a life force driving ahead of us, carrying the Charles Gearys to greater heights and the Vandovers and McTeagues to their deaths. In *Vandover and the Brute*, Norris shows how a greed that goes beyond natural necessity creates a pathological state of mind in which one is willing to murder for an illusion, a mirage. In a culture in which material goods become ends in themselves, what remains in the end will be junk. Thus Norris, like Zola, shows how the farther we are removed from the biological rhythms of nature, of the land, the more grotesque our behavior becomes.

8

Like Norris, Theodore Dreiser felt that natural processes were necessary to the proper functioning of the city. Dreiser's idea of force involved the workings of both nature and economic/social systems. He came by this idea in the summer of 1894, an intellectual turning point in his life. At that time, as a reporter on the Pittsburgh *Dispatch,* he would spend his free time in the public library reading Herbert Spencer and Honoré de Balzac. The experience, he said, "quite blew me, intellectually, to bits."[24] Dreiser made use of Spencer—first in his philosophical essays in *Ev'ry Month* entitled "Reflections" and signed "The Prophet," and later in *Sister Carrie.* In fact, Spencer's *First Principles* serves as a key to Dreiser's *Sister Carrie.* Dreiser's first novel is an exercise in the principle of matter in motion—Carrie embodies rise and generation, Drouet stasis, and Hurstwood decline and degeneration.

Carrie is subject to few emotional attachments. The word "love" is not part of her vocabulary. She says good-bye to her mother with hardly a thought of what is involved in leaving home, has a casual thought about her father when her train passes the factory where he works, is happy to be out from under the authority of her sister and brother-in-law in Chicago, tires of Drouet once she meets Hurstwood, and abandons Hurstwood when he can no longer provide for her. While Carrie is modeled in part on Dreiser's sister Emma, she also is a lot like Dreiser himself at the time he was writing the novel. She is his age, arrives in New York in the same year that he first went there, and once on the stage shares his single-minded desire to succeed. Like Dreiser, she has an idea of what constitutes the good life. Material pursuit defines her very being. Ames points the way toward more intellectual matters, but these seem more ideal than real, especially when they are more or less subsumed to material desire in the coda. The only thing Carrie cares deeply about is herself. The novel leaves us with a cultural truth: in America narcissism—the philosophy of "me now"—can empty reality of all but the self and its material trappings.

All of the novel's characters are caught in this commercial materiality, and the self is defined by its place in this material realm: take away Drouet's clothes and, as Dreiser writes, "he was nothing"; so too with Hurstwood's managerial position, and Carrie's connection with the theater. Characters define themselves by who they are, what they buy, what they wear, and how they display themselves. Carrie moves beyond the factory and shop girls with the wardrobe Drouet buys her; Drouet defines himself as a city sport with his loud suits; and Hurstwood's interest in upward mobility is displayed in his more reserved dress. *Sister Carrie* is a novel of perpetual desire, of persistent longing, in which characters are driven by their pursuit of consumer goods—goods that consume the consumer rather than vice versa.

But despite its thematic importance, Dreiser does not substitute merchandise for the processes of nature: temperament and environment interplay. While certainly the product of their environment, naturalistic characters are also biologically moved by the power of temperament. Characters like Carrie are naturally drawn to city lights where consumer stimuli generate a behavioristic response. Both Drouet and Hurstwood are willing to "display" Carrie, to buy the expensive clothes for her that will reflect their purchasing power. (The twenty dollars that Drouet gives Carrie to make her his mistress does not seem like much until one realizes that a dollar at the turn of the century was worth roughly forty times more than the present dollar.) As Veblen pointed out in his *The Theory of the Leisure Class* (1899), women's fashions serve to display male wealth.

Despite her obsession with material goods and despite her self-involvement, what distinguishes Carrie from the other characters in the novel is her imagination—her ability to reinvent herself, to reach within and display the proper emotion on the stage. Dreiser's most engaging characters bring an artistic temperament to their material desire. His world is a combination of the sublime and the ugly—and the two are sometimes one, like the grim beauty of the train yard with its blinking red and green traffic lights glazed in the rain. Dreiser's most intuitive characters—Carrie and Cowperwood—are sensitive to this synergy, to life's strange combinations.

Dreiser combined the themes of the artist and the crowd in his short story "Nigger Jeff," which he wrote in the summer of 1899, before *Sister Carrie.* Jeff is accused of assaulting a nineteen-year-old white woman and is taken from the sheriff by a mob under the forceful leadership of the woman's father. Dreiser depicts the mob as having a bestial, almost preternatural energy, which cannot be restrained by reason or by appeal to the processes of law. The story is narrated by a young reporter, an incipient artist, who witnesses the struggle of opposites: the courage of the sheriff and the blind rage of the father, the fear of Jeff and yet his love for his mother, which is so strong that it compels him to return and results in his arrest. The reporter is moved by both the violence and the pathos of the situation: he participates in the panorama of life, hoping to write a story that gets "it all in."

In the tradition of Balzac, Dreiser saw life as a composite of opposites, as grimly beautiful, embodying a mysterious power that demanded acknowledgment. The city was a lure and a trap, a magnet attracting young men and women from the small town because only the city offered a way of realizing the fullest sense of self. Dreiser begins *Sister Carrie* with this point: "To the child, the genius with imagination . . . the approach to a great city for the first time is a wonderful thing. Particularly if it be evening. . . . Ah, the promise of the night."[25] Carrie feels this promise, this force, in the fire signs that light the city (images of light and dark infuse the novel, from the city lights to the blackened room in which Hurstwood commits suicide). Carrie also feels the power of the city in the crowds, which she enjoys watching from Hanson's stoop or from the window of a Broadway hotel. The crowd, larger than the self, embodies the power the self seeks.

Carrie's state of mind is the product of her youth (Carrie is eighteen when the novel opens and twenty-six at the end), while Hurstwood's is the product of middle age (he is twenty years older than Carrie, thirty-eight at the beginning of the novel and forty-six when he dies at the end) and of an aging process that seems to accelerate with his decline. (To think of Hurstwood as old at forty-six seems misplaced today, until one remembers that life expectancy in the late nineteenth century was about fifty years.) Carrie looks forward; Hurstwood looks backward; Drouet is unchanging, a mediation between the two, content to live in the present. The main characters illustrate Herbert Spencer's theory of "equilibrium and balance." There is also a correlation between the ages of the main characters and their chemical makeup—between age and "anastates and kata-states," positive and negative bodily energy. Dreiser took this idea of bodily energy from the theories of Elmer Gates, who ran a labora-tory of "psychurgy" in Chevy Chase, Maryland.[26]

Dreiser depicts the causal sequence that takes Carrie to the New York Waldorf and Hurstwood to Potter's Field, forcefully conveying the impression that there is a necessity to the events of the plot. Each scene anticipates the next scene. Reverse any one scene in *Sister Carrie* and the action stops, so causally connected are the elements of plot. If Carrie had met Hurstwood and not Drouet on the train from Columbia City to Chicago, there would have been no story. There would have been have been no story if she had not met Drouet after she lost her factory job and was on the verge of being sent home by the Hansons. And there would have been no story if she had not been disillusioned with Drouet at the moment she met Hurstwood, and if his wife had not threatened Hurstwood when he met Carrie. Each scene is cause for the next effect. The novel moves in spiraling circles (also one of the key images of the novel) from Chicago to New York, a larger city where the laws work with greater force, taking Carrie higher than she could go in Chicago and Hurstwood to the lowest urban depths.

That there is more to know about the city, that there are higher planes of artistic reality than vaudeville and the Broadway stage—this is the lesson toward which Ames points Carrie. Ames's function in the novel is to humanize the city in the same way that detectives like Inspector Bucket or Inspector Heat humanize the city in Dickens or Conrad. In an earlier draft of the novel, Ames calls Carrie's atten-tion to conspicuous consumption at Sherry's, to the way many people lead inauthentic lives by displaying themselves as a commodity. (Later the novel will show Mrs. Hurstwood "displaying" Jessica.) And yet Carrie herself is subject to displaying herself in just such a way—and to a desire for the luxurious goods that she sees around her.

As the coda of the novel states, such desire will never be satisfied: Carrie will dream of a happiness that she will never have. The logic of the city is to excite and overwhelm, pose simultaneous but con-flicting possibilities, each one compelling in its own right but exclud-ing the others, guaranteeing discontent. Longing is built into the system. Carrie and Hurstwood are unaware of the processes they enact. Dreiser's characters, part of an evolutionary system that includes adaptation, are subject to forces of environment, and unconscious of the biology through which this system works.

Norris's *The Pit* had an influence on two of Dreiser's novels—*The Financier* (1912) and *The Titan* (1914). But despite the influence, *The Financier* is fundamentally different from Norris's novel. The story is told against the backdrop of the Civil War when speculative money was being spent on new enterprises, especially in the West. While Norris questioned a system that created wealth out of mere speculation, Dreiser in his Cowperwood trilogy seemed to be in awe of it. Not only could the speculator generate wealth, but the contractor had that power as well. Men like Jay Cooke contemplated a railroad that would connect Duluth with the Pacific Ocean: "Here, if a railroad were built, would spring up great cities and prosperous towns."[27]

As his opening metaphor clearly reveals, Dreiser knew that capitalism involved a kind of economic cannibalism. The lobster lives on the squid; men live off other men. The predator adds another dimension to the idea of self. His use of the double changes in meaning: the second self is no longer the weak and helpless self in the throes of a nervous breakdown that he depicted in the autobiographical *An Amateur Laborer* (published posthumously in 1983) but the strong, self-reliant person that Cowperwood's activity turns him into. While Dreiser's world is a realm of limits, Cowperwood tests those limits. Health and wealth become reciprocal values in his desire to go beyond the conventional.

Both Dreiser and Norris believed in an economic system that took its meaning—its force—from nature, but Dreiser seemed more willing to accommodate the play of speculation in this process. Dreiser knew that the system was larger than the individuals who made it up and that the markets were contingent and interdependent. When the Franco-Prussian War tied up European capital, Cooke's house failed, bringing down with it those who were dependent on Cooke, just as the Chicago fire of 1871 had brought ruin to Cowperwood. Markets work in the realm of historical force, and behave as if controlled by laws of nature as inexorable as the law of gravity. This is the thesis of Dreiser's next novel, *The Titan*. Cowperwood has moved to Chicago.

Having successfully established a gas trust, he decides to act on a plan to monopolize the streetcar system. Cowperwood's aggressive climb into the upper reaches of society creates a swarm of powerful enemies who finally defeat him — one force brings into being its opposite in a realm that sets limits to how far he can go.

Dreiser's view on capitalism, like much of his thinking, was contradictory. He admired the ability of Yerkes to manipulate the money system at the same time as he realized that his extreme wealth left others in extreme poverty. Capitalism as a system allowed economic values to preempt natural values, permitted money to be manipulated by those in power; the wealthy and powerful were able, for example, to preserve the gold standard, which worked against Western farmers. Those who see Dreiser as an ardent capitalist fail to appreciate how, in the final analysis, he doubted the fairness of the process, and how he believed (as the ending of *The Stoic* [1947] reveals) that disappointment was built into the money system itself: perpetual pursuit of money was unending and thus devoid of ultimate satisfaction. Dreiser's commitment to communism stemmed more from his belief that such a global force could help restore an economic "balance" (consistent with Spencer's idea of "equilibrium") than from an acceptance of an ideology.

Dreiser's conflicted thinking, which manifests itself in his use of a second self, can be found in *An American Tragedy* (1925). Clyde Griffiths is the product of two worlds and the victim of two selves. He is destroyed by opposing forces, trapped between his early poverty and a world that lures him on — first the gaudy world of the Green-Davidson Hotel, then the more sedate realm of the Union League Club in Chicago, and finally the prosperous and tasteful world of the Lycurgus rich. As Clyde moves from scene to scene, his world gets larger, more refined, and more luxurious. And as it does, his appetites expand in proportion to what he sees.

Clyde is caught between the world of his impoverished father and his wealthy uncle, between his sense of duty to his family and his desire for a better life outside the family. He is a product of the city but falls prey to the petty values of the small town; he seeks secular values but becomes a victim of the religious mentality that he has tried to escape since childhood. Clyde is also the victim of the different temperaments of the prosecuting and defense attorneys and of the opposing political parties who see the value of his case. His situation stirs deep emotion in others: Mason, the district attorney with his disfigured nose, resents Clyde's good looks and his easy ways with women; Belknap, his own attorney, is more sympathetic, having escaped a situation like Clyde's when his girlfriend was able to get the abortion that was refused Roberta. Clyde's case takes on deeply personal meaning for both, provoking intensity in Mason and a willingness to manipulate the truth on the part of Belknap. The whole trial is an exercise in Spencerian opposites with Clyde in the center.

Clyde has a change of heart when he comes to murder Roberta: technically her death is an accident. He decides he will not murder her, but he will not marry her either—and he pushes her away when she comes toward him, causing the boat to overturn, at which time he swims to safety as Roberta drowns. He explains what happened to Reverend McMillan who, when asked by the governor, refuses to save Clyde from the electric chair because Clyde was not sorry to see Roberta drown and thus had murder in his heart; Clyde's execution is thus the product of legal error and religious belief.

Caught between desire and fear, Clyde's will is negated, suspended in time. In the woods, he wants to both run from and toward Sondra—the effect of which is once again to create a Spencerian "equilibrium or balance," the two emotions canceling each other out, temporarily paralyzing him, keeping him fixed in place until the deputy sheriff arrests him. Otherwise his relationships are dynamic, generating a chemical energy, which further diminishes his will power. When he meets Sondra, the force of her presence is greater than that of any woman he has yet met. Dreiser tells us that there was an "electric" effect, an actual charge and discharge of energy, between Sondra and Clyde: one that negated the power that anyone else might have had over him—an idea probably derived from Jacques Loeb (1859 – 1924),[28] the mechanist whose theories of tropism (involuntary reaction to stimuli) so impressed Dreiser at this time.

As Clyde reacts to his environment and to the presence of other characters, so he reacts to the presence of nature itself, a scene instilling a mood in him that creates a state of mind. In Big Bittern, Clyde is in the hands of an overwhelming psychic force whose power, like that of an Aladdin genie, cannot be denied once it is called into play. As a primitive element resides in naturalistic literature, a subterranean, dark, and inverted force inheres in Clyde's nature. The sublime and the demonic exist side by side; coinciding with this malevolent element is an "insidious beauty" that "seemed to mock him."[29]

The forces at work in nature have two elements—just as Clyde has two selves, a pleasant exterior and a sinister inner self that even frightens him. The two selves are sometimes presented ironically, as when Clyde displays an uncanny resemblance to his cousin Gilbert. The look-alike appearance, consistent with genetic theory, belies different class and legal realities, as Clyde is never quite able to fit into the Lycurgus social world or command the wealth that allows manipulation of the legal system. Clyde is appropriately relegated to the "shrinking room" in his uncle's shirt-and-collar factory, remaining the poor relative from beginning to end in the appropriately named Lycurgus (Lycurgus was a legendary Spartan reformer who rewrote the legal codes in eighth century B.C., instituting restrictive conventions).

The power the novel generates stems from what has been called "repetitive form"; as in modern advertising, Dreiser seeks to make an impression on the reader and then reinforce that impression with repetition. The same thing happens over and over (Clyde's running away from the car accident in Kansas City anticipates him swimming away from the drowning Roberta; his desire to buy Hortense a coat instead of helping his pregnant sister foreshadows his willingness to abandon the pregnant Roberta for Sondra). The repetitive event fixes Clyde's character, makes it predictable, but while Clyde's character remains constant, the consequences of his actions become more extreme.

In Dreiser's world there is often a gulf between reality and appearance. Accidental events, for example, seem to dominate the novel. Yet behind the veneer of accident is causal sequence and inevitability. Given Clyde's conflicting character—his desire for money and pleasure combined with his ineptness and passive nature—it is only a matter of time before he will overreach himself. Dreiser believed that chance was just another name for our ignorance of causes.[30] If Clyde believes himself to be the product of gratuitous events, it is only because he does not fully understand the deterministic nature of his

environment or the darker life forces—especially the power of sex—
at work in him.

The key to Dreiser's literary philosophy is his belief in a cosmic
balance, a mechanistic equation of forces that brings all reality into
physical opposition: ugliness and beauty, poverty and wealth, desire
and guilt, sickness and health, life and death—one is impossible
without the other. Matter in motion described physical processes
that maintained the balance, an idea Dreiser brought to his earlier
work. What went up came down. As we have seen, Dreiser's interests
in political causes like communism stemmed from his belief that
such political systems would help restore the imbalances caused by
capitalism. Dreiser had no trouble reconciling Marx and Nietzsche:
one took as his subject the industrial community; the other the
larger-than-life figure that went beyond that community. They diverged in their thinking about the source of political redemption,
Marx locating it in industrial power, and Nietzsche in the rugged individual. Behind their respective force was mystery, a sublimity the
artist perceived that engaged a more spiritual, even preternatural reality, an idea Dreiser brought to his later work.

Dreiser was, as Eliseo Vivas pointed out in a 1938 essay,[31] an
inconsistent mechanist; his philosophical curiosity was piqued by
theories positing the existence of a spiritual or preternatural realm
characterized by the Unknown and by the play of fate and chance,
which he found in writings of Charles Fort (1874–1932)[32] and in the
doctrines of Christian Science, Quakerism, and Hinduism. Dreiser's
mind was always open to new explanations of reality. His parents,
coming from peasant German stock, shared and no doubt instilled
in him this superstitious mentality, and his thinking was strongly influenced by Spencer, whose concept of the Unknowable left the final
meaning of the universe open to speculation. As a result, a sense of
the supernatural crept into Dreiser's work, evident in a play like *The
Blue Sphere* ([1926] although here, as in the short story "The Lost
Phoebe" [1918], the supernatural may be the product of delusional
thinking). Dreiser's interest in the supernatural, however, can be
overemphasized, especially if one fails to acknowledge the extent to
which he was influenced by the mechanistic side of Spencer's philosophy and if one fails to take adequate account of Dreiser's own

counterstatements—such as his argument that behind fate and chance is an unseen causality at work.

Fate and chance, while often thought of as synonymous, are really the opposite of each other. Fate involves the pregiven from all time; chance involves accident. The safe springing closed in *Sister Carrie*, the Chicago fire the leads to Cowperwood's bankruptcy in *The Financier*, the capsizing of the boat in *An American Tragedy*—might all appear to be accidental events and hence matters of chance. But in Dreiser's world, determinism rules and hence there are no chance events. Thus, the safe springing closed, the fire, the capsizing, they are part and parcel of Hurstwood's subliminal willingness to steal the money, Cowperwood's risky use of city loan funds, and Clyde's desire to be rid of Roberta. If these chance occurrences had not happened, there would have been others that would have caused the same events. While fate and chance are the opposite of each other, and while chance prevails in Dreiser's fiction, they both stem from events that are beyond individual will and reveal a causality that is inseparable from a predetermined sense of character.

If the individual will is a product of temperament, it is also shaped by conventions—by moral laws so strong that they turn society into a prison without bars. In 1918 Dreiser collected a number of short stories in a book entitled *Free and Other Stories*. These stories illustrate the power of conventions, especially the convention of marriage, which proves to be more a trap than a source of human fulfillment. In "Free," a talented architect, regretting his early marriage to a sickly wife, wishes her dead so that he can be "free." But when she finally does die, he realizes that his conventional life has used up his youth and that being free is now meaningless. Another version of this story is "The Lost Phoebe," the account of a man who loses the ideal that led to marriage and in a hallucinatory state pursues his wife's youthful incarnation to his death. In both stories conventions create a destructive state of mind, marriage becomes a social bond robbing these men of youth and hence the vitality of life.

In 1927 Dreiser once again collected a number of stories in a book entitled *Chains* that further reflected his concern with conventions. One story, in which a groundhog thinks praying to a saint can combat the force of the river ("St. Columba and the River"), exposes

Dreiser's contempt for religious convention; in another a woman poisons herself in the hope that her husband's mistress will be blamed for her death, the power of conventions ultimately holding her loveless marriage in place ("Convention"); and in another a morally timid young woman fatally shoots her seducer, gives birth to their child, is exonerated in both legal and public opinion, and then under the weight of guilt and remorse commits suicide ("Typhoon"). Another story that treats the destructive nature of conventions is "The Shadow," in which a woman abandons an illicit affair in fear that she will lose her child if her behavior becomes subject to scrutiny in the course of a divorce. The converse of "The Shadow" is "Marriage—for One," the story of Wray, a young man who marries his girlfriend Bessie after he has transformed her into a "new" and independent woman. Once married, Bessie takes the idea of the liberated woman too far and refuses to become the conventional wife. She rejects Wray's desire for authority, leaves him, returns and has a child only to rebel again at the idea of being wife and mother, leaving him finally for good, even though he is still deeply in love. This story, as well as the portraits in *A Gallery of Women* (1929), reveals Dreiser anticipating feminist causes, advocating women's independence, even when the man is the victim of unrequited love.

Dreiser believed that conventions were unnatural social restraints within which human nature was maliciously bound and that Puritan dictates worked against human desire. He felt that conventions prevented life from being lived to the fullest. In another story, a successful engineer returns to the scene of his early poverty and remembers the drab routine, the suffering of his wife, and the death of their two children. Desiring to be free from the restraints of poverty and the tedious conventions of domestic routine, he had abandoned his wife in pursuit of the wealth and luxury that he eventually attained. Now, twenty-four years later, his first wife and her family all dead (the only constant in Dreiser's world is change), he is eaten up by remorse and guilt. The narrator concludes: "There is something cruel and evil in it all, in all wealth, all ambition, in love of fame—too cruel" ("The Old Neighborhood").[33]

Dreiser's world turns on contradiction: whether one accepts conventions and its chains or breaks the chains and seeks freedom, the end result seems to be the same—guilt and remorse. Conventions hold in place the institutions that characters cannot escape: they are obeyed with regret, broken with guilt. Dreiser seldom deviated from the position expressed in his conclusion to *Sister Carrie*: life was "blind striving," never remedied by "surfeit," always unsatisfying and lacking "content."

From Carrie Meeber to Clyde Griffiths, Dreiser's characters are acted on by an elegant materiality that produces desire but never brings true satisfaction. The forces that activate this desire come more from without than within, are closer to the stimuli of Jacques Loeb than the unconscious of Sigmund Freud, the behavioristic difference between Freud and Loeb being one of mechanistic emphasis. Dreiser's characters walk a tenuous line between freedom and conventions, well-being and poverty, success and failure, domesticity and criminality, their frailty often compounded by seemingly unexpected and accidental occurrences that start a chain of preordained events from the safe "clicking" shut that determines Hurstwood's fate in *Sister Carrie* to Clyde's "pushing" Roberta away that sends both to their death in *An American Tragedy*.

Beliefs this extreme were bound to encounter opposition, and Dreiser's worldview met with resistance on a number of fronts. Not only was he attacked by the neohumanists on grounds that his view of humanity was too harsh, he was also attacked by modernist critics who were unsympathetic to the naturalist method. In his influential essay, "Reality in America," Lionel Trilling (1905–1975) took exception to both Dreiser and his literary assumptions. He began his essay with a rebuke of Vernon Parrington, who, according to Trilling, was plagued by "the chronic American belief that there exists an opposition between reality and mind and that one must enlist oneself in the party of reality." Trilling was annoyed that liberal critics like Parrington were more willing to forgive Dreiser his faults than they were Henry James just because Dreiser was more obviously on the side of the poor. Trilling did not believe that Dreiser's "moral preoccupations [were] . . . going to be useful in confronting the disasters that threaten us." Trilling concluded with the charge that Dreiser's "ideas" (a word Trilling substitutes for "reality") "are inconsistent or inadequate."[34]

In retrospect, Trilling's argument seems overstated. It is likely that neither James nor Dreiser will save or damn us. James and Dreiser portrayed two different kinds of experience, both of which are worthy of being represented and as fiction not mutually exclusive. And then one does not fully understand what Trilling meant when he said that Dreiser's ideas were "inconsistent" and "inadequate." Inconsistent within his fiction or as ideas per se? Inadequate for what purpose? As previously noted, Dreiser was an inconsistent mechanist; but while Dreiser's own thinking is at times inchoate and contradictory, his fiction is not because his fictional aim is to dramatize conflict and not register a coherent philosophical system. Trilling's essay is more than a literary rebuke of Dreiser. It indicates that a new generation of critics was impatient with the naturalist method and its assumptions, and with the preference for the fiction of Dreiser and the naturalists over that of Henry James and the modernists.

9

Another major American naturalist at least indirectly influenced by French naturalism was Jack London (1876–1916). London began his career by filtering Kipling through Zola and ended it by influencing Sherwood Anderson, Ring Lardner, and Ernest Hemingway. His fantasy novels were influenced by H. G. Wells and influenced in turn George Orwell. In his autobiographical novel *Martin Eden* (1909), the Jack London figure comes upon Herbert Spencer's *First Principles* and puts everything aside both day and night until he has finished reading it. London's philosophy shares Spencer's belief in naturalistic force—a cosmic energy that is moving life ahead of it. London was equally influenced by John Fiske and Ernst Haeckel, and his use of naturalistic theory is more tutored and informed than critics often credit it with being.

London once referred to himself as a "material monist," by which he meant a believer in the idea that reality is reducible to material causes. And yet this term is not truly descriptive of his beliefs, primarily because of his interest in atavism and the nature of human origins. Such interests drove him back to prehistory and a Jungian-like unconscious, a Conradian realm of primitive being that might be redemptive rather than destructive. These idealized concerns were not necessarily consistent with his "material monism," creating an opposition between a radical individualism (which accommodated the superman) and a concern with mass politics (an inseparable aspect of his socialist politics). His tales of the South Seas put Polynesia and Melanesia in opposition—the former represented as a kind of pastoral heaven, the latter as an uncivilized hell. He longed for a natural innocence, and yet welcomed American imperialism, especially the takeover of Cuba and the Philippines. His sexual politics were characterized by a kind of androgyny, the idea that the ideal human being was a balance between the masculine (rational, efficient, scientific) and the feminine (affective, compassionate, artistic).

In his own life, he created a balance between the man of adventure—concerned with racialism, heroism, exploration (his fiction drew on his travels in the Yukon, California, and the South Pacific), and the epicene—shy, private, and philosophically curious. Even in his use of material themes, London was not always consistent. While he shared Spencer's view of force, he did not share Spencer's belief that evolution was necessarily a progressive process. Like Spencer, London believed in the survival of the fittest, a belief consistent with his interest in the superman, and yet he also expressed deep sympathy for the poor and portrayed the hobo sympathetically. He could reconcile conflicting beliefs: London wrote for money and sought success as a commercial writer in a capitalistic society while remaining a devoted socialist.

One does not look for consistency in London's work, especially considering that many of the contradictions are built into literary naturalism itself. London can write a story about the call of the wilderness to a dog that heeds that call and ends up running with a wolf pack, and he can write another story tracing the transformations of a wild dog into a tamed animal. In these two stories we have the essence of London's concern—the pull up and down of evolutionary process.

In *Martin Eden,* many of the contradictions that characterize the main character's life were to be found within London's own life. Martin Eden finds himself torn between two women—Ruth Morse, from a genteel background, and Lizzie Connerly, from the working class—and discovers that he wants neither of them. His disdain for the

Morse family turns to contempt, and his interest in Lizzie flags. Martin is also torn between his interest in achieving commercial success and his desire to produce serious fiction, finally solving the problem by writing adventure stories that bring him both public recognition and personal gratification. Once he has proved to himself his ability to succeed as a writer and once he overcomes the perils of romance, life becomes dull. Like London himself, Eden is subject to periods of severe depression; in a depressive phase he commits suicide by climbing through the porthole of an ocean liner deep in the South Pacific. London once again has a main character resort to suicide in his novel about an alcoholic, *John Barleycorn* (1913). Both of these stories anticipate what some of his biographers believe was his own suicide by an overdose of morphine in 1916.

London's adventures into the wilderness and chronicles of the urban poor, his struggle with poverty and disdain of success, his belief in the Nietzschean superman and his tolerance for the weak, his euphoric outbursts followed by bouts of serious depression—all this suggests that he lived the contradictions that characterized his writing. In London's stories we see clearly the interconnectedness of human experience. We start with basic assumptions about human nature (the evolution of primitive instincts, the drive to live and propagate, the desire to gain power over the environment and others) before we move to social relationships and systems (the tenuousness of love and friendship, the infusion of the primitive in civilized systems, and the embodiment of natural drives in the tribe, the mob, and the nation-state, where it is expressed as imperialistic reach).

London's tales of the Yukon, set as they are at the ground zero of nature's forces, deal with the limits of humanity, the individual defined against the extremes of nature. In "To Build a Fire" (1910) a novice to the Yukon adventures fatally out in seventy-five-degrees-below-zero weather. He had no understanding that man was "able only to live within certain narrow limits of heat and cold."[35] As in naturalism in general, London brings a zero-sum game to bear in his story. A zero-sum situation arises from oppositions, whether the opposition of economic and social classes or the opposition of man and nature, and there is always a winner and a loser. In London's struggle between man and nature, humanity functions within fixed mechanical limits; one cannot exceed those limits anymore than one could live without oxygen: naturalistic truths are a matter of built-in laws. Those who are still in touch with their natural feelings know these laws—and the limits they set—by instinct.

London gives expression in his story to a certain line of thinking in Darwinian thought—promulgated by Spencer, Huxley, and Fiske—that conventional knowledge was passed down from generation to generation. The man, unlike his dog, was no longer in touch with rudimentary nature. A primitive survival instinct was lost because the man and his ancestors had alienated themselves from rugged nature, but his dog, still in touch with nature, knew the danger: "the dog knew; all its ancestry knew, and it had inherited the knowledge" (148). When a cascade of snow from a tree puts out his fire, the man is too weakened by the cold to light another and eventually perishes in the snow, while his dog instinctively heads for the nearest human camp.

A related story is "Love of Life," the adventure of a man who goes into the Klondike in search of gold and then is brought to the edge of death as he tries to return to civilization (the passage between the civilized and the primitive is always fraught with danger in London). Abandoned by his partner after he sprains his ankle, London's survivor finds himself lost in the white wilderness. As he searches unsuccessfully for food, he gets weaker and weaker, until he is on the verge of death. But his desire to live is strong: "It was the life in him, unwilling to die, that drove him on."[36] As death nears, his cache of gold loses all value. Although surrounded by animal life, he realizes that he does not have the strength to compete with the other animals, and Spencer's idea of the survival of the fittest takes on specific meaning. About to expire, he finds himself confronting a sick wolf, which follows him patiently, and each waits for the other to die. When the crew of a ship on a scientific expedition to the Arctic finally saves him, he cannot reconcile himself to such good fortune and hordes biscuits to stave off future hunger. No story by London better grasps how transparent the line is between life and death or better depicts the urgent desire to live in the face of imminent death. The power of London's story lies in the way it focuses on a matter of ultimate significance—a man's desire for survival when faced with his immediate extinction.

Living by the laws of nature and not those of man often leads to an inversion of traditional values. In "Diable—a Dog," a man and dog are held together unto death by a mutual hate that is stronger than love. And in "To the Man on Trail" the law turns on a kind of fairness (a man steals back the money out of which he was cheated) and on the ability to remain strong and fleet (as he pursues revenge at the same time as he stays ahead of the mounted police). Indeed, law in this realm is customarily an individual and not a communal matter, values strength over weakness, and is often dispatched from the barrel of a gun. The laws of the wilderness and of civilization have little in common and those of the former legitimize the Nietzschean superman as a matter of necessity.

Another story that contrasts primitive and civilized life is "An Odyssey of the North." If the title is meant to suggest Homer's epic (at one point the central character is likened to Ulysses), London's narrative reverses the Homeric happy ending. The story is set in the Alusian Islands, the bridge between Asia and the new world, where Native and Caucasian life have long intersected. Naass has the blood of kings in him and is in line to rule the island of Akutan. He falls in love with Unga and wins her with the bounty of wealth he can give her family. But before their marriage is consummated, Unga is kidnapped by Axel Gunderson, a Swede, who has come to the North in search of gold and other bounty. Gunderson is one of London's supermen: seven feet tall, weighing three hundred pounds, with blond hair that gives him the look of a lion, he creates the laws by which he lives. Naass, sorely injured by the loss of Unga, goes in search of Gunderson, seeking revenge. When he finally catches up with them, he discovers that Unga has been won over by Gunderson. When Naass hatches a plot that kills Gunderson, Unga tries to kill Naass and chooses death by remaining with Gunderson.

In this story, London portrays the way a man and woman from a primitive island are so transformed by ways of the white man that there is no return for either of them to their former life. Gunderson, who embodies the spirit of territorial conquest, is the agent of this transformation. Even in death he is stronger than Naass, who at the end of the story is a persona non grata, a fugitive from his own land and a stranger in a new one. As in Conrad's *Heart of Darkness* (1902), the journey is through time as well as space; the journey takes us back in time to basic human truth. Conrad sends Marlow into the dark jungle; London sends his seekers into the white snow. Conrad depicts civilization giving way to primitivism; London depicts primitivism giving way to civilization. Both depict the destructiveness inherent in each transformation.

10

Among the last of the naturalists, Upton Sinclair (1878–1968) came the closest to being an American Zola. Like Zola, he addressed the biology of economics and wrote novels dealing with the major events of his day. Sinclair was the son of an alcoholic liquor sales-man and a mother from Virginia wealth. He knew firsthand the ad-vantages of wealth and the travail of poverty. This divide in his own life was later reflected in his fiction made up of wealthy protago-nists who often became involved with the lower classes. His major achievement was *The Jungle* (1906). Sinclair spent seven weeks inves-tigating the meatpacking industry, especially the Parkington district of Chicago. Teddy Roosevelt read his novel, which was instrumental in creating the Pure Food and Drug Act of 1906. His work won the respect of major international writers like George Bernard Shaw and Arthur Conan Doyle.

Along with *The Jungle,* his other major novels are *The Metropolis* (1908), a depiction of New York high society; *King Coal* (1917), deal-ing with a Colorado miner's strike; *Oil!* (1927), an analysis of the Tea-pot Dome scandal; and *Boston* (1928), concerning the Sacco-Vanzetti case (just as Zola protested the fate of Dreyfus, Sinclair protested the execution of Sacco and Vanzetti). He also wrote novels dealing with speculative finance (*The Moneychangers* [1908]), journalism (*The Brass Check* [1919]), and education (*The Goose-Step* [1923]).

For a decade, between *King Coal* and *Oil!,* Sinclair produced little of literary significance. His major literary achievement comprised the historical novels listed above, whose subjects concern contem-porary events. As such, they direct attention outward to a temporal reality rather than inward to a subjective reality. This has led to the legitimate charge being brought against him that the theme of his novels is often more complex than the characters who embody that theme—that is, his novels fail as radical fiction because his characters never attain a complexity that does justice to his political ideas. His novels accept a naturalistic reality at the same time as they present a left-of-center solution to the narrative problems they pose. As a result, his fiction has a morality-play quality—fictional characters take on historical villains in a confrontation between good and evil.

Van Wyck Brooks insisted that Sinclair's novels were formulistic: his workers good, his capitalists evil, his women diminished by money or dissatisfied by their wealthy husbands, especially when their men were patriots. A worker like Jimmie Higgins is portrayed as so helpless—crude and illiterate—that his defeat is inevitable: he becomes a martyr to the progressive cause, more symbol than a real person. But Robert Cantwell has pointed out that the protagonists in Sinclair's novel are more often wealthy young men whose aristocratic values are tested—and found wanting—by the radical movement. Hal Warner in *King Coal* and Bunny Ross in *Oil!* are wealthy converts to Sinclair's radical cause, as is Carmelia, who embodies New England gentility in *Boston*. With the exception of *The Jungle*, Sinclair's fiction takes the moral and political conversions of a wealthy character as its subject.[37]

Like Zola's, Sinclair's novels represent the world in which he lived—and the power that emanated from invisible channels. He saw the struggle between capital and labor as being at the center of modern industry. He believed that social justice was inseparable from economic equality, and did not surrender his beliefs even when he was accused of being an anarchist. There was a jungle within and a jungle without—change the latter and you change the former. Their topical concerns partly explain the popularity of Sinclair's novels when they were written; concomitantly, the passage of time has made them irrelevant and has rendered them outdated today. This is true of much literary naturalism—for example, Dos Passos's *USA* (1930–36) series and the novels of John Steinbeck, especially *The Grapes of Wrath* (1939).

In 1927, Sinclair wrote *Money Writes,* a caustic survey of American literature accompanied by an attack on Hollywood. In 1934, Sinclair ran unsuccessfully for governor of California on the EPIC platform

(End Poverty in California), a socialist program. When he proposed that Hollywood should pay higher state taxes, the movie industry turned against him with a "Stop Sinclair" slogan. This was among the first of the mass-media political assaults and swung the election from Sinclair to Frank Merriam, his seventy-three-year-old opponent. His relationship with Hollywood, however, was not totally hostile. In 1932, Metro-Goldwyn-Mayer adapted to his satisfaction his protemperance novel, *The Wet Parade* (1931).

In the forties and early fifties, Sinclair wrote eleven novels that make up the Lanny Budd series—contemporary historical novels in which his hero comes into contact with world figures (Hitler, Stalin, Roosevelt, etc.). *World's End* (1940) deals with the years 1913–1919; *Dragon's Teeth* (1942) treats the rise of Nazi Germany; and the last novel in the sequence, *The Return of Lanny Budd* (1953), treats postwar American attitudes toward the Soviet Union. Lanny Budd is by Sinclair's own description politically schizophrenic, caught between a commitment to the principles of liberalism and a desire for the expediency of pragmatism. His state of mind becomes a credible metaphor for the reality of Cold War politics. Sinclair wrote an autobiography, *American Outpost* (1932), which he revised and updated in *The Autobiography of Upton Sinclair* (1962). By the time he died, he had published forty-two major works.

Sinclair's fiction reflected the reality of his era. The journey to the city often brought the naturalistic character into contact with the slums, a product of the industrial world, and into contact with illicit work and sanitary practices. All of these elements can be found in his *The Jungle,* the story of an immigrant family that comes from Lithuania and settles in Chicago. As in most naturalistic novels, poverty leads to degeneration, although the novel ends on a note of sympathy for the working class.

Sinclair's novel treats a number of naturalistic themes. There is the plight of the immigrants, still part of the peasant world, who come to an industrialized, urban America, where they have to adapt to a new environment or be destroyed. The novel also exposes in detail the unsanitary conditions of the meatpacking industry (the slaughtering of diseased—often tubercular—cattle, the packaging of spoiled with good meat, the free play of rats next to the slaughtered meat), which led to federal legislation regulating the industry. Despite being a close-knit family in Lithuania, once they come to America the family breaks. As key members of the family die, Jurgis, the central character, sets out by himself. And as the family becomes poorer, a process of degeneration sets in.

An intelligent and informed examination of the naturalistic and socialistic novel in terms of the part-whole relationship is L. S. Dembo's *Detotalized Totalities* (1989). Dembo argues that socialist novels like those of Sinclair's are failures because their central characters cannot find the means to totalize—that is, give coherent meaning to—a world beyond capitalism. This is different from the charge, mentioned above, that Sinclair's themes are more complex than the characters who embody them, and Dembo's complaint can be answered by pointing out that the realist/naturalist novel is not able to go beyond history.

Literary naturalism is informed by determinism, by the idea that society is a function of the workings of heredity and environment. And yet the politics of literary naturalism are unpredictable, consistent with the belief that the particulars of future adaptation and survival are unknown. Socialist realism is both closed and open-ended: closed in that it is inseparable from the history of socialism; open-ended in that a socialist solution may rectify the imbalances of capitalism. The politics of socialist realism are thus predictable, consistent with the (mistaken?) belief that history is unfolding in sync with the evolution of communism.

A problem of ideological compatibility thus arises when a novelist like Sinclair writes a naturalistic novel and then appends a socialist solution to the problems it poses. Sinclair's socialist desire for equality as a remedy for the plight of the poor was inconsistent with the Darwinian belief in a natural hierarchy and the naturalist's belief in the deterministic workings of heredity and environment. From a naturalistic point of view, limitations are built into history itself: they stem from the imbalance between the rich and poor, the powerful and disenfranchised. The fate of the Jurgis's family, especially its loss of solidarity, embodies the inevitably destructive existence of an agrarian, immigrant family in the new, industrial world. From a socialist point of view, such problems will be corrected by the politics of the future. Despite the insurmountable odds against Jurgis, the novel ends on a note of hope, although it certainly does not the supply a resolution with the kind of specificity that Dembo would like to see.

Like London, Sinclair overlaid naturalism with socialist doctrine, moving his fiction to the Left. While socialism may have been inconsistent with naturalism, it was, however, consistent with the desire to prevent putting the public at risk for the sake of profit and with the desire to see labor better benefit from the industrial process. Despite the contradiction, it was not unusual to find naturalists—from Dreiser to Sinclair, from London to Richard Wright—giving voice in their writing to utopian socialism or communism or some other philosophy of hope.

5

A Field of Force:
The Cosmic Model

1

Belief in a realm of force added another dimension to literary naturalism: the contention that events extrinsic to the characters rather than their will were determining their fate. A sense of cosmic play runs through the works of Joseph Conrad, Stephen Crane, and Thomas Hardy. Conrad's works can conveniently be divided into three periods: *Heart of Darkness* (1899 [published in book form with *Youth* in 1902]), *Lord Jim* (1900), and *Youth* (1899) were completed before 1900. *The Rescue* (1920), *Victory* (1915), and *The Shadow-Line* (1920) were written after 1914. *Nostromo* (1904), *The Secret Agent* (1907), *Under Western Eyes* (1911), and *Chance* (1913) came in between.

Conrad's novels depict a test of self against the emptiness of the universe. The test is carried out in three dominions: the sea, the jungle, and the political arena. Each of these dominions is riven by a great divide, whether between land and sea, city and jungle, institutions and revolution, a divide often intensified by the geographical and cultural divide between East and West. In a novel like *Almayer's Folly* (1895), the East-West divide structures the plot. Almayer's daughter Nina, a half-caste born to Almayer's Malaysian wife, refuses to accept her diminished status and runs away with Dain Maroola, a Malaysian rajah, to regain her ethnic identity.

The divide is human as well as geographic. In "The Secret Sharer" (1912) a newly appointed captain encounters a second self, a mate from another vessel swimming out of the darkness to take sanctuary aboard his ship. This other self, a Cain figure, knows evil: in a state of exhausted desperation, hoisting the sail needed to save the ship in a violent gale, he has strangled an uncooperative crewman. The captain immediately identifies with this mysterious stranger; he sees how easy it is to become an outcast from humanity and accepts his murderous presence as an extension of himself. He eventually endangers the safety of his own ship by sailing too close to land so his secret sharer (who comes out of and then disappears back into darkness) can safely swim to shore—risking his own destruction in the name of this secret self.

Conrad's divide also separates youth from maturity, the natural from the supernatural, the healthy from the sick, the calm from the storm. In *The Shadow-Line,* the central character sheds his youth and tests his maturity on his initial voyage as captain when his ship is becalmed at 8°20′ north with his crew disabled by an outbreak of typhoid fever. His chief mate insists the previous captain of the ship, dead and buried at that point on the compass, is at the bottom of this calamity, putting a curse on the ship, wishing its crew dead. The captain refuses to accept a supernatural explanation of a natural event and sustains hope with the help of an Apollonian figure, who maintains a semblance of order while assisting him in getting the ship back to port. In his preface to the story, Conrad denies any intention of giving credence to the supernatural, insisting that the workings of the cosmic are part of a natural process: "I could never have [made use of the supernatural] because all my moral and intellectual being is penetrated by an invincible conviction that whatever falls under the dominion of our senses must be in nature and, however exceptional, cannot differ in its essence from all the other effects of the visible and tangible world of which we are a self-conscious part. The world of the living contains enough marvels and mysteries as it is; marvels and mysteries acting upon our emotions and intelligence in ways so inexplicable that it would almost justify the conception of life as an enchanted state."[1]

However mysterious the process, chance is a part of the workings of nature: cosmic events have a natural explanation. Conrad participated in what was one of the main issues of debate in the late nineteenth century—that is, whether primitive culture was in the process of advancing toward or in decline from some ideal notion of civilization. In a thorough discussion of this controversy, John W. Griffith believes Conrad opted for "regression," probably under the influence of Cesare Lombroso and Max Nordau.[2]

Reality in Conrad's fiction is the opposite of that in Jack London's. The call of the wild brings a number of naturalistic factors into play. In London, the call can lead to regenerate experience. In Conrad, it can lead to a degenerate process—that is, to contact with a destructive element that begins to weaken what holds civilization together. Conrad's thinking was Janus-faced: his fiction looked back to literary naturalism as an end product of an era and forward toward literary modernism with its newly formulated impressionistic reality.

Science had assumed that the earth had originated as an incidental by-product of cooling gases from the sun; now the second law of thermodynamics, formulated by Lord Kelvin in 1851, postulated that the earth would eventually freeze through the diffusion of heat-energy. The understanding of entropy took on cosmic relevance: the universe could run down like a machine, like a tightly wound clock. In 1897, Conrad himself spoke of the universe as a machine that had "evolved . . . out of chaos . . . and behold!—it knits. . . . It knits us in and it knits us out. It has knitted time, space, pain, death, corruption, despair and all the illusions—and nothing matters."[3] (In *Heart of Darkness,* Conrad suggests the idea of the "knitting machine" with his description of the knitting women in the director's office in Brussels.)

Such cosmic pessimism led to the belief that civilization was grounded in a contradiction. In his *Romanes* lecture in 1893, Thomas Huxley claimed that a cruel divide exists between the ethic perpetuated by civilization and the laws of nature. One suggested the perfectibility of man; the other insisted on base human limitations. Freud carried this idea even further, arguing that modern man became more civilized only by suppressing the baser instincts. Such instincts could never be completely repressed, and they would eventually express themselves at the expense of civilization. Kurtz himself is an embodiment of these ideas. In the city, Kurtz—a poet, a painter—embodied civilization; in the jungle he reverts, in a devolutionary way, to primal savagery, consistent with a theory of evolution. Lower animal instincts competed with higher human instincts. While Herbert

Spencer argued that evolution would lead to progress and improvements, Max Nordau insisted that it could lead to degeneration.

The romantics collapsed the natural and the supernatural into each other. As J. Hillis Miller has pointed out, the mid-Victorian poets then separated God from nature, leaving an absence in the physical world. Conrad filled that absence and the realm beyond with darkness. "The darkness is in the heart of each man, but it is in the heart of nature too."[4] The moment of truth in a Conrad novel involves a character's encounter with this pervasive darkness. The darkness is further spread by imperialism, revealing "society [as] an arbitrary set of rules and judgments, a house of cards built over an abyss." Imperialism "becomes the expansion of the will toward unlimited dominion over existence" (6), resulting in a corrupt society such as the city of London with its hidden connections.

Human consciousness tries to validate this reality: "nothing exists except as it is seen by someone viewing the world from his own perspective" (4). Conrad's multi-perspective point of view suggests the existence of multiple realities, all of them tenuous and diffuse. In *Youth,* Conrad first makes use of a subjective perspective in the person of Captain Charles Marlow, a stand-in for himself. Marlow, speaking to a group of men sitting around a table drinking, describes the series of troubles (from a disabling leak to an explosion and fire) that eventually sink the *Judea*—this on his initial voyage as second mate on the ship, which was carrying coal to Bangkok. The voyage is one continuous disaster, which youth nevertheless imbues with romance.

Conrad would later complicate even more this point of view. In *Chance,* for example, Powell tells the story to Marlow, who in turn tells it to an unnamed narrator: this complex structure superimposes subjectivity onto subjectivity, distances the reader from events, and creates a sense of variable reality: this emphasizes the element of chance that determines the lives of Flora de Barral, her husband Captain Roderick Anthony, her father, the Fynes (all caught up in a power struggle over Flora), and Powell himself, whose chance position as second mate aboard the *Ferndale* makes him a central observer to the larger forces at work in the story.

Conrad outlined his theory of the novel in the preface to *The Nigger of the "Narcissus"* (1898). There he distinguishes among the tasks of the scientist, philosopher, and artist: the first seeks facts, the second ideas, while the third plumbs the self in search of emotional truths. It is the artist who "speaks to our capacity for delight and wonder, to the sense of mystery surrounding our lives; to our sense of pity, and beauty, and pain; to the latent feeling of fellowship with all creation—and to the subtle but invisible conviction of solidarity that knits together the loneliness of innumerable hearts, to the solidarity in dreams, in joy, in sorrow, in aspirations, in illusions, in hope, in fear, which binds men to each other, which binds together all humanity—the dead to the living and the living to the unborn" (*Tales of Land and Sea*, 106). Conrad's novel itself gives meaning to these humane sentiments. It involves the fate of James Wait, a black man whose terminal illness (here human infirmity is inseparable from blackness) at first provokes and then unifies the crew of the *Narcissus*. Wait embodies the human predicament, and the crew eventually displays solidarity in the face of that predicament.[5]

Ian Watt has read Conrad's preface as a Pateresque statement of aesthetics. The chaos and unpredictability of life leaves us vulnerable to experiencing the world as merely an accumulation of Paterian impressions (Watt, 86). But Conrad, as Allan Hunter has suggested, is also interested in "the permanence of memory,"[6] in the journey back into time and into the processes of degeneration. Conrad takes us beyond civilization to the origins of existence. There we find the primitive forces still at work in civilization, but which it tries to conceal.

Human consciousness is thus the source of two realities: reason produces the light of civilization, and a more atavistic consciousness engenders the darkness. In the center of Conrad's world is a cosmic emptiness. Miller sees the function of the modern poet—from Yeats and Eliot to Stevens and Williams—as that of filling Conrad's "emptiness" with "being": "If there is to be a God in the new world it must be a presence within things and not beyond them" (10). Conrad thus becomes a mediator between the Victorian and the modern world, his nihilism challenging Victorian faith, his skepticism providing a starting point for a new concept of reality. Put differently, Conrad's fiction moves in two directions: back toward the spiritual emptiness of post-Darwinian thought, and forward toward a philosophy of modern being—regeneration thus turns on degeneration.

The thin line in Conrad's fiction between civilization and the primitive suggests the tenuousness of the force of order when exposed to the degenerative force of chaos. The idea of such degenerative force is especially evident in Conrad's major fiction, dealing with the process of imperialism. *Heart of Darkness, Lord Jim, Nostromo,* the Malay novels—all are concerned with colonization, especially as it involves the relationship between civilized and primitive life.

Heart of Darkness recounts Marlow's journey up the Congo River in search of Mr. Kurtz. The journey not only takes him up the river but also back in time: Marlow enters a prehistorical realm, where the laws of civilization no longer apply. A prized agent of the trading company, Kurtz has not been heard from for over a year. An accomplished musician, Kurtz at one time was sensitive to the best in culture. "All Europe contributed to the making of Kurtz," Marlow concludes.[7] In his origins, Kurtz embodies imperial Europe with its ties to a civilized reality that has been abrogated by its encounter with the primitive. The Inner Station, desolate and decaying, is the physical center of the heart of darkness, where Kurtz—in his isolation from the modern world and his proximity to the savage jungle—physically and culturally degenerates. Kurtz had consolidated the natives, whom he organized for his attacks on elephant herds and other tribes. His camp is piled high with ivory, and the skulls on the fence that face his hut are both homage to his misused power and symbolic reminder that greed and death often go together. Marlow further learns that Kurtz had the power to "electrify" large meetings and to organize the tribes for his own purpose. Such insight into the connection between the charismatic leader and his followers moves us from the realm of empire to the edge of totalitarianism. Conrad's story contains the kernel of modern political history.

Marlow comes to see that savagery is the common denominator of history and that civilization only conceals it. Kurtz is able to organize such savagery and turn it into power. Once Marlow gets deep into the jungle, he sees in Kurtz the rapaciousness that drives life. Cities are a function of institutions that transform this primal struggle into a daily business routine. Just as the city uses technology and bureaucracy to do its work, both Marlow and Kurtz find the means to control the natives: Kurtz by becoming their god, Marlow by frightening them with the boat's steam whistle. From the beginning of time, rulers have reigned by suggesting they have access to supernatural powers.

Chinua Achebe, the Nigerian novelist, has challenged how Conrad depicted the natives in *Heart of Darkness*. Achebe argues that native Africa went through three stages: in the first, a native culture existed that belies the modern idea of the primitive; in the second, colonizers exploited the land, succeeding in this endeavor in great part by dehumanizing the natives; and in the third, postcolonialism led to the displacement of tribal authority as it gave way to emerging nation-states. Achebe reads Conrad's story as creating imperial stereotypes, contending that the natives in their passive submission to Kurtz and in their naked savagery fail to do justice to the historical reality of the Congolese tribes.[8] But Achebe's argument has slightly less point when we recognize that Conrad is depicting a destructive element that both civilization and primitivism share—a dark side that reveals itself more clearly at the primitive level because there is less institutional concealment. The point is not that the people of Brussels are more culturally sophisticated than or morally superior to the natives of the Congo—only that they have used the institutions of civilization to conceal a rapaciousness they share with the Congolese. Kurtz is stripped of his civilized pretenses when he succumbs to this destructive element—an experience, from the knowledge of which, Marlow tries to save Kurtz's fiancé, preserving the tenuous sentiment on which civilization rests.[9]

Achebe's criticism raises a fundamental point involving the distinction between civilization and culture. The idea of civilization combines a belief in historical progress with that of biological evolution—a belief that human behavior advances as a result of adherence to codes preserved by social institutions that regulate human nature. Civilization is primarily the product of urban development and its institutions designed to regulate lawlessness. Culture is more specific, the product of philosophical, moral, and religious beliefs, technology, art, legend and lore, customs, superstitions, and the like. Art works and weapons manufacturing share cultural commonality, different expressions of the same communal mind. A theory of civilization looks generically at a people as an evolving product of social codes restraining human nature; a theory of culture looks specifically at a people as the product of a particular time and place. Civilization involves teleology; culture, historical accident. In a civilization, tragedy is looked on as a universal human experience; in a culture, it is looked on as an indigenous one, unique to a specific time and place. Conrad's story is universal, drawing on the absolutes of civilization; Achebe's critique is historicized, drawing on the idea of the relativity of culture. The two views involve different assumptions about the nature of reality and slide by rather than engage each other.[10]

In his depiction of Lord Jim, Conrad once again tests the universal against the particular—that is, tests the limits of human nature. The sea, in its total emptiness, becomes the testing ground of self, where an essential humanness confronts existential reality. Jim became a kind of cosmic wanderer when he jumped into the darkness of the sea—that is, jumped from the *Patna* when it collided with the debris of a sunken ship, damaged its bulkheads, and took on water. The crew believed that the ship would soon sink. Jim joins three other crewmembers in a lifeboat, leaving eight hundred pilgrims sailing for Mecca to drown. When the *Patna* is rescued by a French vessel that tows it and its passengers into port, the cowardly deed becomes widely known. Jim's desire to be heroic is shattered forever. Marlow becomes interested in his case when he attends the inquest that relieves Jim of his officer's certificate, and he follows Jim's fate as Jim tries to stay one step ahead of his lost honor.

When Jim becomes Stein's agent on Patusan, a trading post on one of the minor islands of the East Indies, he feels that he has finally found sanctuary. In the course of time, Jim wins the friendship of the natives, who call him Tuan Jim—Lord Jim. His closest friend is Dain Waris, the son of Doramin, the native chief. All would be well except, as in most Conrad stories, evil comes in pursuit in the person of a second self, Gentleman Brown, a renegade thief, who has come to steal what he believes is the emerald jewel that rumor has it is in Jim's possession. Brown is confronted by Dain Waris, who would have deflected Brown's treachery. But Jim is persuaded by Brown's promise to leave the island and so calls off the blockade, only to see Brown murder Dain Waris. Accepting the responsibility for his friend's death, Jim offers himself in sacrifice to Doramin. Marlow believes Jim has long been waiting for this moment of redemption. Conrad has once again written a novel dealing with inevitability.

Like most of Conrad's fiction, the meaning of *Lord Jim* emerges in the telling. Marlow sees Jim as an embodiment of human fate, his ideal, the achievement of honor, undone by the unpredictability of a hidden self in a world where the unpredictable is the only certainty. Innocence, when tested, proves to be weak and gives way to cunning: darkness is stronger than light. Brown, like Jones in *Victory*, is the embodiment of that darkness: the inevitable link in a chain of fate. As in both novels, the source of evil is greed—for money in *Victory*, for a precious jewel in *Lord Jim*—and in both novels the treasure does not exist. Like most novels, the resolution in both *Lord Jim* and *Victory* comes at the end but is often built into the beginning; Conrad, however, uses this fact about fiction to convey a philosophical point, the idea that what comes at the end in the real world is likewise built into the beginning: sequence becomes consequence.

Lord Jim is brought down by a hidden self—an aspect of his being that reveals itself in crisis and betrays his idealized persona. When the idealized self comes in contact with the darkness, with the emptiness of the universe, it is subject to life's unpredictability. *Nostromo* is Conrad's most detailed portrayal of this theme. The story is told against the backdrop of a revolution in the Republic of Costaguana, a fictitious country in South America. Pedrito Montero has taken control of the eastern part of the country and is about to advance on Sulaco, the principal city in the western section, where in the nearby mountains is located the San Tomé silver mine, for two generations under the supervision of the Gould family. In his hope to save six months of silver excavation from the rebels, Gould has entrusted the silver to Gian' Battista—known as Nostromo ("our man")—and Martin Decoud, the editor of the local paper, who has a utopian vision of the western section becoming an independent state, the Occidental Republic. Nostromo is known for his integrity and Decoud for his intellectual rigor. But both become subject to a second self that reveals unknown things about themselves. Nostromo leaves Decoud on the island of Isabel, where he has deposited the silver, while he goes to sink their lighter. Here Decoud intuits the emptiness of the universe and takes his own life: "After three days of waiting for the sight of some human face, Decoud caught himself entertaining a doubt of his own individuality. It had merged into the world of cloud and water, of natural forces and forms of nature. In our activity alone do we find the sustaining illusion of an independent existence as against the whole scheme of things of which we form a helpless part. . . . A victim of the disillusioned weariness which is the retribution meted out to intellectual audacity, the brilliant Don Martin Decoud, weighted by the bars of San Tomé silver, disappeared without a trace, swallowed up in the immense indifference of things."[11]

Nostromo is now tempted by the circumstance that Decoud's suicide presents him with and does the unexpected: he conceals the silver treasure, selling it ingot by ingot hoping to become rich. Because Decoud has weighted himself with four of the silver bars to drown himself, Nostromo rationalizes that he cannot return the silver because it is likely he will be accused of stealing the missing ingots. Like Lord Jim, he reveals that his integrity is no match for the temptation he is faced with. It is not until Nostromo is accidentally shot by Giorgio Viola—who confuses him with Ramirez, his daughter's suitor, of whom he does not approve—that Nostromo, on his deathbed, realizes what he has done. When Mrs. Gould declines his offer to return the silver, it goes unclaimed; in a mirror image of the situation in *Victory* and *Lord Jim*, where there is greed for money and a jewel that doesn't exist, here the silver exists, but absent a greed for it. Once again the object of greed in a Conrad story turns out to be empty of value. Viola's daughters—Linda and Giselle—are left with their conflicting impressions of Nostromo, and Dr. Monyghan, whose corrupt past still pursues him, survives by the power of that corruption and shuts out the emptiness of existence.

Isolated in this empty universe, Conrad's characters become the source of their own reality. Conrad's other fiction further explores the fragile nature of modern civilization. His *The Secret Agent*, dealing with a terrorist plan to blow up the Greenwich Observatory, aims at undermining the source of bourgeois order—time itself. Conrad's world is ruled by chance—what he called cosmic irony—and his characters, stumbling blindly, are often frustrated in their attempts to give meaning to their lives. When the bomb goes off by accident,

Stevie blows up himself instead of the observatory, and Winnie, his sister, is so outraged that she murders Mr. Verloc, her husband. Inspector Heat (the name is significant, given Conrad's entropic universe) is the modern equivalent of Dickens's Inspector Bucket—now faced with an anarchistic society that has changed the rules of the crime game.

The law depends on predictability; terrorism on unpredictability: Verloc has changed the terms of the relationship between crime and law. For the detective to function, he must be able to identify with the mind of the criminal, which in Conrad's fictional world is now more difficult to do. Conrad was perhaps thinking here of impressionistic claims: if each individual, like Pater's Marius, constructs a reality out of personal sensations, how can communication be possible? Like the sun giving way to heat-death, communication was giving way to solipsism. Both revealed a process of decline.

Under Western Eyes, a sequel to *The Secret Agent,* examines moral nihilism in the context of a more politically extreme situation, dealing as it does with Russian revolutionaries in St. Petersburg and Geneva. This novel draws on the failed Russian revolution of 1905 and anticipates the Bolshevik Revolution of 1917. Razumov, a philosophy student at the university, becomes involved in terrorist activity when Haldin, a fellow student, assassinates a czarist minister and then takes refuge in Razumov's room. When Razumov goes to the authorities, Haldin's fate is sealed—and so is Razumov's. Drafted into the employ of the secret police, Razumov is sent to Geneva to spy on the exiled revolutionaries. Among this group is Nikita, the sister of Haldin, with whom he falls in love. Trying to escape his guilt, he confesses to Nikita his involvement in Haldin's death, guaranteeing his own death. Once again Conrad wrote a story that supposedly reflects the laws of the universe: it begins with a chance occurrence (Haldin going to Razumov's room) and then plays itself out from there as a sequence of seemingly inevitable events.

In *Victory* Conrad again treats the connection between chance and inevitability. Axel Heyst is the manager of the Tropical Belt Coal Company on Samburan, one of the Malaysian islands. Although the principal island in the archipelago is Sourabaya, Heyst remains in isolation on Samburan after the coal company has gone bankrupt,

living in a house with his father's furnishings, including an intimidating portrait of the now dead father. At the center of the novel is
the gratuitousness (the Cause of causes) that characterizes Conrad's
fiction: Heyst has unwittingly provoked the animosity of Schomberg, the innkeeper on Sourabaya, who whets the appetites of a Mr.
Jones and his henchman, Martin Rodman, by allowing them to believe that Heyst has hidden "plunder" on Samburan. As a guest at
Schomberg's hotel, Heyst has met and then run away with Lena, the
violinist in an all-women orchestra. Jones and Rodman come in pursuit, intending to pillage. Heyst, who has been trying all his adult life
to escape the bleak philosophy of his father, finds his life controlled
once again by dark forces when Lena, who embodies the optimism
he has long sought, dies at the hands of Jones.

Conrad sets a childlike innocence against an abiding greed from
which there is no escape. The isolation of the setting, the introspective passivity of Heyst, the loneliness of the principal characters, the
gratuitous evil that pursues them—all combine to reinforce the sense
of inevitability that runs through the novel. The power of the novel
also stems from the way it is told; Conrad uses a telephone-game
device involving a narrator informing another narrator, the story
told from several points of view, each trying to come to terms with
Heyst's inherent goodness in contrast to the malice of Schomberg
and the evil of Jones and Rodman. The novel is an inverted Adam-
and-Eve story, with Heyst's father as a god-like presence and Schomberg and Jones as the embodiment of evil. Heyst and Lena find that
their innocence can not confront the destructive element that is built
into reality.

Evil is a given in Conrad's world, inseparable from human nature,
and the difference between order and chaos can turn on sexuality,
which Conrad connects with the jungle. In *The Rescue* (begun 1898,
published 1920), Captain Tom Lingard is summoned out of the
darkness by Carter, the captain of a yacht that has foundered off the
shore of a Malaysian island. The island secretly houses a group of
chiefs, who are attempting to restore a young prince to power—a
plan Lingard supports. Fearful that the yacht will expose the planned
coup, Lingard goes out to help Carter in the hopes of freeing the
grounded ship. Literally out of the darkness comes Mrs. Travers, the

beautiful but dissatisfied wife of the yacht owner, whose sexual temptations are too hard to resist and lead to Lingard's downfall.

Characters like Razumov, Heyst and Lingard are confronted with the element of the unpredictable that is part of the workings of the universe—a destructive principle that conflates fate and chance, order and chaos, good and evil, civilization and primitivism. These characters encounter the forces of darkness, participate in the cosmic masquerade, and are driven toward introspection before it overwhelms them and becomes self-destructive.

2

Stephen Crane (1871–1900)—a friend of Conrad's, who inspired Crane to adopt the impressionistic technique that added a new dimension to the naturalistic novel—died at the age of twenty-eight, and yet he left an impressive amount of work. Almost all of his fiction, with the exception of *The Red Badge of Courage* (1895), grew out of personal experience. He knew firsthand the slums he depicts in *Maggie* (1893) as well as the West of "The Blue Hotel" (1898) and "The Bride Comes to Yellow Sky" (1897). He struggled in the shark-infested sea off the coast of Florida as the shipwrecked victim he described in "The Open Boat" (1897). His impressions of war from Cuba and Greece found their way into *Wounds in the Rain* (1900), stories like "Death and the Child" (1897), and novels like *Active Service* (1899). In his desire to have lived the experience of a story, Crane anticipated Ernest Hemingway—was, in fact, a bridge between Hemingway and Twain, whom he admired. Influenced by Conrad, Crane was one of the first literary impressionists, giving a subjective dimension to an otherwise realistic story and thereby anticipating neorealism.

Added to these achievements was the fact that *Maggie* was perhaps the first naturalistic novel published in America. In an inscription to Hamlin Garland, Crane wrote that his story "tries to show that environment is a tremendous thing in the world and frequently shapes lives regardless." Maggie is certainly the victim of her environment. She is born into poverty, raised by drunken parents, trapped in the slums of New York, a victim of Christian scruples, and ultimately condemned when, lured by the more elevated world of her brother's friend, Pete, she gives herself to him. Her story is a matter of destiny, the outcome of which is determined from the beginning. Her act is more a matter of compulsion than will, pre-ordained rather than thought out.

In addition to the debilitating effects of the physical environment on Maggie is the equally unfavorable influence of a middle-class moral environment. From the sentimental songs Maggie hears at the dance hall to the obsessive desire of her mother for respectability, Maggie is the victim of middle-class values that instill a desire in her to escape the slums. Added to this is the confusion she experiences when confronted by contradictory imperatives, such as Jimmie's demand that she remain a virgin, on the one hand, and Pete insistence that she give herself to him, on the other. The poverty of the slums undermines a sense of community and locks each character into an isolated realm of desolation, but this desperation produces a subliminal state of mind receptive to a false promise of hope. Middle-class and Christian imperatives create a desire for respectability—a desire that in the slums is as lethal as the poverty that controls the Johnsons' lives.

Crane's novel works on two levels: he depicts a physical environment and a state of mind that work together destructively. As in *The Red Badge of Courage,* where a romantic vision conceals the horror of war, an irrelevant code of respectability informs Maggie's life in the slums. Added to this social code is a religious code that intensifies the effects of environment and further determines Maggie's fate. For Maggie, the wages of sin are literally death. In addition to being the product of poverty and the ignorance that goes with it, she is also the product of an amoral, irreligious life. Thus Maggie's fate as a suicide in the East River is determined by what is most irrelevant to her life—the middle-class social values she never knew and the Christian moral scruples she never had.

Crane's *The Red Badge of Courage* challenges the idea that heroism exists per se, as an inherent quality that one brings to war. Henry Fleming, a young farm boy, joins the Union army with expectations of achieving glory in battle. But during the first attack, Henry throws down his rifle and runs. He tries to rationalize his cowardice as natural instinct when a squirrel in the woods runs away from him. Fight or flight was the law of both nature and battle, and he acted instinctively when he fled in fright. In his attempt to return to his regiment, Henry is bloodied when hit in the head by another soldier, and he returns with a "red badge" and no mention by his comrades of his panicky flight. In the next battle, Henry holds his position bravely. As other battles loom, Henry feels he has proved his mettle: he has been transformed from coward to a man of courage who can take pride in his behavior.

In *The Red Badge of Courage*, Crane questions whether there can be such a thing as heroism in a naturalistic world. Henry Fleming acts cowardly and then courageously in battle, but this behavior is the result of automatic responses—first of fear, and then of egoism and pride—and not of willed action. Henry's behavior is more instinctual than rational—that is, more a matter of weighted than willed motives. In the first battle, cowardice overwhelmed pride; in the second, pride outweighed cowardice. Henry is acted on when he both runs and stays in battle. The difference between a hero and a coward is thus a matter of behavioral stimuli, weighted in this case toward the desire to win the approval of his comrades. Men face each other in war not as friends, or even as enemies, but as programmed machines. That much of the action in the novel is related impressionistically from Henry's point of view creates a sustained irony: we think he is making events happen, when in reality events are happening to him.

Crane is as well known for his short stories—especially "The Open Boat," "The Blue Hotel," and "The Bride Comes to Yellow Sky"—as he is for his novels. And like the novels, the stories place characters in settings in which false codes of behavior often conceal the true nature of reality. "The Open Boat" is Crane at his best, and here a sense of man confronting cosmic forces is clearly at the very center of the story. Four men, survivors of a shipwreck, struggle for two days and nights to reach the shore. The sea is violent with huge waves that threaten to swamp their ten-foot dinghy. As they approach the shore, the survivors see a windmill, which the narrator suggests looks like a giant and they as ants. In Crane's fiction, the windmill comes to symbolize cosmic force, underscoring the ants' humanity. Reality becomes a state of mind: the windmill seems to get bigger the closer they come to it, the sea larger, the men smaller. Nature is at best indifferent to their predicament, but as they come closer to land, nature's indifference turns to cosmic play, as if fate brings them so close to being saved only to drown them. The narrator comments: "When it occurs to a man that nature does not regard him as important . . . he at first wishes to throw bricks at the temple . . . [but] there are no bricks and no temples."[12] A common plight leads to a comradeship that supplies the only source of meaning in the story. But when the boat swamps and they struggle for shore, that sense of comradery is lost: each man must confront the raging sea by himself, caught in the unpredictable play between sea and land that parallels the struggle between man and the cosmos. It is ironic that the oiler, perhaps the strongest of the four men, is the only one to drown; the land, welcomed by the others, becomes his grave. One cannot know the meaning of the universe—the fragile difference between life and death—until such experience offers a look behind the veil. As the last words of the story tell us, only then can one become an "interpreter"—a mediator between man and the cosmos.

In "The Bride Comes to Yellow Sky," Crane inverts the code of the West. Jack Potter, the town marshal, returns with his bride to Yellow Sky, Texas, from San Antonio. In Yellow Sky is Scratchy Wilson, harmless when sober, a terror when drunk. Wilson sends fear through the whole town, embodying the familiar turned strange under the influence of alcohol. Wilson, when drunk, is intent on revenge in his desire to kill Potter, but his malice evaporates when he learns that Potter is newly married. Human beings have little recourse in war or the sea against death, but death can be prevented by the romantic sentiment of a drunken gunslinger. In "The Bride Comes to Yellow Sky," Crane again demonstrated the whimsy that controls our lives as well as the code of the West.

"The Blue Hotel" reverses the plot of "Yellow Sky." The Swede that comes to Scully's hotel in Nebraska has read too many dime novels and believes that he will be killed in keeping with the code of the West. At first nervously passive in the face of his fears, his personality changes when drunk, the story being yet another of Crane's that turns on the effects of alcohol. Now looking for a fight, he accuses Scully's son Johnnie of cheating at cards, beats him in a fistfight, and then is stabbed by a professional gambler in a nearby saloon. In "Yellow Sky" we move from potential violence to calm resolution; in "The Blue Hotel" we move from the calm of a card game by a warm stove on a cold, windy night to the violence of murder. In Crane's world, a thin line divides peace from violence, and the slide from one to the other is not willed. Everyone participates passively in the Swede's death: Johnnie for cheating, the Easterner for not challenging Johnnie, the cowboy for encouraging Johnnie, Scully for opening the whisky, the Swede himself for seeking the death he fears. Each act individually is harmless, but collectively, each act is lethal. It is fitting that death results from a card game and ends with the act of a professional gambler. Crane found exactly the right metaphor—life as a gamble—multiplying individual acts into a collective realm of determined force to convey the way chance builds on itself.

An inexplicable causality, perhaps carried over from his interest in Tolstoy, is at work in Crane's fiction. As previously mentioned, Tolstoy adds an epilogue to *War and Peace* (1865) in which he explains that historical causes are too complex to be fully understood. Crane also coveys a sense of a complex multiple causality that makes what happens seem like a cosmic mystery. The idea of a cosmic force is, of course, an extrapolation from naturalistic theory. Logically, nature is no more hostile than it is beneficent. Man is a part of, not separate from, nature and thus subject to nature's laws. The inimical play of events that one finds in Conrad, Hardy, and Crane is as much a part of nature as the hawk's swooping to catch the field mouse. Life feeds on life—that is the way the system works.

But logic is not always at work, and the idea of the cosmic has many origins. The cosmic, for example, can stem from a sense of inevitability, as we find in Hardy and Faulkner. Another source is the obsessive temperament, which, when it acts compulsively, evokes the idea of being controlled by outside forces. Still another source is life's accidents: the letters that go astray in Hardy suggest some kind of will inimical to human welfare. And lastly, the inconsistencies of life, like Crane's oiler drowning in sight of land, allow whimsy to take on ironic, at times cosmic, meaning.

The cosmic is another aspect of the determinism that informs naturalistic literature, and though it is represented as mysterious, it is not that there is no explanation for it (this would make it the transcendental force of romanticism); rather human reason is not yet developed enough to understand it. Man is thus posited to be the source of the cosmic but then, ironically, the cosmic is considered to be too complex for human understanding.

3

Cosmic irony adds another direction to the novels of Thomas Hardy. Chance, accident, coincidence—"Hap," as Hardy called it— dominated such novels as *The Return of the Native* (1878), *The Mayor of Casterbridge* (1886), *Tess of the D'Urbervilles* (1891), and *Jude the Obscure* (1896) and sealed his characters' fate. Near the end of his career, Hardy turned to poetry. *The Dynasts* (1903–8) is a poetic drama about the Napoleonic Wars in which history is rendered as a series of accidental events. Hardy's novels involve another version of naturalism. Seemingly uninterested in hereditary or even environmental matters, Hardy sets his fiction against the backdrop of a cosmic realm and a world of chance. Behind the chance events that control the novel is a sense of mystery, of larger forces at work.

Hardy's *The Return of the Native* is a representative example: the story of Eustacia Clym-Wildeve née Vye seems fated from the beginning. She chooses a false happiness when she marries Clym and then falls back on Wildeve, who had previously demonstrated his faithlessness. Her sense of what she wants is clouded by a reality that she cannot comprehend. Added to this is a string of accidents that work to seal Eustacia's fate. She would have gone back to Clym if his letter had not gone astray. And she and Clym would have had the financial means to move to Paris if Diggary had not mistakenly given Mrs. Yeobright's money to Thomasin. Such continued apparent mishaps reveal Hardy's belief that life is mere whimsy, governed by chance, reinforcing the cosmic sense of events being beyond the characters' control.

Hardy's *Tess of the D'Urbervilles* is also dominated by a sense of the cosmic. Hardy's novel takes realism/naturalism in a new direction. The story of Tess has little to do with Darwinian theories of heredity, albeit a bit more with environment, and considerably more with temperament, an unacknowledged aspect of heredity. The main theme in this story is how accident determines the characters' destiny. Jack Durbeyfield becomes self-important when he learns by chance that he is related to the long-vanished D'Urbervilles; and Tess's fate is sealed when the letter—a familiar Hardy device—that she writes Clare Angel, confessing her affair with Alec D'Urberville, goes under the rug, where he does not find it. Chance determines the course of the novel, but chance seems to stem from cosmic sources. Despite their opposite meaning, chance and fate seem intertwined in Hardy's fiction.

Another novel in which life is depicted as determined by accidental events is *Jude the Obscure*. Jude Frawley's one mistake—his marriage to Arabella—produces Father Time, whose very name suggests the inevitability of fate built into time. The novel is obsessed with the past. Jude's task of repairing the medieval cathedrals suggests the anachronistic. Ironically, he desires to enter the church and works to keep it in repair, while the dictates of the church work against his common-law arrangement with Sue. Hardy and William Faulkner share much in common: both novelists construct a past that works on and determines the present. Characters are the blind victims of their past, products of choices that spring from incomplete understanding. As in the traditional naturalistic novel, there is always a more informed force working beyond the limited comprehension of Hardy's cosmic victims.

As previously mentioned, Jude is a more determined version of George Eliot's Adam Bede; one a carpenter, the other a stone mason, the tragedy of their lives stems from chance events set in motion early on by mistakes they make in their romantic pursuits. But the stakes are higher in Hardy's novel, the consequences more serious. Perhaps the difference in meaning can be explained by the thirty-five years between the novels. During that span there was a growing sense of misdirected force that came with the industrial machine. Both novels have rural settings, but even the countryside now is part of a larger, more complex realm. A diminished humanity confronts a larger, seemingly cosmic force. Determinism plays an important role in both novels, but in Hardy it is more overriding.

Like the naturalists, Hardy created a world where the will of the individual is dominated by forces from without. Like Conrad's characters, Hardy's characters define themselves against a cosmic realm that, if not hostile to their well-being, is at least indifferent to it. Hardy never thought of himself as a naturalist, but there is little doubt that his narrative world owes much to the battle between cosmic force and individual will that informed one variant of the naturalistic novel.

6

A Field of Force:
The Social/Political Model

Darwin's conclusions challenged the old religious truths and engendered a feeling of cosmic homelessness that in turn spawned human anxiety. The works of Marx and Freud sprang in part from this anxiety, from the fear of an unknown future. If God was absent from the universe, He was also absent from human affairs, which explained this new sense of political loneliness. This condition was key to the rise of a social and political novel that had its roots in literary naturalism. One subgenre of the social/political novel was utopian fiction, the hope of a new world; another was a fantasy literature that projected both the best and the worst kind of future.

1

Like Jack London, Knut Hamsun (1859 –1952) spent his early years as a vagabond, first in Norway and then in America. His first novel, *Hunger* (1890), is a sympathetic portrait of the urban downtrodden. Another major work, *Mysteries* (1892), is the story of an outcast, Johan Nagel, and a study of degeneration, ending in suicide. Hamsun believed in the superiority of national "blood" and in the idea of the sacred soil and the "rooted" life of the people, ideas that connected him both with Nietzsche and Hitler, the latter of whom he visited in 1943.

Growth of the Soil (1917) is a naturalistic story of life on the land, an existence that is constantly being threatened by modern, commercial, urban life. Isak, a Norwegian peasant, leaves his village and starts a farm deep in the wilderness. During this time, the land changes. As in many naturalistic novels, the story treats another generation in the person of Alex Strom. The community is now dependent on the welfare of a copper mine and the profits from the store that services the mine. Isak, however, remains faithful to the land, which both supports and vitalizes him. Hamsun depicts a withering agrarian life at the same time that he celebrates the soil as something mystical, even sacred. Tragedy looms, however, in the inevitability of its imminent loss.

Hamsun's *Hunger* is the other side of the narrative coin from *Growth of the Soil*. In *Hunger* he treats two well-established realistic themes—urban hunger and the artist in the city. The two come together in the person of the unnamed narrator, who is the impoverished artist in the city, totally at the mercy of the commercial whims of editors. When the novel opens, he has not eaten for days and is delirious with hunger. His hunger makes his behavior so erratic that many people think he is a madman. The narrator's relationship with people is conditioned by whether or not he has money; with money, he is tolerated; without, he is treated as a criminal outcast.

Another social commentator was Gerhart Hauptmann (1862–1946). Despite winning the Nobel Prize for literature in 1912, Hauptmann's importance in Germany was much greater than his literary reputation in Europe and America. He wrote about everyday life and common people—farmers, miners, and weavers, the lower class in general—who responded enthusiastically in turn to his sympathetic portraits of them. His first play—*Before Dawn* (1889), a portrait of farm life—makes explicit use of naturalistic, environmental, and hereditary theories. His next play, *Lonely Lives* (1891), depicts the disillusionment that awaits a young intellectual class. His best-known play, *The Weavers* (1892), in great part based on accounts by his grandfather, a former weaver, depicts the exploitation and living conditions of the Silesian weavers in the 1840s. The owner Dreissiger intimidates all the weavers with the exception of Becker. Joined by Jaeger, a returned soldier, Becker leads a rebellion against Dreissiger. By the end of the play, the army has arrived, shots are heard, and the uprising is destined to fail. Hauptmann creates a spectrum of characters whom he plays off each other: the plight of the weavers is ultimately contrasted with the well being of Dreissiger and those who uphold the social and religious institutions that preserve the status quo. Time has been kinder to Ibsen whose literary reputation has outlasted Hauptmann's. Ibsen's early plays were so controversial that he had to leave Norway for Germany, where from 1877 to 1882 he wrote his most purely realistic plays: *A Doll's House* (1879), *Ghosts* (1881), and *An Enemy of the People* (1882).

Maxim Gorky anticipates the social causes that came with the Russian Revolution of 1917. *The Lower Depths* (1902) takes place in a cellar apartment, where an assortment of derelicts uses and abuses each other. These characters share two things: each other's misery and the tyranny of Kostilyoff, the landlord. After the landlord dies, there is expectation of change for the better, but nothing of the sort happens. These characters are locked into a process of degeneration and decline so extreme that it cannot be broken, even when the symbolic embodiment of their predicament is eradicated. Like Hauptmann's *The Weavers*, Gorky's *Lower Depths* treats a group caught in a situation from which there is no escape. They are determined from within as well as without. Their character—what the naturalists reduce to temperament—has become their fate.

Giovanni Verga gives us an Italian version of literary naturalism. His *The House by the Medlar Tree* (1881) treats the decline of a once prosperous family. In the village of Trezza on the island of Sicily, the Malavoglia family has fallen on hard times. Hounded by the loan sharks, the family is forced to sell their ancestral house. Seeing no future in the village, the oldest grandson leaves home. On the surface, Verga's novel is an Italian version of degeneration. The decline of the Malavoglia family is the main subject of the novel, but this decline is portrayed against a historical background. One sees that an old way of life in Sicily is passing. Conscription officers, tax collectors, and process servers pursue the family. As the government gets more powerful, even the strongest members of the family are weakened. The novel, however, ends on a note of hope. When the youngest grandson, Alissio, takes on the responsibilities of the family, their finances improve to the extent that he can pay off their debts and buy back the family house.

2

Jack London's incursion into the naturalistic political novel was *The Iron Heel* (1908). At the beginning of the novel, the United States is under the control of a capitalistic oligarchy that protects its wealth with a police force and army (though these are not needed so long as the people give consent to a system of religious and cultural ideas that reinforce the status quo). The novel is told from the perspective of Avis Everhard, the wife of a die-hard socialist, Ernest Everhard. Avis comes to see "fearful realities" beneath appearances. As she becomes more committed to the revolution, she transforms herself, creating a second, revolutionary self. The novel begins with a series of lectures that establish London's ideological positions: Ernest, London's superman, insists that inductive reasoning avoids metaphysical speculation and is superior to deductive reasoning, especially when reinforced by pragmatist philosophy. He also believes that the capitalists put profits ahead of the worker's and public's well being. The interests of the lower-middle class are preempted by those of the upper-middle class, and their interests in turn are preempted by the trusts. The trusts produce an abundance of goods, which leads to a surplus. Everhard does not want to destroy the machines of the trusts (that would be to turn back the historical clock); instead he advocates that the workers take control of the means and the distribution of production. As for the surplus, Everhard points out that the way capitalism solves the problem is through imperialism, where the raw material of the colonies is brought into the production process and the surplus of goods are disposed of among the colonies; under socialism, he explains, there would be no surplus because there would be no profits. (Another solution regarding the surplus had come from Edward Bellamy, who advocated the general distribution of surplus goods.)

In London's novel, the United States, Germany, and Japan vie for imperialistic superiority. Eventually the United States and Germany engage in a war that reduces the surpluses of each country and ends unemployment by creating the need of an army. The imperialist countries struggle for control of the Pacific, and London not only anticipates World War I and II but also the attack on Pearl Harbor.

The war ends when labor in each country calls a general strike. But the labor unions become part of the problem rather than the solution when they are bought out by the oligarchy, forcing the socialists underground. Events come to a revolutionary head in Chicago (the ur-city of literary naturalism) in a scene that London adapted from Zola's description of the communard revolution in *La Débâcle* (1892). After four days of revolutionary slaughter (unlike Bellamy, London believed the transfer of wealth between the classes would necessarily involve violence), Ernest and Avis find their way back to New York, where Avis's story ends in mid-sentence, suggesting that she hid the manuscript before she was arrested or once again escaped into the underground. The fact that the manuscript is recovered and published in a distant future further suggests that the socialist revolution has succeeded or that a government sympathetic to its cause has replaced the oligarchy.

London's novel is an ideological mix of Nietzsche and Marx, an attempt to reconcile the superman leader to the collectivist state. London was wrong in his Marxist belief that the middle class would be absorbed into the proletariat and that eventually there would be a viable international labor movement. But he was correct in connecting capitalism, the nation-state, and imperialism. Behind it all was the working of power as a mechanical force in a world of limits.

Another attempt at political fantasy was Edward Bellamy's *Looking Backward* (1888), a visionary utopia. Julian West, with the help of a mesmerizer, goes to sleep in Boston on May 30th, 1887 and awakens 113 years later on September 10th, 2000 to find the city and its institutions totally transformed. There are now no stores or banks. There is instead an industrial army made up of the nation's citizens who use modern technology to produce an abundance of goods that are shared equally among the nation's citizens. Each citizen is given a job that best suits his or her aptitude and is on call for twenty-four years, from the age of twenty-one to fifty-five, although most work only to the age of forty-five. There are no laws in this new state, no legislature, no military army or police force because there is no war or crime; institutions are self-regulating, and surplus goods are consumed by the citizens, thus avoiding a surplus market that leads nations to compete hostilely with other nations. Bellamy's plan influenced Howard

Scott's doctrine of Technocracy, which Dreiser tried to get Upton Sinclair to incorporate in his EPIC political platform. Sinclair dismissed the idea because behind the system was an industrial engineer who could easily become a totalitarian dictator.

There are two ways of looking at political institutions: holistic and progressive. The holistic view assumes that human society is by nature conservative and as such that there are limits on how much change it can tolerate; the progressive view looks to an ideal that justifies radical change. In theory the naturalistic view was holistic, but in practice it was often progressive. Both London and Bellamy look to a radically different future. The novels of Bellamy, Donnelly, and London begin where Zola's novels end—with the power of a commercial/industrial class about to be transformed. The utopian writers fantasize what is implicit in naturalism, often resorting to science fiction to do so.[1]

Like George Orwell's *Nineteen Eighty-Four* (1949) that came after them, Bellamy's and London's novels deal with a future that has already passed. The predictive aspect of their visions is thus moot. But if one puts in perspective the opposition they saw between socialistic and capitalistic prescriptions, it can be seen that they anticipated in a real way the forty-four year conflict between capitalism and socialism that constituted the Cold War. The socialism they desired was never to be. Capitalism and its major institutions were too powerful to be destroyed. There are differences between nineteenth- and twentieth-century capitalism: institutions like the World Bank have created a dependency between what had been imperial countries and their colonies, and global financing has created an international labor force and market. But capitalism as an investment system powering the production and distribution of goods has remained intact.

3

The anxiety over where science and technology were heading led to fantasy projections of a culture gone astray. H. G. Wells in *The Time Machine* (1895) describes the earth cooling and man devolving as the time traveler journeys farther into the future. Wells makes use of the oppositions built firmly into the naturalistic novel. He reworks the dialectic between material and aesthetic pursuit, the battle between man's animality and the desire for beauty. When the time traveler arrives in a new realm he discovers two forms of life that have moved further and further away from each other: the Eloi, who have become so aestheticized that they are near extinction; and the Morlocks, who have become so brutalized that they have sunk beneath the animals.

In *The Island of Dr. Moreau* (1896), Wells recasts this plot, showing Dr. Moreau actively engaged in vivisection, through which he has transformed the island animals surgically, giving them the rudiments of humanity (that is, the ability to think and to use language). Moreau's experiment recapitulates the naturalist's belief that evolution and degeneration are two sides of the same coin. As the animals lose their human attributes, they revert to their original nature, revolt against Moreau, and kill his assistant. Despite the fate of Dr. Moreau, Wells came to believe that evolutionary progress could be made under the enlightened leadership of a scientist leader. His fantasy expression of this idea was *When the Sleeper Awakes* (1899) a futuristic story that contrasts totalitarian and Enlightenment ideas.

In *A Modern Utopia* (1905), Wells connected his belief in Darwinian evolution with his idea of utopia. But Wells modified Darwin's ideas because he did not believe that nature was working for humanity's benefit; instead man had to inform nature with a directing intelligence that might come from the built environment. He believed the way out was a World State. "As against the individual the State represents the species; in the case of the Utopian World State it absolutely represents the species."[2] Hope lay with the race, not the individual, and he came to believe in what he called the "Mind of the Race," which involved the merging of the individual mind into a collective mind that preserved a racial memory. Thus, like Samuel Butler and later Aldous Huxley, he adopted a vitalist position—a belief that matter was informed by mind. By this point in his thinking, he had sacrificed democracy to authority.

In *Mind at the End of Its Tether* (1944), written two years before his death, Wells not only repudiated the efficacy of a racial memory, he predicted the end of the universe, as we know it, and the end of man, as we know that species.[3] Wells's thinking ended in doubt. He questioned two powerful constructs: the Enlightenment construct, which he ended up rejecting, and the Darwinian construct, which he radically revised. Wells's fantasy fiction parallels the rise and fall of naturalism as a literary mode.

A close friend of Wells who shared many of his reservations about the future of modernism was George Gissing. Gissing's *The Private Papers of Henry Ryecroft* (1902) also asked where modern industry and science were taking us, pushing even further the antidemocratic theme that Gissing had expressed so clearly in *Demos* (1886) and *The Nether World* (1888). Both Wells and Gissing raise the same naturalistic questions that we find in George Orwell, especially in Orwell's fantasy projection *Nineteen Eighty-Four*.

Orwell (1903–1950) had a sense of history that allowed him to see the interplay between and among the nation-state, imperialism, and totalitarianism. Everything in Orwell's world, as in literary naturalism, comes back to the realm of force—in Orwell's case force expressed as political power. Orwell's superstate begins as an Enlightenment construct, intent on the need to control nature, and then seeks to extend this control over the general population. The superstate is part of the evolutionary development of capitalism. Power is the end product of the superstate, and explains its need to control minds, manipulate the past, and contaminate language. The rise of the superstate destroys individualism. For Orwell, modern history went wrong when socialism failed to make a difference. Instead of the state achieving individual equality, it created another kind of inequality based on hierarchy: Big Brother took the place of wealth; superpoliceman replaced the business tycoon. Control became an end in itself, and hope for a community gave way to the masses under the dictate of a master. As O'Brien tells Winston: "The party seeks power entirely for its own sake. We are not interested in the good of others; we are interested solely in power."[4]

Orwell believed that the failure of modern political systems stemmed from the breakdown of liberalism with its faith in individuality and then the additional breakdown of socialism and communism: individual greed splintered the state; totalitarian power dehumanized it. Neither political system produced a community. What Orwell saw so clearly was how power structures all else—subsumes consciousness, language, sex, history, even nature, reducing the landscape to the vistas it allows to be seen. Power in the form of

Newspeak destroys difference: war is peace, slavery is freedom, and ignorance is wisdom. Language means what Big Brother tells us it means. What went wrong at the level of the state infects everything—the city, the masses, art. Like Wells, Orwell took us to the end of the Enlightenment legacy. The state began by organizing power and ended by being consumed by the power it organized.

4

Both Wells and Orwell saw that power taken to an extreme resulted in political tyranny. But in another naturalistic fantasy, William Golding (1911–1993) suggests that the loss of authority leads to anarchy. *The Lord of the Flies* (1954) is a moral fable that answers Ballantyne's *Coral Island* (1913). Golding portrays a band of boys stranded on an island who degenerate from rational beings into primitive savages. Golding's novel is the reverse of a utopian novel like *Robinson Crusoe* (1719). Instead of those marooned on a deserted island learning to cope with and control nature and to progress toward civilization or forms of authority, they devolve, reverting to an instinctual primitivism. They become hunters and turn lethally on each other. As in Conrad's *Heart of Darkness* (1902), Golding's novel suggests that atavistic forces are freed when one is cut off from the authority of civilization. When the marines arrive, they bring authority and civilized order to bear on the chaos of the jungle.

Anthony Burgess's (1917–1993) *Clockwork Orange* (1962) picks up where *Lord of the Flies* leaves off. *Clockwork Orange*, about a violent gang leader in an equally violent futuristic society, voiced Burgess's fear of what a totalitarian future might bring. The novel portrays naturalistic violence confronting a corrupt, authoritative government intent on brainwashing a sociopath hoodlum through a behaviorist method of rewarding behavior that conforms with the dictates of the establishment and punishing behavior that deviates from it. While not excusing sociopathic behavior, Burgess suggests that an important aspect of human nature is lost when one is cut off from basic human instincts, even when those instincts lead one to engage in acts of primitive violence. This is especially true when deviant human behavior is used to justify a totalitarian show of power. Burgess highlights one of the main dilemmas facing naturalistic theory: the conflict that exists between natural instincts and socially marginable behavior.

No literary mode was more concerned with the opposition between primitivism and technology, culture and civilization, than literary naturalism though the thinking here, as the above discussion reveals, was not of a piece. Burgess, like Freud (along with Norris and London), believed that modern humanity had lost contact with a residual natural self and was instinctually diminished. Golding, on the other hand, believed that forms of political authority were necessary if civilized life was to be sustained.

The transformation from a coal-burning smokestack culture to an electrically-powered, computer-driven information culture involved exponential change. Each phase of technology creates new ways of seeing the world and new forms of control. Dreiser saw such control as corrosive: it impinged on the natural realm and created an artificial society ruled by puritan values and a commodity culture. The debate here was primarily political. In between these extremes—and on another thematic level—Joseph Conrad (along with Stephen Crane and Thomas Hardy) maintained that a more ironic turn of events and a cosmic destructive element contaminated the workings of both the jungle and civilization. There was thus a variable response to what should have priority—the primitive or the technological.

Descending the evolutionary ladder can bring one face to face with savage impulses, climbing the evolutionary ladder can result in restraints that curb natural instincts or forms of state power that destroy individualism. The balance between the savage and the civilized, the primitive and the decadent, anarchy and authority is precarious. Both the individual and the state are the product of evolutionary forces. The modern state needs to exercise authority to prevent anarchy; at the same time such authority needs to be restrained to prevent the slide toward totalitarianism.

5

The origins of totalitarianism in Europe are not easy to chronicle. Movements like fascism stem from failed democracies. Totalitarianism is the product of a mass movement: it appeals to different classes but mostly to the middle class, is deeply suspicious of international movements, often resorts to terror and the threat of war, asserts the primacy of the nation, demonizes its enemies, and favors a one-party system under the control of a charismatic leader who can eliminate dissent; it takes its being from emotion and myth, especially the myth of the nation-state and the belief in national destiny. This sense of destiny is often connected with a mystique of the land. Totalitarianism attacked liberalism, asserting that maintaining order and control was more important than preserving liberty and individual rights. It promised vengeance for wrongs inflicted by others and suffered in the past—depressions, military defeats, reparations, challenges to national borders. It accepted the marketplace, so long as it was subordinated to the state, and held out the promise of better economic times.

Historically, the movement found support among those disillusioned with the new secular society, who felt something important had been lost in the decline of religious authority and the elimination of the monarchy. In France, Louis Napoleon's Second Empire (1851–70) capitalized on these grievances, but not as blatantly as the Action Française, an organization founded in 1899 that supported a new nationalism based in part on anti-Semitism. By 1917 the movement had gained a military component and extended itself to the masses. Under the leadership of Charles Maurras and Leon Daudet, its position became so extreme that by 1925 the Pope had condemned it.

An undercurrent in this movement was a distrust of rationalism, positivism, and materialism—combined with hostility toward bureaucracy, the parliamentary system, and the idea of democratic equality. Nietzsche and Bergson challenged Bentham and Comte: positivism gave way to a vitalism that affirmed a life force, often grounded in the idea of the power of native (read nationalistic) soil and the people. New theories of the unconscious (Sigmund Freud), a new psychology of the crowd (Gustave LeBon), and the import of revolution through violence (Georges Sorel) encouraged a notion of the masses as primordial force.

In 1906 Georges Sorel (1847–1922) wrote *Reflections on Violence*. Sorel supported the new movement of socialism, which aimed for a classless society and the public ownership of industrial production. The work of Marx and Engels, especially the *Communist Manifesto* (1848), helped the movement. As the movement developed, it split into various camps: two important factions were anarchism and syndicalism. Anarchism was the political belief that government defended injustices and that all government should be abolished. Early anarchists were William Godwin (1756–1836), Mikhail Bakunin (1814–1876), and Pierre Joseph Proudhon (1809–1865). Syndicalism supported the idea of seizing control of industry through general strikes, sabotage, and violence. Along with Proudhon, Sorel was a leading syndicalist. Another splinter group was the Fabians (who sought gradual, peaceful reform) and the revolutionaries (who wanted immediate change through violence). Sorel's book was an argument for the latter option and lent support to movements on the Left and the Right that felt violence was justified in attaining their political goals.

The old nineteenth-century conception of liberalism, democracy, and egalitarianism gave way to a new scientism based on doctrines of the overman, elitism (involving a hierarchy of those who governed), and the glorification of war and violence. These trends were reinforced by social Darwinism, the rise of anthropology and zoology as academic subjects, and the appeal of new racial doctrines. A book that addressed these new concerns was Ernst Haeckel's (1834–1919) *Riddle of the Universe* (1899), which in Germany had enormous sales. Haeckel is best known for his theory that ontogeny recapitulates phylogeny—that the development of an individual organism involves duplicating its evolutionary stages. Thus history became biology. The new sociology of Max Weber (1864–1920) promoted the idea of a charismatic leader as an alternative to bureaucratic rule. These men, along with Nietzsche and Spengler, should not be held responsible for the way their key ideas would later be misused.

Fascism tapped into many intellectual sources. Enlightenment ideas, especially the concept of the nation-state and the rise of a destined people, would be taken up by the Right. These doctrines were later reinforced by naturalism, which rested in turn on social Darwinism—the notion of a natural force, in particular, was the basis for the romantic belief of *Völkisch* nationalism. In Germany there was a national resistance to urbanism, bureaucracy, and technology. A Nazi antiurbanism connected the land with cultural health—and the city, bureaucracy, and technology with degeneration and cultural decline. And yet the need to marshal support from the masses, the rise of regulating agencies, and the connection between the preparation for war and the demand for an advanced industrialism brought about the dominance of cities, the development of bureaucracy, and the advance of technology.[5]

Embedded in Oswald Spengler's (1880–1936) philosophy of history was a forerunner to these ideas. Spengler's theory of history stemmed from a belief in the organic nature of society and is consistent with modernistic theories of history (such as Toynbee's). But, as in literary naturalism, he reduced each culture to its biological basis, its pattern of growth and decay. The process of decline began when we moved from a landed to urban society. Destiny and countryside were at the heart of Spengler's theory—a national destiny and a vital countryside. As one moves away from the natural rhythms of the land, instinct gives way to reason, myth to scientific theory, and marketplace to abstract theories of money that is processed by banks. When all this happens, a primitive sense of race is lost. It is not hard to see how these ideas might have given rise to the belief that modern, urban civilization had interrupted a process of German destiny and that the dominance of the city—with its heavily Jewish population—was contaminating an Aryan racial line. These ideas nurtured the belief, left unstated by Spengler, that a strong central government and a charismatic leader could redeem the state from this process of decline. It all came back to the state. Fascism rejected economic activity separate from the state and thus rejected both nineteenth-century laissez-faire and socialism. It advocated an organic social order wherein the individual would find his or her place in the society based on ability. The new leader would exploit a new ideology held fast by nationalism and militarism.

The word "fascism" comes from the Italian word "fasces," which refers to a bundle of rods carried by the Roman lictor. The idea behind fascism as a political movement is that a bundle of disconnected grievances and demands are heard and answered by a leader of the party. Fascism can play itself out in a paroxysm of violence, as happened in Hitler's Germany, or it can gradually lose popular support, as in Franco's Spain. In every case, for fascism to succeed, the demands must have social urgency and the support of a vital leader.

In 1919 Mussolini (1883 –1945) founded the *Fasci Italiani di Cambatti-mento*, composed mostly of ex-soldiers who sought the overthrow of the government by violence. By 1922 most of the ideas that constitute fascism had taken hold in Mussolini's Italy, as they would in Germany a decade later. Soon almost all of Europe and even parts of South America would have an active fascist party. Dollfuss and Schu-schnigg headed a fascist movement in Austria from 1933 until its incorporation into Germany in 1938, Horthy led one in Hungary, Pil-sudski in Poland, Metaxas in Greece, Franco in Spain, Solazar in Portugal, and Perón in Argentina.

Nineteenth-century liberalism—the triumph of the individual as defined by John Stuart Mill—was attacked from both the Left and the Right. Modernism with its emphasis on subjectivity and later existentialism with its emphasis on unrestrained individualism would try to reinstate the autonomy of the self. But in the meantime, naturalism transformed the idea of the individual: it did away with the idea of the heroic, substituted the politics of mass man and the power of industrial technology for freedom and independence, and replaced romantic dreams with a theory of cosmic and social force.

The theme of force was translated into political, mostly proto-totalitarian terms, by naturalistic authors and presented realistically as in need of correction (London, Sinclair, and Farrell) or depicted via fantasy as threats to humanism and liberal individualism (Orwell, Donnelly, and London). But there were other authors who went beyond their writing, became activists, and engaged the political moment. Two such writers were Knut Hamsun in Norway, who moved toward the political Right, and Theodore Dreiser in America, who moved toward the political Left.

6

Knut Hamsun's reputation in the West was diminished by his sympathy for the far Right, especially his support of the Nazi party in Norway and his sympathy for Hitler's causes. Robert Ferguson has analyzed the source of Hamsun's beliefs in his biography of him, *Enigma*.[6] The most significant element was Hamsun's dislike of

England and affection for Germany. Added to this was his distrust of socialism, which he felt encouraged "endless strikes," and his hatred of communism. He supported the use of the army to put down the 1931 strike at the Norsk Hydro plant at Menstad, in Telemark. The troops were ordered in by Vidkun Quisling (1887–1945), the Defense Minister, who was executed in 1945 for his leadership in the Norwegian Nazi party and his participation in the German occupation of Norway during the war. When in 1932 Quisling viciously attacked the Labor party in the Storting, Hamsun was one of the signatories in a petition of support. In that year he also contributed a foreword to a book, *The Politics of Revolution and Norwegian Law* by Herman Harris Aall (1871–1958), in which Aall contended that the Labor party's activities were illegal. Aall was the leading political theorist of the Norwegian Nazi party and a close friend of Quisling. Aall's influence on Hamsun was ongoing.

Despite (or perhaps because of) the fact that he lived in or near big cities much of his life, his sympathies lay with a rural, landed population. He believed the vitality of the land could energize a people and curtail the spread of urban liberalism. Hamsun had an aristocratic distrust of the mob and of democratic process. He admired the charismatic leader—Mussolini and Hitler—who could lead the mob toward the political Right. In the early thirties, Hamsun proclaimed that fascism was inevitable in Norway as well as Europe in general. Hamsun also joined the attack on Carl von Ossietzsky (1889–1938), a German veteran of World War I, who later became a pacifist and who warned Europe of the military buildup in Germany, for which he was jailed and later interred in Sachsenhausen concentration camp. In addition, Hamsun supported racist notions to protect the presumed purity of the German race. He lent support to Jon Alfred Mjøen (1860–1939), a Norwegian biologist, who propagated a theory of "racial hygiene" that was endorsed by the Norwegian Nazi party.

Hamsun's wife, Marie, even more committed to Nazism than her husband, was a member of Quisling's NS Party. Their children were all educated in Germany, and both sons were members of the Norwegian Nazi party. Hamsun visited Hitler in 1943. After the war he was accused of treason, but like Ezra Pound in America, he was declared mentally deficient. Nevertheless, he lost his country estate, was fined eighty thousand dollars, a bankrupting amount at the time, and his last years were spent in poverty.

On the opposite end of the political spectrum was Theodore Dreiser. Dreiser shared Hamsun's dislike of England and affection for Germany. But unlike Hamsun, Dreiser had long been sympathetic to Russian communism. In 1927 he visited Russia and recorded his mostly favorable response in *Dreiser Looks at Russia* (1928). He was impressed with the benefits pledged to workers, the emancipation of women, and the absence of lawyers, but he complained about the unsanitary conditions and governmental spying. Dreiser's support of Russian communism stemmed from his belief in social and political forces: he felt communism from the Left would help balance the forces of capitalism from the Right. Dreiser joined the John Reed Club and, in the thirties, gave himself to such political concerns as the defense of the Scottsboro boys (nine black men who were sentenced to be electrocuted for allegedly raping two white girls who had been riding a freight train in Scottsboro, Alabama). He also supported the Harlan, Kentucky, coal miners' strike, and he protested the conviction and imprisonment of Thomas J. Mooney for supposedly bombing the San Francisco War Preparedness parade in 1916.

In the late thirties, he supported the Loyalist cause in Spain, traveling to Barcelona and visiting the Ebro River battlefield. Dreiser even sided with Stalin when Hitler signed his nonaggression pact with Russia. And he advocated that America stay out of the war at this time. In *America Is Worth Saving* (1941), Dreiser outlined a capitalistic plot to take over Europe. He insisted that England plotted with Hitler to conquer Russia, but Hitler had "double-crossed" England before England could double-cross Hitler. In June of 1941, three months after the publication of Dreiser's book, Hitler broke his nonaggression pact with Russia, and Dreiser suddenly found that he was for American intervention.

Dreiser did not turn officially communist until about five months before he died, but he probably would have if Earl Browder, who found Dreiser's politics unpredictable, had not refused his request to join the party. Between 1940 and 1945, Dreiser continued to support communist causes. His interest in Russian communism never waned:

he was deeply moved by the courage of the Russian people during the war. His novels were more read in Russia than in the United States, and just before his death Stalin deposited a royalty check for $34,600 in Dreiser's Los Angeles bank account, in great part as a token of appreciation for Dreiser's political support. In July of 1945, William Z. Foster, Dreiser's old friend, succeeded Earl Browder, and on August 7, 1945, Foster officially welcomed Dreiser into the American Communist party.[7]

Both Hamsun and Dreiser believed in a universe of force, often embodied as political power. Hamsun thought the force could be redemptive if organized from the political Right, Dreiser if the force was organized from the political Left. As a result, Hamsun and Dreiser—on opposite sides of the political spectrum—shared common ground. Hamsun's sympathy was with a rural population, Dreiser's was with urban dwellers, and while they may have bewailed the fact, both recognized that the age of liberalism—John Locke's idea of Enlightenment natural rights, Mill's doctrine of liberty, and Emerson's belief in self-reliance—had passed. Individualism had given way to mass culture, and the idea of the masses was only one step away from the idea of the need for a master. Certainly Hamsun was wrong in his support of Hitler, as Dreiser was wrong in his support of Stalin. But everything in their thinking—conditioned by theories of force and power—had led to such commitment.

7

Thematics and the Conventions of the Novel

Naturalism has roots in biological assumptions: it deals with transformations in living systems. As such, a set of dichotomies structure naturalistic fiction. We have, for example, the dichotomy between the primitive and the civilized and between regeneration and degeneration. No narrative mode was more concerned with the transformation of the self; thus in the novel of compulsion we find a second self or double that takes over, and in the family saga we see each generation becoming more incapable of adjusting to its environment. The subject of environment in turn leads to the dichotomy between the land and the city—one of the key themes in naturalistic fiction. In the city novels we get a host of subthemes: the effect of industry, the rise of the slums, the threat of the crowds, the rise of political strongmen who can persuade the crowd—now a mob—to embrace dangerous ideologies, such as totalitarianism, that are often put into practice via war. Given our dual nature, when political conflict cannot be resolved peacefully, it is usually resolved violently—by combat or war.

Archetypal expressions of each of these themes can be found within the naturalistic canon. The power of the primitive, for example, is revealed in Jack London's *The Call of the Wild* (1903). The transition from an overcivilized, sybaritic state to rugged individualism is depicted in London's *The Sea Wolf* (1904) and Kipling's *Captains Courageous* (1897). The novel of compulsion finds ur-expression in the Goncourt brothers' *Germinie Lacerteux* (1864). The decadence of generational decline is the concern of Thomas Mann's *Buddenbrooks* (1901). The contrast between the land and the city is the subject of

Zola's *La Terre* (1887), Frank Norris's *The Octopus* (1901), and Willa Cather's stories of the lost frontier. The city novel treats the rise of new industries with their willingness to put profits ahead of public welfare as in Upton Sinclair's *The Jungle* (1906) or Dreiser's Cowperwood trilogy. The new industries quickly turned much of the city into slums—a situation depicted starkly in Zola's *L'Assommoir* (1877) and a bit less graphically in Stephen Crane's *Maggie* (1893). Out of the slums came the professional prostitutes like Zola's Nana. Out of the provinces into the city came the ambitious young woman like Dreiser's Carrie in search of greater self-fulfillment. And out of the masses came an energized labor force as in Zola's *Germinal* (1885) or the discontented mob ready to riot as in Nathanael West's *The Day of the Locust* (1939). When misled, the mob, now an army, played a significant role in national catastrophes as in Zola's *La Débâcle* (1892).

Along with supplying insights into the new urbanism, the naturalistic novel illuminated two major cultural and historical events: the development of the idea that there is a hidden self at work, its origins stemming perhaps from human animality and of the idea that there is a realm of force—cosmic and political/social force—at work in the world. The workings of cosmic force can be found in the fiction of Conrad, Stephen Crane, and Hardy; the workings of political force in the fiction of London and Norris, Hamsun and Dreiser.

1

One of the main themes of literary naturalism is the conflict between barbarity and civilization. Many naturalists feared that the more civilized we become the further alienated we are from a residual, primordial beauty and a life energy. We find this theme most emphatically expressed in Jack London. While his primitives have a firm love of life, many of London's civilized heroes seek death. The story in which London most clearly treats this theme is *The Call of the Wild*, the story of the dog Buck, part Saint Bernard and part Scottish shepherd. Stolen from the estate of Judge Miller, Buck is sold into captivity, ending up as a sled dog in Alaska. As Buck moves from civilization to the wild, he reverts to an atavistic or primitive self, feeling closer to his ancestors the wolves than to the humans for whom he runs the sled. In *The Call of the Wild*, London depicts the duality that is characteristic of literary naturalism. Animality versus humanity, the savage versus the civilized, the travails of the North (Alaska) versus the comforts of the South (California)—such doubling infuses the novel and generates narrative tension. London depicts a spectrum of reality from the primitive world of wild wolves to the civilized world of modern man. Appealing to the naturalistic assumption that man is descended from animals, London moves us to a state of origins and makes a dog his central character. London, however, gives the dog human qualities—memory, intelligence, and a capacity to adapt to a hostile environment—and allows Buck the range of the evolutionary chain. As a devolutionist, London portrays the lower levels of being—the world of wolves—as more "pure" and enlightened than the world of civilized man. The wilderness for London was always therapeutic and redemptive for both man and animal.

Freud repeats a naturalistic truth in *Civilization and its Discontents* (1930) when he argues that the further we move away from our natural or primitive origins, the more displaced we feel as human beings. One of the narrative devices in naturalistic fiction was to make use of a plot that displaced an overcivilized person from the urban realm into a more primitive setting. Rudyard Kipling does this in several stories, especially *Captains Courageous*, Jack London in *The Sea Wolf*, and Frank Norris in *Moran of the Lady Letty* (1898). In London's *The Sea Wolf*, when Humphrey Van Weyden is thrown into the sea after a clipper ship accident, he is picked up by Wolf Larsen, captain of the *Ghost*. Larsen is clearly bipolar, a manic-depressive with a cruel streak that stems from his mental condition. It is the task of Hump (as he is called) to adapt to this hostile environment, which he does by shedding his civilized self and descending to an atavistic, primitive realm. In Larsen, London portrays the man of power who has lost all capacity for restraint and runs a ship to its destruction. London suggests that, like a totalitarian leader, Wolf Larsen knows no limits, and his destructive tendencies are only exacerbated when his brother, Death Larsen, appears. London describes what can go wrong when the powers of nature are destructively tapped. But he also shows in the transformation of Van Weyden the redemptive aspect of those powers. In *The Sea Wolf*, London takes us into the realm of the primitive, a realm that encompasses both degeneration and redemption.

2

The theory of evolution presumes that we are conflicted—a rational self competes with an irrational self, a remnant of human evolution. This second self embodies a Dionysian element, making us the unpredictable beings that we are, and manifesting itself in various ways in naturalistic fiction. First, it can appear as the romantic self, searching for some kind of essential meaning. Second, it can manifest itself in the form of the artist, sensitive to both the beauty and the chaos that underlies material reality. Thirdly, it can express itself in the form of compulsions, desires and events that cannot be turned off. And lastly, it can emerge as a destructive element, a kind of chthonian impulse, capable of moving an individual to commit some extreme crime or of initiating physical or moral decline in him or her.

In *The Social History of Art* (1951), Arnold Hauser described "the inner strife of the romantic soul [that] is reflected nowhere so directly and expressively as in the figure of the 'second self.'"[1] Dreiser's characters are compulsively attracted to an idea of romantic possibility at the same time as they are restrained by their own physical limits. Carrie has hidden acting talent, potential that neither Drouet nor Hurstwood has. This ability, activated by and revealed in the city, is something that she was unaware she possessed when she lived in Columbia City and that she discovers when she goes on the stage as an amateur actress in Chicago. All kinds of mysteries lie buried in the city, including the layered depths of humanity. The city and its mechanical extensions energize Carrie and allow mobility. She intuits the power of the train, feels its flow embodied in the crowds that she watches from Hanson's doorstep, feels a glamorous presence embodied in public space (avenues, parks, restaurants, hotels), and is aware that it is creating in her a romantic state of mind. Ames encourages her to take this new sense of self as far as her abilities allow. But her abilities have limits—just as the novel graphically shows Hurstwood's limits—and at some point Carrie's desire will give way to frustration, a point the novel leaves for the coda.

3

The mediator between nature (the call of the wild) and the new (commercial) city was the artist. Zola treated the artist in the person of Claude Lantier in *L'Oeuvre* (1886) and Dreiser in the person of Eugene Witla in *The "Genius"* (1915). Dreiser also endows Cowperwood of his trilogy of desire with an aesthetic sense. In both Dreiser's and Zola's fiction, there is a redeeming vitality beneath the ugly surface of the industrial world. Those who intuit this sense of beauty often fall victim to the ideal, miscalculate mechanistic reality, and, disillusioned, perish. Such was the fate of Claude Lantier, Cowperwood, and Eugene Witla. The naturalist artist challenged the assumptions of romantic art, treating the work as a craft and the profession as a commercial process. One of the novels that brings both of these concerns into focus is George Gissing's *New Grub Street* (1891).

In *The New Grub Street*, George Gissing (1857–1903) portrays a world where the achievement of artistic ambition is tied to material success. Gissing turns the generational novel (with its vertical sweep) into the novel of artistic and monetary success (with its horizontal movement). The emphasis is on the way Grub Street (the center of English publishing) functions. While the novel depicts two generations of characters, the emphasis is on the second generation and their desire to succeed on Grub Street. Gissing concentrates on how money creates a publishing system at the expense of a literary system, defines the publishing world to the exclusion of artistic integrity.

One might not want to connect a work like *New Grub Street* with literary naturalism at all, except for three aspects. First, there is a sense of chance at work that prevails throughout. Much of the novel turns on matters of death and inheritance, matters against which more traditionally naturalistic characters define themselves. Second, Gissing creates in *New Grub Street* an environment that draws out the essential meaning of character. Grub Street, the place, becomes a kind of litmus test of self: as in the naturalistic novel, it exploits whatever weakness one might bring to it. And third, the main characters have a fixed nature, and while this is not ascribed to heredity, it does mimic that aspect of naturalistic fiction in which characters are fated to play out a certain destiny.

4

Less uplifting than the story of romantic longing or of the dual artistic vision is the story of compulsive love. As we have seen, the Goncourt brothers conceived the story of fated love in their *Germinie Lacerteux*, a work that greatly influenced Zola's *Thérèse Raquin* (1867) and in turn Tolstoy's *Anna Karenina* (1875) as well as Hardy's *Jude the Obscure* (1896). Anticipated by Flaubert's *Madame Bovary* (1857), this genre of story had a seemingly pathological hold on the novelist's imagination. Told against a realistic background—sometimes urban, sometimes rural—the story is always somber, revealing the seeming power of a second self bent on self-destruction. As in most novels of compulsion, will power is helpless in the face of uncontrollable sexual urges. The naturalists believed that the existence of such sexual urges were evidence that the human condition is inseparable from drives rooted in chemistry and repudiated the Enlightenment assumption that the individual was free to behave in an essentially rational manner.

The best portrayals of compulsive love owe much to Zola's depictions. *Sappho* (1884) by Alphonse Daudet is such a story—a narrative that depicts the other side of the *Nana* story. Instead of seeing the world through the eyes of a high-class prostitute, we see it through the pathetic eyes of a man who is obsessed with her. Another story involving the compulsions of love is *A Woman's Life* (1883) by Guy de Maupassant (1850–1893), the story of Jeanne de Lamare who transfers an unreturned love for her husband into a pathological affection for her son, Paul. Maupassant's novel is actually in the "slice of life" tradition, despite the fact that it covers a time span of over twenty-five years. Adultery plays a major role in the story—along with the obsessive love of Jeanne for Paul. The novel ends with the promise of Paul's return from Paris, but the reader knows that his returning home will simply exacerbate Jeanne's problem, not solve it. Love-out-of-control is a theme that dominates the nineteenth-century novel.

Zola's influence went beyond his French contemporaries, and in Ireland George Moore used the same kind of plot in *Esther Waters* (1894), which also brought into narrative play such elements as the compulsions of love, the struggle for survival, and the processes of degeneration. Like so many naturalistic novels—*Nana* (1884) and *Sister Carrie* (1900) come to mind—*Esther Waters* centers on the fate of a young woman in a hostile world. In *Esther Waters*, Moore writes his equivalent to Zola's *Nana*, but he puts less emphasis on hereditary matters than Zola does and more on the trials of a young woman coping with her illegitimate child and the fact that she has been outcast. As in Zola's fiction, most of the story is told against the backdrop of degeneration—the degeneration of individuals, such as William Latch, and the degeneration of places, such as the Woodview estate. Esther does not seem as self-reliant as Nana or Carrie at their independent best, but she does have enough instinct to escape her hostile predicament. Even if she is more of a victim than either Carrie or Nana, her persistence in the face of adversity is a trait she shares with other naturalistic women.

In America, the battle between the sexes was the subject of a number of feminist writers concerned with the desire of women for sexual freedom, although one of the subthemes of this fiction dealt with what to do when such freedom was won. Kate Chopin (1851–1904) treated both of these themes. Born Katherine O'Flaherty, the daughter of a prosperous Irish immigrant (killed in a railway accident when she was four) and a French Creole mother, she was educated at the St. Louis Academy of the Sacred Heart. She married Oscar Chopin in 1870, by whom she had six children. Oscar died of swamp fever in 1883, and in 1888 she took up writing fiction at the suggestion of her family doctor, Frederick Kolbenheyer, who also persuaded her to read Darwin, Huxley, and Spencer. Influenced in great part by Guy de Maupassant, she wrote about failed love.

In *The Awakening* (1899) Edna Pontellier, a New Orleans businessman's wife, awakens to a desire for sexual liberation. Like Emma Bovary, she read high romantic literature in her youth. In her maturity she finds herself being suffocated by her jaded emotions and her authoritative husband, Leonce Pontellier, twelve years her senior, to whom she has been married for six years. After a moonlit swim, Edna returns from the beach with Robert Lebrun and reclines in a hammock outside her cottage. When her husband orders her inside, she refuses to go and "awakens" to the fact that she is not her husband's property.

Before her awakening, Edna had confused infatuation with love. Chopin raises the question of what a woman is to do with the new-found consciousness that dispels such romantic illusions. Both Edna's sexual awakening and her death occur in the sea and are symbolically equated with the power of the sea, from which in evolutionary (that is, naturalistic) terms all life comes and to which her life returns. The sea is a natural force—a source of power, a means of release—from which her marriage has separated her. Her suicidal swim thus can be seen as a means of satisfying a desire to be reunited with this force. But since the swim takes her life, it is not an answer to the question of how Edna's new sexual freedom can be reconciled to the social conventions that circumscribe such freedom.

Put differently, Edna's suicidal swim seems more an escape from than a solution to the question of how her newfound consciousness can be employed, and the novel never really answers the question of how the modern woman is to use her sexual freedom. Chopin raises the same question that Dreiser raised about conventions. When accepted with regret, broken with guilt, they create a no-win situation, becoming the invisible chains that set limits to the impulse for sexual freedom.

Although Chopin's novel met with conventional disapproval, the representation of the desire for sexual liberation persisted in the works of Edith Wharton, Willa Cather, and Gertrude Stein, who sought alternative narratives to the urban, industrial, scientific, male bildungsroman. Edna's plight also anticipated that of Fitzgerald's Daisy Fay, who likewise awakens to the death of love but is unable to imagine a plausible alternative to her life with Tom Buchanan. It would take feminine resistance several generations to break the chains. In the meantime, conventions would get the better of disgruntled lovers like Edna—often self-destructively, as Chopin's ending suggests.

Edith Wharton's (1862–1937) *The House of Mirth* (1905) and *The Custom of the Country* (1913) are novels that like Dreiser's *Sister Carrie* tell the story of an ambitious young woman who crosses class lines intent on becoming a success in her own right. *The House of Mirth* is the story of Lily Bart. Born into wealth and comfort, Lily loses her social position when her father dies, leaving the family financially destitute. Lily Bart finds herself between classes. No longer part of the upper class and unable to reconcile herself to the lower class, she finds herself in a nowhere zone in which she loses her identity, her sense of self, and she responds accordingly. When faced with the option of marrying a man she doesn't love, blackmailing Bertha Dorset, or returning to poverty, she ends her own life by consuming a bottle of chloral. *The House of Mirth* reveals the pretensions of the times: the false codes of marriage, where reputation is more important than love, and the desire for status is at any price, even the ruination of a friend. Once more the force of conventions is stronger than individual resistance to them.

Wharton's The *Age of Innocence* (1920) is a study of a society that encourages sexual repression: it depicts a man who is totally alienated from his instincts and feelings. Newland Archer, a handsome young attorney, is engaged to May Welland when he meets Countess Ellen Olenska. He falls in love with Ellen, but cannot summon up the courage to act on his instincts. In *The Age of Innocence*, Wharton anticipates Freud's *Civilization and Its Discontents* (1930). Newland Archer, like Henry James's overcivilized John Marcher and T. S. Eliot's inhibited Prufrock, cannot act in the name of sexual desire. If Kate Chopin portrayed a form of sexual awakening, Edith Wharton portrayed a form of sexual death. The two stories complement each other: female sexuality cannot find an outlet while male sexuality is still subject to conventions; female love cannot find a means of expression so long as male love offers an inhibited response. The stories depict the frustrations that came with liberated love, the stifling of desire that plagued the post-Victorian society. In the tradition of the French realistic fiction that she knew so well, Wharton gives us another version of unfulfilled passion, of love gone awry.

Another novelist who writes from a feminist perspective is Charlotte Perkins Gilman (1860–1935). She was born in Hartford, Connecticut, the great-niece of Harriet Beecher Stowe. When she was nine, her father (the grandson of Lyman Beecher, the influential preacher) abandoned the family. Gilman's own childhood was marked by loneliness, anxiety, and rebellion against domestic conventions. Devastated by the loss of a close female friend, Martha Luther, she married Charles Walter Stetson in 1884. Soon after she went into a severe depression. Like the woman in "The Yellow Wallpaper," Gilman felt oppressed by her husband and the loss of her own identity. Moving alone to Pasadena, California, Gilman took up again her old careers as painter and writer, finding much-needed therapy in her work. She became a prolific writer and capable editor. In 1900 she married her first cousin, Houghton Gilman, a Wall Street attorney, and they lived agreeably as husband and wife until he died in 1934. She died the following year.

"The Yellow Wallpaper" (1892) is a story told from the point of view of a woman in the throes of a mental breakdown. Cloistered— perhaps "imprisoned" would be a better word—by her physician-husband in an airy attic room, she is repelled by its yellow wallpaper, part of which is torn off. The fungus-like discolored wallpaper rebukes her state of mind. She comes to believe that women are imprisoned in the wallpaper and at night she helps release these "prisoners" who then crawl about. Most critics see the wallpaper as a symbol of the narrator's imprisonment in her husband's (read male) world.

The story is an autobiographical depiction of Gilman's own mental illness brought about by the depression connected to her first marriage and intensified by the post-partum depression that followed the birth of her daughter. Her ailment was more common than is often thought and went at the time by the name of "neurasthenia" (neura=nerve, asthenia=weakness). George M. Beard connected this condition to physical and emotional symptoms (restlessness, anxiety, insomnia, backache, indigestion, and headache) that led to chronic fatigue. Middle-class men in a commercial-industrial society were especially prone to such an ailment, although women experienced the same symptoms. The more civilized the culture, the greater the emotional stress, and the more common mental illness. While the cure for men usually was activity (travel, avocation, and exercise), that for women was a passive "rest" (or bed) cure.

The leading authority in this matter was Silas Weir Mitchell, to whose care Gilman was subjected. Mitchell's influence at this time was great. He successfully treated Frank Norris when he was in the throes of a nervous breakdown, and Edmund Wilson's father, who was a chronic depressive. Mitchell concurred with Beard that psychological problems stemmed from the speeded-up pace of American life and that the emphasis on money and property as the basis of so-cial position led to obsessive anxiety. He also believed that women were naturally inclined toward the duties of wife and mother and that the acceptance of such responsibilities would bring about men-tal stability. Mitchell persuaded Gilman to emphasize the "domestic" aspect of her life, to give up her career as a writer, and to devote her-self totally to husband and baby. But Gilman, like the woman in the story, became more ill under this treatment. Close to suicide, Gilman eventually broke with Mitchell, an act that saved her sanity even as it led to her divorce.

Once again Dreiser's career is relevant to this topic: Gilman's ner-vous breakdown bears many similarities to Dreiser's nervous col-lapse after Doubleday tried to break their contract with him to pub-lish *Sister Carrie* and after the death of his father in the same year. Both Gilman and Dreiser were incapacitated by their illness, experi-enced a kind of vertigo in which things seemed askew, and were aware of a second self—a kind of helpless observer who was watch-ing a more vital and healthy self deteriorate. When not plagued by insomnia, they suffered from nightmares and even hallucinations—as well as a host of physical ailments. Both saw writing—first the keeping of a diary, then writing involving their own mental illness (Dreiser's *An Amateur Laborer* (1983) and Gilman's "The Yellow Wallpaper")—as an attempt to understand and move beyond their illness. Each illness could be considered the result of a failure to live up to gender expectations: the male was not aggressive enough to hold his own in a competitive society, and the female was not passive enough to reconcile herself to her domestic duties and to her place in the social hierarchy—a mirror-image parallel. But there the parallels stop. Dreiser went to Muldoon's health farm where he was subjected to a sturdy daily physical routine that eventually restored his health; Gilman was put under a rest cure that further incapacitated her.[2]

Gilman challenged Mitchell's medical assumptions in works like *Herland* (1915) and responded in different terms to his theories in her *Women and Economics* (1898), in which she discussed the conse-quences of women being economically dependent on men: men pro-duced wealth, which was then bestowed on women, establishing an all-determining social convention. As a result, women became totally

dependent on men and had to use their sexual attributes to win husbands and secure a family. Gilman believed that women needed to
develop their own sense of identity separate from men, a position
that turned her against the traditional idea of marriage and the conventions that made women economically dependent on men.[3]

Gilman agreed with Bellamy's socialist doctrine in *Looking Backward* (1888) and Thorstein Veblen's suggestion in *The Theory of the
Leisure Class* (1899) that domestic activity perpetuated the subser-
vient status and led to the limited opportunities of women. The
feminist perspective was often reinforced by male writers like Sinclair Lewis when they were able to identify with a Madame Bovary-
like character as Lewis did in *Main Street* (1920). While the theme
of uninhibited love dominated the European, in particular the
French novel, the theme of inhibited sex played a significant role in
American realism. Sherwood Anderson treated this theme at length
in *Winesburg, Ohio* (1919), as did Edgar Lee Masters in *Spoon River
Anthology* (1915).

There is not always a consistency between modern gender theories and the way women and men were depicted in literary naturalism. In recent gender theory, there is a reluctance to see gender as
a fixed principle of identity. Consistent with the current general
theoretical distrust of master narratives and universal assumptions,
many contemporary feminist critics treat gender identity as fluid, as
constantly changing, depending on time and context. Women are
separated by class, race, and other differences, and therefore not seen
as being part of a homogeneous group. There is no single feminism,
no political party. Recent feminist critics have rejected Freud's biological determinism, which divides the species into men and women,
each desiring the opposite sex.[4]

Realism and naturalism stressed the desire for a general freedom
and independence rather than create an agenda of feminine liberation. In this context, realism has been seen as a response to female
sentimental fiction[5] in its tendency to depict masculine rather than
feminine reality; it emphasized the perils of nature and society to the
extent that Frank Norris even celebrates masculine women over
more feminine types. However, the realism of Henry James accommodated a specifically feminist point of view. And even among the

naturalists there were significant exceptions to subsuming women's freedom to the idea of universal freedom: Dreiser's story "Marriage— for One" anticipates a feminist agenda, as do the many works that question the way conventions inhibit sexual love. Moreover, Dreiser's Carrie and Norris's own Trina offer a female perspective. And the writings of Kate Chopin, Edith Wharton, Charlotte Gilman, along with those of Willa Cather, added indelible portraits to the realist/ naturalist canon of women defining themselves in a male-centered world.

5

The double self in realist/naturalist fiction thematized the war between social conventions and the desire for sexual independence, also that of the struggle between the rational and animal aspects of character. The idea of a double self here is grounded in the evolutionary suggestion that mankind is a product of a dual nature: the animal self, an atavistic power waits to assert its degenerative effect within the human self. As we have seen, such a view is given expression in both Frank Norris's *McTeague* (1899) and *Vandover and the Brute* (1914). Like Zola's, Frank Norris's novels are informed by a naturalistic biology steeped in Darwinian theory modified by his reading of Asa Gray and Joseph Le Conte. The major difference between Norris's ideas and Darwin's is that Norris adds a life force to his philosophy. This force, especially evident in a novel like *The Octopus* (1901), was thought by Norris to be immanent in nature and to push life ahead of it, an idea that anticipates Henri Bergson's *élan vital*.

Poverty has the same degenerative effect on Trina and McTeague that it has on Gervaise and Coupeau in *L'Assommoir*, and it brings to the surface the same homicidal tendencies that we see in Jacques Lantier in *La Bête humaine* (1890). What we see in Norris is the biology of greed, a desire for money and gold so extreme that it can create an illusionary reality and incite men to murder. A degenerative process is latent in both the individual and the environment. Once that process begins, social and physical decay reinforce each other, accelerating individual decline.

The process of degeneration not only takes place on the individual level, it also takes place on a generational level. In an industrial family, this often leads to characters becoming more decadent or debased than their elders—in each case more unsuited to their environment and less capable of carrying on their inherited responsibilities. Mann's *Buddenbrooks* (1901) owes much to the structure of the generational novel and has often been compared to Galsworthy's *The Man of Property* (the first novel of *The Forsyte Saga*, published in 1906). It also carries on the tradition of the Goncourt brothers and Zola's *Rougon-Macquart* (1871–93) series.

The novel traces the process of decline in the Buddenbrooks, a high-bourgeois family, from Johann senior, who brings the family business to its pinnacle in 1875, down to Jean, who holds the business together until it is passed on to his son Thomas. Thomas embodies the middle class at its disciplined best. Restless, tense, and ambitious, he forces himself, conquering temptation and overcoming the hedonism and indolence that corrodes his brother and sister. But Mann believed that, just as the aristocracy began to decline in the seventeenth century, the high bourgeoisie began to decline at the end of the nineteenth century. Thomas's obsession with material pursuits becomes self-destructive, limits his capacity to love, and isolates him from his wife and son. Mother and son become inseparable, substituting the pursuit of beauty for the love that Thomas never gives them. In time, Hanno becomes unfit to take over the family business, spending his days with his mother listening to music. He is so weakened physically and emotionally that at the age of fifteen he dies during a typhoid epidemic. For Mann the pursuit of beauty also leads to a process of decay. The passing of the merchant heralds the birth of the artist, whose search for the beautiful leads to an often fatal decadence. The theme of *Buddenbrooks* also informs *Tonio Kröger* (1903) and *Death in Venice* (1912). The pursuit of fulfillment beyond material comfort gave rise to an aestheticism that could be deadly.

The Forsyte Saga (1906, 1920, 1921) by Galsworthy chronicles the years from 1886 to 1920. Like most generational novels, it treats three generations—a long enough period of time to reveal the links and breaks between predecessor and descendant. The principal characters, Soames Forsyte and his beautiful wife Irene, are torn between a desire for money and the pursuit of the beautiful. Galsworthy's novel, in the tradition of Mann's *Buddenbrooks*, depicts the evolution of a family from the materialistic obsessions of the first generation to the more selfless concerns of the third generation. At the end, Soames realizes that the age of the Forsytes has passed. Like Mann, Galsworthy shows the failure of money to satisfy human and aesthetic concerns. Also, like Mann, Galsworthy creates a novel in which what happened in the past determines the present—thus the impossibility of Jon and Fleur's to carry on in the face of their parents' history.

The emphasis on external circumstances to the exclusion of an inner reality led Virginia Woolf to attack the generational novel. The brunt of her wrath was directed at novels like *The Old Wives' Tale* (1908) by Arnold Bennett. *The Old Wives' Tale* covers fifty years of time and once again deals with three generations of characters. The plot centers on two sisters, Constance and Sophia Baines. Constance is plain and conventional; Sophia is beautiful and rebellious. Constance's life is stable and ordered; Sophia's is unpredictable and disordered. *The Old Wives' Tale* uses almost all the elements of the generational novel. The story presents a panorama of late-nineteenth-century European life, setting Constance's and Sophia's lives against the backdrop of events of the times, such as the siege of Paris that followed the Franco-Prussian War and the transition from an agrarian to an industrial society. It features a character, Gerald Scales, whose degeneration becomes a metaphor for the decline of the times. And it contrasts the material success of Sophia with the artistic inclinations of her nephew, Cyril, once again employing a dichotomy that seemingly is a fixed element in this kind of story. One would expect a novel with this range to emphasize heroic characters participating in major historical events. Instead, Bennett uses his sweep to tell a story of two ordinary women. His novel, in other words, gives epic importance to the commonplace.[6]

The Clayhanger Trilogy (1910, 1911, 1915) was another Bennett story dealing with commonplace people in a commonplace world in which the quality of their lives was gauged by endurance. Set in the industrial Midlands of England, the novel charts Edwin Clayhanger's life from adolescence to old age. His early years are marred by two frustrations: his unfulfilled wish to be an architect and his unfulfilled desire to marry Hilda Lessways. Bennett's novel takes us slowly through the ordinary life of a middle-class entrepreneur in industrial England. *The Clayhanger Trilogy* was typical of the new British realism: there was nothing extraordinary about Edwin or Hilda or their world, and it was this representation of the ordinary and the staid passing of years that gave the novel both its shape and meaning. When transformed in such Virginia Woolf novels as *The Years* (1937), the generational novel will compress time and depict an interior reality.[7]

6

Although the generational model depicted the decline of the high bourgeois, an agrarian world was giving way in the face of an urban, industrial revolution. By 1920 there were more people living in cities than in rural areas, even as some cities were still defined by their relationship to the land. The main function of Chicago, for example, was to process the products (crops and cattle) that came from the land.

At the center of *Sister Carrie* is the city, first Chicago and then New York, Dreiser revealing a more complex entity in his depiction of the latter. Chicago has become a self-contained entity, now distinct from the prairie, full of a Promethean energy that lights up the sky at night. All of the novel's characters are caught up in an urban materiality and defined, as we have seen, by their rise (Carrie), fall (Hurstwood), and stasis (Drouet) within the city. They turn to the city lights for warmth and encouragement, and to money for the means to satisfy their desires.

Since the city takes its being from the production and consumption of goods, the people who make up the city are subjected to the laws of production and consumption. Dreiser depicted factories (production) in Chicago and lavish shops (consumption) in New York. Dreiser's New York scenes are set mainly in or around 1894, the depression year in which he went to New York and was confronted by an army of jobless men that he was soon to join. All of Dreiser's characters embody a larger process at work. He believed that for every Carrie living in luxury and elegance, there was a Hurstwood sleeping in a flophouse or worse. The city was both a lure and a trap. He told the story of people whose lives were inextricably bound up with the city, the laws of which he believed in as faithfully as the most deterministic urban historian.

The theme of the double plays into the theme of the city, because the city is large enough to better entertain the possibilities of a second self. In the tradition of Balzac, both Dreiser and Norris send their characters to a major city to realize what potential they may have. Often this journey leads to their demise rather than their success, but all of their stories unfold against the backdrop of the city, the rhythms of the land now sounding only in the far distance.

As in realism/naturalism in general, Dreiser's fiction makes use of the contradictions between Enlightenment optimism and naturalistic pessimism. His characters long for self-fulfillment but are caught in a spiral of counterforces that frustrate their desires. They are thus unable to reconcile romantic aspirations with a world of physical limits. They desire an essentially unattainable self-fulfillment. Dreiser's characters are restless but also directionless; they long for stability but are caught in flux. They are victims of their temperament and of a society that they cannot fully accept or totally reject. Most of all, they are victims of their romantic illusions: their belief in the possibility of self-fulfillment and purpose when life in reality is like the rocking chair in *Sister Carrie*—going nowhere.

In some ways, *Sister Carrie* anticipated *The Great Gatsby* (1925). We have in both novels a sweet-and-sour story that thematizes success and failure, self-realization and degeneration, desire and decline, ambition and lost hope. Gatsby tends to embody in himself what Dreiser divided between Carrie and Hurstwood. To be sure, Carrie is more passive than Gatsby, but when she decides to reinvent herself, she is as intense. And all of the major characters fail to come to terms with what is delimiting, whether those delimitations be defined naturalistically, as in Dreiser's fiction, or aesthetically or neorealistically, as in Fitzgerald's. Both novels examine in a fascinating way the whole question of a distinctively American identity and the consequences of narcissism and materialism, especially in the city.

Another version of the city is that of Nathanael West's, who depicted Los Angeles as both the final frontier and an urban hell. As one critic has demonstrated, Van Wyck Brooks's concept of Puritan versus Pioneer is critically to the point of West's novel, his narrative pursuing the desire for freedom in a world of restraint.[8] The lack of an American identity is reflected in the architecture of the city, an amalgam of different styles that violate the principle of organic unity. West represents Hollywood as the end of a dream in which the unfulfilled, restless self strives for success and material gain. West does not concentrate on what is glamorous in this pursuit, but on shabby apartment houses, the loneliness of the displaced aspirant, the burlesque that goes along with grubbing a living, the misery of trying to survive in the prelude to the dream. Desiring the good life, finding its opposite, West's disillusioned pilgrims become angry, their anger erupting into a riot at the end of the novel. Like Conrad, West believes that beneath the surface of civilization, in this case beneath the false glamour of Hollywood (both the place and the industry), is a brutal violence waiting to express itself. West edges toward apocalypse: his neorealism, like that of Sherwood Anderson's, takes us into a realm of the grotesque and approaches the antirealism of Gogol and Kafka.

8

Literary Transformations

1

A recent study argues that there were two modernisms, one stemming from postromantic aestheticism, the other from laissez-faire liberalism. Eliot and the high modernists embraced the first, avantgarde modernists like Marinetti the second. High modernists rejected liberalism, and their distrust of it led to a reactionary literary politics; they also treated mass culture with contempt, although a desire for a large audience qualified their disdain.[1] By 1910 distrust of reason and mechanistic theory had set in, especially in Europe. Freud in Vienna, Pareto in Lausanne, and Sorel and Bergson in Paris had given expression to antirationalist ideas. Burckhardt's historicism, as transformed by Nietzsche, eventually gave way to the organic history of Spengler. Nietzsche's "will to power" anticipated Freud's "libido," Bergson's "élan vital," and Pareto's cyclical authority.

Both naturalist and modernist literature reveal a surface and a subsurface in their works. Naturalism went beneath the surface and uncovered an evolution that bespoke a primitive past. Modernism went beneath the surface and discovered a symbolism that reflected the universality of time. The context of the subsurface in naturalism is an atavism (a throwback to remote ancestors); in modernism it is aesthetic (the repetition of time, the constancy of the beautiful, the uniformity of the universe).

The modernist's comparison of present and past rested on historical correspondence, the belief that all time was one, which explained the layering of modernist writing that Joseph Frank termed "spatial form." Nietzsche's idea of "eternal recurrence," Spengler and Pareto's cyclical theories, Pound's belief in the "repeat" of history were all expressions of this idea. Faulkner's story of the Sutpen family follows the model of generational naturalism, until Faulkner superimposes on his story the Absalom myth, creating a timeless correspondence between the present and the past, giving universal meaning to what for T. S. Eliot was the chaos of history.

Naturalist and modernist symbolism reinforced the *idea* of their respective narratives. While naturalist symbolism compressed and individualized evolution, modernist symbolism globalized the literary work. The difference between naturalist and modernist symbolism lies in their use of time and history. While the naturalist writer emphasized the sequential plot, the modernist writer tried to conceal it. While naturalism exploited causal connections, modernism questioned the process of causality.

While modernism and realism/naturalism as literary movements overlapped, they were informed by opposing ideas of reality, and the transition from realism/naturalism to modernism effected a radical change in the novel. A reader today can chart that transition by comparing the way Joyce rewrote *Stephen Hero* into *The Portrait of the Artist as a Young Man* (1916) or the way Proust rewrote *Jean Santeuil* into *A la recherche du temps perdu* (1907–19). The rewriting makes apparent the change in narrative point of view from one in which characters are seen from the outside to one in which consciousness and memory dominate the telling.

Zola believed that reality was directly accessible to the novelist. Proust believed that consciousness gave meaning to memory, and memory made art possible. The difference between Zola and Proust is the difference between the naturalist and modern novel. Proust de-emphasized the depiction of physical reality in the novel, portraying instead characters' subjectivity by fusing time present and time past. Once the present and the past are interconnected, consciousness—often in the form of memory—creates both the meaning of time and reality. On his return from Cambray, Marcel, Proust's narrator, remembering his aesthetic vows, suffers from doubts about his artistic ability. As he looks out the train window, he imbues the trees with the emotion he is experiencing. Marcel tells us, "Here I am in the midst of nature's beauty, yet it is with indifference, with boredom, that my eyes note the line that separates [the trees'] luminous foliage from [their] shadowy trunk."[2] Memory—the past infused with consciousness—creates reality, a dictum at the heart of modern literature. When Gatsby finally realizes that he has lost Daisy Fay, his newfound consciousness changes reality in a Proustian way. Nick Carraway, Fitzgerald's narrator, tells us in words similar to Proust's, that Gatsby "shivered as he found what a grotesque thing a rose is and how raw the sunlight was upon the scarcely created grass."[3]

As in Bergson, the connection between the past and the present in Proust is contingent on the mind. The emotions that we bring to our memories create the reality of those memories. The connection between past and present creates a third order of meaning, the past providing insight into the present and vice versa, and out of this interpenetration of meaning comes the epiphany, which is what the modernist believed was the ultimate function of art. Memory heightened by resplendent emotion can transform physical reality. When the emotion changes, so does memory, and so also reality. We can find this same phenomenon in Virginia Woolf, whose sister-in-law, Karin Stephens, wrote one the first critical books on Bergson. The modernists thus repudiated what they saw as Balzac's and Zola's naïve belief that we have direct access to the real.

Another difference between literary naturalism and literary modernism was that the former had a mechanistic and the latter an organic view of physical reality. A mechanistic view combines materialism and determinism: the first reduces life to a material base, rejecting spiritual or vitalistic (mind over matter) grounding; the second postulates that life is governed by causality. Both theories reject the miraculous and the fatalistic. The mechanists maintained that all natural phenomena could be explained in terms of matter in motion. It all came back to the working of physicochemical process: the heliotrope must turn toward the sun. The naturalistic character must seek forms of pleasure and power—must seek material comforts, sex, drugs, alcohol, and the material goods that confer status and the pride of ownership. The mechanistic universe is fixed, based on the unfolding of matter, subject to physical laws like the law of gravity or thermodynamics that disavow the supernatural.

The organicist, on the other hand, believes the relationship between mind and matter and between human beings and environment is less determined. The organic universe is self-contained, self-energized, capable of growth, marked by an ability to assimilate diverse material. The organic view is holistic: the parts cannot be understood except in relation to the whole. The organic universe is living and unfolding, revealing itself symbolically. When extrapolated, a theory of organicism confers an organic unity on things that are not living and thus not literally organisms—for example, a literary text, a work of art, a nation- state, and the universe as whole, as in absolute idealism.

Naturalism as philosophical system was informed by both the organic and the mechanistic. The theory of evolution involved organic process—the transformation of living matter into a different form, such as the metamorphosis of the modern caterpillar into a butterfly or a tadpole into a frog. But living matter is also subject to physical laws, to such things as genetic makeup and environment, responding mechanistically to immediate stimuli as they act on chemicals that make up the nervous system.

The literary modernists (like the romantics) insisted on the organic, regarding matter as infused with spirit, energy, and life. And, unlike the naturalist who affirmed the animality of life, the modernist refused to model humanity on animal forms. H. G. Wells embodied the former position, D. H. Lawrence the latter. Others expressed the idea of the organic in their own way: Joyce with his "yes" to feminine replenishment, William James with his belief that a religious state of mind gave matter direction, Bergson with his theory of vitalism, Samuel Butler with his idea of creative evolution, Bernard Shaw with his belief in a life force. Henry Adams connected his idea of the Virgin to the organic, his idea of the dynamo to the mechanistic. Adams believed history was now a product of the brute violence of irrational energies. The masculine principle (the Dynamo) had overcome the feminine principle (the Virgin): technology, urbanization, the corporation and other money institutions had led to this destructive change. "Chaos was the law of nature; order was the dream of man,"[4] he wrote. Modern man forced his mechanical will on the land, turn-ing technological control into forms of wealth.

Literary naturalists, on the other hand, tended to reduce reality to mechanistic terms, although the fact that organicism had a place in the philosophy of naturalism gave rise to contradictions in their thinking. Theodore Dreiser, for example, the most adamant of the mechanists, could not completely expunge organicism from his worldview, leading to the charge that he was an inconsistent mecha-nist. The organicist aspect of naturalistic philosophy admitted that it was possible to pursue and achieve an idealized self, but the mecha-nist side asserted the existence of physical limits. These two beliefs found expression in literary naturalism in the form of characters who experienced a sense of intellectual and physical displacement, a feeling that he or she had an ideal place in the world but could not find it. Dreiser saw how these competing ideas gave rise to a problem in modern culture: such characters are born to yearn and yet live in a world of limits. They are born to be one step behind themselves, urged on by a desire that generates a destructive counterforce. They believe that they are independent, creatures of free will, and yet they are mere tools of their appetites, of physical needs, of other persons, and of the universe. They are creatures of idealism in a world where force and circumstance cancel out ideals. Such characters are the products of physical limits. They are rootless, preyed on, and subject to injustice. They unwittingly aspire to goals that are transient and beyond their grasp, are never satisfied with their family situation or their position in society, and struggle for wealth and recognition. In more sensitive moments, they intuit the beauty of life and experi-ence the tensions between a physical and an idealized reality, which only makes them more discontent with their materialistic society and limited sense of self. The contradictions built into naturalism differentiate it from other narrative forms and conventions—like the romance and melodrama.

2

In his magisterial *The Gates of Horn* (1963), Harry Levin tells us that the "epic, romance, and novel are the representatives of three successive estates and styles of life: military, courtly, and mercantile."[5] In this study, we have examined the novel as a composite of subgenres or narrative conventions and defined it by the way that it depicts various modes of reality. In both pursuits, we have worked outward from the text, connecting subgenre and modal reality with historical events and process. There is, however, as Levin suggests, a third way to look at the evolution of the novel and that is in terms of its narrative (that is, plot) pattern and the audience that narrative accommodated.

The epic, tragedy, comedy, romance, and melodrama can all be defined in terms of plot. The epic is the adventurous account of heroic men, who often fight to preserve the pride of the clan or national identity. Tragedy in the Aristotelian sense features a flawed hero, who destroys the harmony of his world through a catastrophic mistake that brings about his suffering and leads before his death to his moral awareness and to a feeling of both pity and fear on the part of the audience. Comedy is the inverse of tragedy, involving more ordinary characters whose conflicts are resolvable. In classical comedy, the authority that opposes happiness is undermined, mismatched couples are properly paired, frivolity gives way to order, and the comedy ends with a happy marriage or the righting of a social wrong. The romance was the medieval version of the epic, centering on a heroic leader and his band of knights who were often in pursuit of a sacred object (e.g., the grail) or an ideal (the achievement of which required moral testing), set against backdrop of the realm of the aristocracy and its conventions of courtly love. By the nineteenth century, the romance began addressing more middle-class concerns but still sustained the use of noble characters whose pursuits had symbolic, even allegorical, qualities as in, for example, Melville's *Moby Dick* (1851).

Melodrama is the more recent trend in literary genre. The word itself means "theater with music," suggesting that forms of music (a drum roll or the play of the violin) can underscore the difference between dramatic good and evil. Instead of noble heroes concerned with divine law, national themes, or social order, melodrama uses more ordinary characters caught in the throes of love, lost identity, family crisis, or class conflict. (Most soap operas are melodramatic.)

Melodrama portrays the conflict between virtue and villainy, good and evil in black and white terms, simplifying the moral conflict of the earlier forms at the same time as it embraces sentimentality, even in the face of violence. It thereby seeks to lead an audience toward an awareness of social villainy that necessitates eradication. Melodrama takes the romance to its inevitable conclusion, rewarding good and punishing evil.

Critics like Peter Brooks believe melodrama is a more secular version of a religious plot. Brooks's definition is mainly stipulative and of his own invention. He sees melodrama as a product of the French Revolution and as a response to the demise of tragedy in a secular era. In that context, mythmaking became individual and personal. Melodrama shared qualities with the gothic novel: for both, evil is real, an irreducible force. But unlike the gothic—in which there is a loss of belief in the idea of the sacred, fear without worship—melodrama reasserts the existence of a moral universe.

Brooks goes on to suggest that literary naturalism is an extension of melodrama.[6] His desire to heighten romantic content is similar to that of other critics who have linked naturalism with the romance. To be sure, these plots share a narrative formula: the use of sensational incident, virtuous protagonists versus villainous antagonists, forces at work beyond a character's control, an inability to escape the past. But these critics fail to consider an essential difference between and among the romance, melodrama, and naturalism: naturalism empties the romance and melodrama of its moral dimension, collapses good into evil, and destroys the moral center that guarantees the victory of good over evil. Indeed, in the naturalistic novel, power, represented as a form of evil, often triumphs.

We can trace this movement through to the morally ambiguous narrative of Henry James, whose late novels turn on more personal than established choices. We can see the evolution of this idea by comparing Dickens's *Great Expectations* (1861), Dreiser's *Sister Carrie* (1900), and F. Scott Fitzgerald's *The Great Gatsby* (1925). In Dickens's novel good and evil are clearly demarcated (Magwitch vs. Compeyson, Joe Gargery vs. Orlick, Pip vs. Bentley Drummel) and "good" does win out, although even Dickens had trouble at the end with the idea that the victory of goodness was total.

In *Sister Carrie,* one could argue that Carrie initially—but not for long—is the personification of innocence. But it certainly is more difficult to read Drouet and Hurstwood as villains. Finally, the resolution of the novel is far from one in which virtue is rewarded. In fact, Dreiser empties *Sister Carrie* of any moral imperatives to which Carrie can appeal for guidance, and his novel ends on a note of moral ambiguity that Howells felt pushed moral relativism too far.

The Great Gatsby actually carries this relativism further. Both Gatsby and Nick have their faults and are guilty of misperceptions. Gatsby believes that he can realize an old ideal in an exhausted past and that his "roughneck" background and criminal money can break down the walls of the established rich. Nick thinks that he can move with the amoral rich with impunity—that participating in the world of the cruel rich does not have consequences, that he can lie to himself and call it honor. But Gatsby and Nick have redeeming qualities that Tom Buchanan lacks. The morally careless realm in the novel, embodied by Tom, wins out in the end. The villain has triumphed in a neorealistic world in which moral imperatives are no longer relevant. The novel moved from an obvious contrast between good and evil in the melodrama of Dickens to a far more morally ambiguous use of character and plot in the modernism of Fitzgerald. This change was mediated by literary naturalism.

In its origins the novel was closer to the comic mode than to the tragic. Early fiction made use of a moral universe to which an author could submit narrative conflict for resolution. Realism/naturalism changed all that and was an important movement in the development of the novel. Naturalism supplanted the sentimentalism of a Fielding's Squire Allworthy or a Dickens's Mr. Brownlow or Esther Summerson when it was no longer convincing to have commercial and industrial conflicts resolved by men and women with the capacity to do good through the power of their human heart. In the evolution of the novel, there is always a residue of earlier forms in later works, and it is true that one can sometimes find an element of sentimentality in naturalistic fiction: the novels of John Steinbeck come to mind. But most of the naturalists saw the world in terms of competing forces that could not peacefully coexist, and they went to the very source of what was corrupting modern society.

Zola exposed corrupt financial markets that made men like Saccard millionaires. He created sympathy for the mineworkers in Lille who labored from morning to night in dismal conditions for stipends that could not support even the meanest life. He revealed the pitiful state of life in the slums, the origins of high-class prostitutes like Nana, and the general corruption and decadence of the aristocracy, who were able to live the good life by exploiting an impoverished labor class. Frank Norris revealed the machinations of the Chicago produce exchange, the deceit of big railroads who encouraged the ranchers to improve their land before running them off it. And Dreiser depicted the travail that a young woman faced in the new city as well as the financial scheming that went on in the money markets and in the public transportation system.

Naturalism also reassessed the dominating cultural values: the naturalists questioned the belief in an all-knowing God, faith in an Horatio Alger formula of success, and trust in romantic love and the virtues of heroic behavior. The naturalists intuited turbulence beneath the surface of civilization. From Zola to Stephen Crane, we have the inextricability of violence and the everyday. From Zola to Jack London we see the ambiguous play between good and evil, chance and design, accident and purpose. A chance occurrence may start a process, such as Clym's letter going astray in *The Return of the Native* or Hurstwood finding the safe unlocked, but then the process plays itself out as a predictable sequence—a chain of events fatalistic or determined, over which we have no control. Naturalism broke with traditional social and ethical values, leaving a far more ambivalent reality.

The way was cleared for the neorealism of Ernest Hemingway and John Dos Passos—and of literary existentialism, which had to work through what was limiting in literary naturalism in order to come out the other side. Naturalism also depicted the animal/sexual instincts being suppressed by the authority of civilization and coming back in a repressed ways as forms of the grotesque.

Literary naturalism created a technique of its own. It established a direct connection based on a theory of environment between the meaning of character and the meaning of setting. It depicted the displaced character, caught between romantic aspiration and mechanistic limits; it brought to light the contradictions, inherent in the transition from an Enlightenment to an industrialized world, between a belief in progress and a sense of entropy, between a trust in evolution and a fear of degeneration; and, relying on the scientific assumption that the mind functioned empirically and that history could be documented, it created a plot held together by cause and effect sequence. The naturalistic novel often made use of a double perspective that resulted in narrative irony, the play between what the characters anticipate and what the reader or narrator knows. The naturalistic hero was usually inarticulate, lacking a deep inner life and the capacity for moral reflection or expression. He or she was subject to poverty and suffering that stemmed from biological makeup and the workings of environment, culminating in an inevitable sequence of determined events, usually triggered by chance.

3

A residue of naturalism could be found in modernism, even as naturalism was transformed into a new realism. Traces of literary naturalism can be found in such films as Michael Cimino's *The Deer Hunter* (1978) and Martin Scorcese's *Mean Streets* (1973) and *Raging Bull* (1980).[7] But after World War II the literary imagination revised its emphasis on race, heredity and blood lineage, and behavioristic ideas involving the environment. As naturalistic ideology thinned, its literary aspects changed as well, resulting in neorealism. The work, for example, of Ernest Hemingway falls into this category: it looked back to the realism of literary naturalism at the same time as it manifested his iceberg theory of language—the idea that nouns in motion could produce emotion, that language could depict an objective reality and yet appeal at the same time to the emotions of the reader.

Critically not much has been said about neorealism as the bridge between naturalism and modernism. The new realism involved a confluence of nineteenth- and twentieth-century intellectual and artistic movements: Darwin and Bergson; William James's theories of the mind; the avant-garde, especially Dada and Surrealism; Gertrude Stein's theory of language; and Walter Pater's theory of sensation.

Pater's ideas led to Conrad's impressionism, which in turn, influenced the work of Crane and then Hemingway, in whose characters we see the residue of literary naturalism. F. Scott Fitzgerald began his career as a transformed naturalist: "May Day" (1922) is a study in both national and personal degeneration as is *The Beautiful and Damned* (1922). There are naturalistic elements in Fitzgerald's fiction as late as *Tender Is the Night* (1934).

Neorealism was, in fact, literary naturalism without its documentation. The benefactors of this blending, beside Hemingway and F. Scott Fitzgerald, were John Dos Passos, Nathanael West, and James M. Cain, whose *The Postman Always Rings Twice* (1934) was a perfect example of literary naturalism devoid of commentary. Literary experiment transformed literary naturalism, introducing a subjectivity and a surrealism to it. Dos Passos created a continuum of contemporary history in his *USA* trilogy, giving an intensity to key events via both a personal and historical perspective. As Edmund Wilson has contended, the neorealism of West, especially in his earlier works like *The Dream Life of Balso Snell* (1931), owed much to surrealism, to early modern writers like Rimbaud and Lautréamont, while *The Day of the Locust* (1939) combined a modern grotesque and a naturalistic element moving toward violence.[8] And the experimental language of Gertrude Stein's *Three Lives* (1909) perpetuated a subjective dimension in the new realism of Sherwood Anderson, Ernest Hemingway, and Ring Lardner.[9]

In its use of self-involved, elemental characters set against a cosmic background of ironic events, neorealism also anticipated literary existentialism. And while it goes back to the Middle Ages and Rabelais, the grotesque is also relevant here. A subgenre in which the workings of nature are inverted, it connects Gogol and Kafka with Sherwood Anderson and Nathanael West. The grotesque in modern literature, in which the familiar became strange and uncanny, was often informed by Freud's theory of repressed desire. When the grotesque led to a "fantasy realism," a fantasized situation that was then treated realistically, it anticipated magic realism.

Cain's transformation of the naturalist novel made it suitable for the philosophical uses to which Albert Camus put it. For *L'Étranger* (1942), Camus needed an "elemental" character, someone that lived by his senses, but not naturalistic reality. Camus found such a character in Cain's Frank Chambers. There are other similarities: the climax of each novel is a murder, followed by a court hearing; the novels conclude in a murder cell in which the principal characters, waiting to be executed, are talking or writing to a priest. The most obvious parallel between the two novels is that both Frank Chambers and Meursault are misfits, passive heroes who respond to immediate stimuli. Like naturalistic characters they are described in terms of their behavior; and also like naturalistic characters, they react rather than act.

Even earlier novelists like Ernest Hemingway depicted characters in contact with nature. They did this not to demonstrate the truth of theories like evolution or degeneration, but to test their characters, using the big-game hunt, deep-sea fishing, or the bullfight as the means of gauging their courage. Hemingway created a natural aristocracy outside of society, which allowed more individual will and self-determination than one would find in naturalistic fiction. Like Kipling in *Captains Courageous* (1897) or Jack London in *The Sea Wolf* (1904), Hemingway places his protagonist outside of modern history, especially outside a mechanical urban order, on a boat or on an island, where a code of primitive values rules. Such a narrative maneuver allowed Hemingway to contrast elemental and civilized man. Another device involved locating a story in a moment of transition, like that of the Spanish Civil War, in which two ways of life—primitive and modern—confronted one another. And lastly, Hemingway set up geographical opposites: in *The Sun Also Rises* (1926), for example, he contrasts Jake Barnes in Paris and Jake in Burguete. Hemingway struggled to situate his pre-urban vision in a realm of idealized action and rituals that partake of the land and the sea, until finally he displaced urban reality with the extended arena.

Hemingway not only contrasted the primitive and civilized, but he depicted his naturalistic world impressionistically. Impressionism dictated the move from naturalism to modernism—from an objective to a subjective reality. The distinction between descriptive detail (in which the detail controls the mind) and impressionistic detail (in which the mind controls the detail) is objectivity on the way to becoming subjectivity. Hemingway's is a naturalistic world seen through a Paterian prism in which the emphasis is on a recording consciousness rather than biology, heredity, or environment.

John Dos Passos also adapted literary naturalism to a new realism. There is a direct connection among the works of Dreiser, Dos Passos, and Norman Mailer. Dos Passos helped transform literary naturalism in his *USA* trilogy (1930–36), anticipated by his own *Manhattan Transfer* (1925), by combining the narrative elements of Dreiser and James Joyce. Dos Passos's early novels came out of an aesthetic tradition.[10] His *Three Soldiers* (1921) positioned a sensitive, misunderstood artist in a hostile, philistine world—as if Joyce's Stephen Dedalus had narrated Dreiser's *The "Genius"* (1915). He further developed this method in his *USA* trilogy by multiplying the number of characters caught in the social matrix and by adding a subjective dimension. Newspaper headlines and biographical insertions contributed both a topical and historical aspect to the social background. His newsreel technique combined topical events and real people like J. P. Morgan and Thomas Edison, and a device known as the Camera Eye supplied a personal point of view.

Dos Passos thus sustained a narrative about a sensitive individual caught in an indifferent, materialistic society. He shared Henry Adams's belief that atomistic multiplicity threatened human progress. Dos Passos initially believed that individual welfare was threatened by the misuse of power by big business, which led him early in his career to an align himself with the Left. Late in his career, he came to think that the misuse of power now arose out of big government, which switched his allegiance to the Right. While some have seen this as an exercise in political contradiction, there is common ground between these extremes, and his position today, with its insistence on the overriding importance of individual freedom, can best be described as libertarian. His characters came to embody the vortex of activity that was modern America, all seemingly headed for failure, more the victims of social forces than biological necessity.

A number of modernist characters manifested this degeneration : Mann's Buddenbrooks family, Faulkner's Compson family, Fitzgerald's Anthony Patch and Dick Diver. But no naturalistic explanation of their decline was offered. The scientific observer was gone, the ironic point of view was modified, and the emphasis was more on a state of individual consciousness than naturalistic reality.

4

Naturalism and existentialism are in a number of ways polar opposites: one insists on the workings of determinism, the other stresses individual freedom. And yet naturalist and existentialist literature do share common ground: both, for example, depict a hostile universe to which the main characters must adapt or be destroyed. As in naturalistic fiction, when existential characters philosophize about the nature of existence, they ultimately become aware of a void, a cosmic emptiness that overpowers them. The naturalistic novel often depicted this force as either destructive (Conrad) or redemptive (London). The existential novel usually depicts a gulf between this force and civilized life, the former questioning the latter. As in Camus' *L'Étranger*, this discrepancy engenders moral contradiction.

According to critics like Joseph Wood Krutch and Herbert J. Muller, literary naturalism lacked the "nobility" and the "dignity" to be tragic; unlike the characters in classical tragedy, its characters lacked the ability to participate heroically in their own fate.[11] In both naturalism and existentialism, tragedy is no longer a pattern of action that pits a character against a moral universe, but a pattern of action that negates both community and a moral center, leaving a void or a realm of chaos as the defining element. Sartre questioned the very idea of a human nature, and hence the idea of tragedy, by insisting such fixity was a matter of individual engagement. (This idea anticipated the deconstruction of Jacques Derrida with its loss of textual fixity.) There would have been no existentialist novel if realism/naturalism had not repudiated the existence of moral imperatives, thereby creating the antihero and leaving both a moral and cosmic hole, which becomes the basis for existential dread and leads to either the cosmic courage or the cosmic fear that characterizes so much existential fiction.

The wedge that separates naturalism and existentialism is Nietzsche (1844–1900). Nietzsche pushed Kirkegaardian principles to their limit. Once an all-embracing moral order was lost, Nietzsche's philosophical subject stood outside society and political institutions. In *The Birth of Tragedy* (1871), Nietzsche claimed that in classical tragedy Apollonian order (civilizing, measured, sublime) gave contrast to unruly Dionysian energy (primordial, orgiastic, chaotic); he despaired of the modern tragedy of his time, which he believed had abandoned the Dionysian in favor of the Apollonian. However, after Nietzsche, Dionysian forces reigned in modern tragedy to the exclusion of Apollonian principles. Dostoyevsky's Kirillov exemplifies this paradigm: he destroys himself out of the obsessive desire to prove that he is his own god, beyond divine mandate. Camus' Meursault shares Kirillov's state of mind. He acknowledges the absurdity of the first shot by firing four more shots into the prostrate Arab, knowing this will cost him his life. Meursault and Kirillov are inverted Christ-figures: they desire to be their own god; they are products of a demonic urge for self-authority. The philosophy of Jean-Paul Sartre contains the same Nietzschean destructive principle. Sartre sees life as a struggle between mutually exclusive states of being—matter and consciousness. But to be pure fixity and consciousness at the same time is to be both god and dead. The Sartrean heroes—Mathieu and Hugo, for example—destroy themselves when they achieve a kind of self-completion.

No one has illustrated the destructive nature of existential thought better than Paul Bowles. Bowles's novels are set against the backdrop of a hostile environment within which the main characters choose their mode of destruction. Rather than drawing his fictional world along Darwinian lines, however, Bowles posits the existence of a cosmic realm that brings this fiction closer to that of Conrad than that of Zola. The principal characters in *The Sheltering Sky* (1949) are Port and Kit Moseby, both ineffectual and overcivilized Americans who discover new depths of being after several months of primitive life in the desert. The novel takes place in North Africa, in and around the borders of the Sahara. The land is completely antihuman: the sun burns without mercy; the sky cracks with heat; the wind singes the skin; and the red earth burns like an ember. These elements are manifest extensions of the destructive power lying above the protective shield of the sky. The sky is a thin veil protecting one from the cosmic violence beyond: it "shelters the person beneath from the horror that lies above."[12] Port and Kit find new depths of being as a result of their contact with the elemental desert before the vital but destructive forces eventually consume them.

Let It Come Down (1952) repeats almost exactly the plot of *The Sheltering Sky*. Nelson Dyar (dire, dare, die?) comes to Tangiers to escape the limitations of life in America. He also finds new being in a physical and elemental relationship with the natural life. Dyar wants to be so self-involved that nothing from the hostile world can harm him. When Dyar commits a gratuitous act of murder, he bolts the door between himself and humanity and seals himself within his own consciousness. Once there, his being has all the fixity of death. Like other existential heroes, Dyar's self-completion is a form of self-destruction.

The Spider's House (1955) takes place in Fez, at the time in a state of siege. Morocco is being torn in half by two factions: the relentless French colonists and the greedy Istiqlal nationalists. Once again Bowles's central character, John Stenham, retreats from the hostility of the physical world into the void of his own mind. Bowles's characters embrace solipsism, and in so doing cut themselves off from the physical world of causality, replacing the naturalist's environment with a cosmic consciousness. But interestingly, Bowles could never have created characters who achieve this state of being if he did not have realism/naturalism as the starting point from which to go beyond.

As the emphasis on heredity gave way to a concern with environment, the naturalistic novel turned to a study of political power. Norris and Dreiser had created the model, which was then developed by London and Sinclair. In *The Naked and the Dead* (1948), Mailer resurrects this subtype, connecting microcosm and macrocosm, individual and group behavior, to show men driven by a lust for power in a world that is as ferocious as the jungle.

While Mailer treats more than a dozen characters at some length, three main characters emerge. General Edward Cummings is an ambitious, authoritarian, power-hungry leader. He believes that history "has been working toward a greater and greater consolidation of power," and that "the only morality of the future is a power morality."[13] He contends that fascism will eventually control the world and is pleased that it will be an American rather than a German fascism. Cummings believes in the idea of the survival of the fittest, and maintains that the Second World War led to the triumph of a right-wing totalitarian order in America. Cummings explains his ideas to Lt. Robert Hearn, a Harvard graduate from a wealthy Midwest family, who has repudiated the ideas of his father and become a liberal. Hearn is more passive than Cummings, less convinced that the Left has the answer, even as he fears the Right. He is unaware that what is true of the relationship between individuals is also true of the relationship between political groups and between nations—that life is one unresolved power struggle. The character who is intuitively aware of this truth is Sergeant Croft from Texas, whose lust for power is sadistic. In many ways, Croft embodies the blind power of America. He has a cruel, ambitious desire to succeed, undeviating in its intensity. He willfully allows Lt. Hearn to be killed so that he can take over command of the platoon and complete Cummings's instructions. He is in effect the unenlightened extension of Cummings—blind energy without morals or conscience waiting to be directed.

In *The Naked and the Dead,* Mailer tells us that liberals like Hearn are really helpless in the face of Cummings and Croft, who embody the ruthless power of America. This idea is a legacy of literary naturalism and an idea that Mailer develops again in such political works as *Cannibals and Christians* (1966), *The Presidential Papers* (1963), *The Armies of the Night* (1968), and *Why Are We in Vietnam?* (1967) By going through a version of American naturalism, Mailer prepared himself to write an existential novel. *An American Dream* (1965) is an existential allegory—an open-ended journey into primitive psychic energy that took Mailer into the megalomania of Nietzsche at his most extreme.

A second generation of naturalist writers made good use of the first generation. Richard Wright, for example, rewrites Dreiser's *An American Tragedy* (1925) from the point of view of black experience. *Native Son* (1940) deals with the growing consciousness of Bigger Thomas after he commits two murders. Up until the murders, Bigger, held in place by economic forces, is unable to escape his black environment. Mr. Dalton, for whom he is a chauffeur, owns the tenement house in which he and his fatherless family live. Located on the south side of Chicago, these tenements become a line that Bigger cannot cross. He accidentally murders Mary Dalton to keep her from revealing to her blind mother that he has put her to bed because she is too drunk to care for herself. He then decapitates and burns her body in the family furnace, later murdering his girlfriend Bessy in fear that she may reveal his crime.

Wright constructs an extreme scenario—here the two murders—to show the naturalistic influence of race, heredity, and environment on black reality. Bigger Thomas, Wright wants us to believe, is more the victim than victimizer. His acts are primal, driven by atavistic (ancestral) fears that plumb naturalistic theory and create the context for a purely sociological discussion in the courtroom scenes that follow, similar to Dreiser's *An American Tragedy* and to the later *Knock on Any Door* (1947) by Willard Motley. When Bigger is finally brought to trial, he is represented by a communist lawyer whose ideas become the frame of reference against which Bigger's story unfolds. Bigger's sense of despair is tempered by Max's political hope. As Jack London, Upton Sinclair, and Edward Bellamy offered versions of socialism as a solution to their narrative problems, Wright moves easily from naturalistic assumptions within which he states the problem to communist theory within which he offers a solution, following the tradition in allowing leftist politics to offer a way out of a naturalistic predicament.

Native Son is naturalism at its most tendentious, directly bringing to the surface ideas that are often submerged in other naturalistic fiction. Wright, for example, brings everything back to Bigger's primal fears—fear of the white man and of the even greater taboo, interracial sex. As his lawyer tells the jury: "the hate and fear, which we have inspired in him, have become the justification of his existence."[14] But Wright also gives Bigger more insight into his predicament than we see in the most purely naturalistic novels. Bigger's insight brings him a freedom seldom realized elsewhere: "I didn't know I was really alive in this world until I felt things hard enough to kill for 'em," he says (333). One expects naturalist novelists to be sympathetic to their downtrodden characters, but in *Native Son* Wright's sympathy seems misplaced. Dreiser changed the details of the Chester Gillette-Grace Brown murder in *An American Tragedy* to make Grace's death appear

as an accident and to keep the reader from turning unsympatheti-
cally on a heartless murderer. Wright depicts Bigger as both a passive
and active murderer, freed from his mental prison by his murders, violence a source of racial release. Wright believes that African Americans are held in place by fear that stems from taboos and a mindset
that constrains them. One escapes that mindset by an act of violence
so extreme that one becomes an "outsider," a social exile who goes
beyond conventional morality.[15]

Native Son was completed in 1939 and published the next year.
Between 1942 and 1944, Wright broke with the American Communist
Party. In 1942 he published a long story, "The Man Who Lived
Underground," which revealed the influence of Dostoyevsky and influenced in turn Ralph Ellison's Invisible Man (1952). Wright's story
involves Fred Daniels, falsely accused of murder, who escapes from
the police and takes refuge in the sewer through which he crawls,
digging a network of tunnels through buildings that take him into
the black community. Once underground, his whole perspective
changes. The people in the church and the movie theater seem
strange to the point of being grotesque. What he comes to realize is
that his life is different from that of other people. Like Bigger
Thomas, he had been conditioned by the fears that control the black
man in the white man's world and now is freed by his new understanding from that world. Fred Daniels anticipates Wright's most
existential character, Cross Damon of The Outsider (1953). Once
Damon strays beyond human limits, he can find no means to return
to the ordinary. Like Bowles and Mailer, if Wright had not had the
benefit of naturalism, he could not have written his version of the
existential novel. One literary experience made possible the other. By
voiding the novel of its moral center and creating the antihero, naturalism allowed protoexistentialists to fill their fiction with Nietzschean overmen.

5

If there is an American city that supplies a terrain for literary
naturalism, it is Chicago. Norris, Dreiser, Upton Sinclair, Richard
Wright, James T. Farrell, Willard Motley, Nelson Algren, and Saul

Bellow—all set major works in Chicago. The reason is perhaps evident: Chicago came to embody many of the elements essential to naturalism. Located on the edge of the plains, it was defined by the land before it was transformed into an industrial city—primarily by becoming the center of the meat processing industry, the subject of Upton Sinclair's *The Jungle* (1906). Chicago also became the center of the produce exchange, depicted in Norris's story of the wheat business. Dreiser also saw it as a money exchange and the source of private speculation and public wealth in its commitment to a public transportation system. He also saw it as a magnet attracting the ambitious young, like Carrie Meeber. James T. Farrell saw it as a proving ground for the young—the cause of Studs Lonigan's degeneration, Bernard Carr's regeneration. The great wealth produced by Chicago was matched by the great poverty it left behind—the subject of stories by Motley and Algren. More recently came writers like Bellow who, with the exception of perhaps elements from *Augie March* (1953), elected to depict the city in terms distinct from literary naturalism.[16] No other city perpetuated naturalistic assumptions as well as Chicago.

Built into naturalism, especially the naturalistic political novel, were the realities of the industrial age: the capitalistic-industrial process created two extremes—the powerful and helpless, the profiteer and the wage slave. Any literary representation of industrial capital and labor inevitably tended to portray the extremes—that is, to depict a more good-versus-evil situation. James T. Farrell (1904–1979) was well aware of this dichotomy and of the fact that the odds were against the disenfranchised succeeding. Farrell drew directly on his own life in his three major cycle novels. Born near the turn of the century, Farrell depicted key events mostly in terms of the chronology of his own life. His *Studs Lonigan* (1932–35) trilogy (covering the years from 1916 to 1931) is the study of a young man Farrell knew in Chicago and tells the story of a process of deterioration, decline, and ultimately death. His second pentalogy, the O'Neill-O'Flaherty sequence (1936–53 [covering the years from 1909 to 1927]), is his most autobiographical writing and in some ways answers the *Studs Lonigan* novels. His third trilogy, the *Bernard Carr* novels (1946–52) (covering the years from 1927 to 1936), follows Danny O'Neill, who moves from Chicago to New York where he becomes a successful writer, art substituting for his earlier commitment to Catholicism and later sympathy for the Communist party.

The *Studs* trilogy is a story of spiritual poverty; it is not really a story of the slums but of the "near" slums: Studs is not poor; his father owns an apartment building and a housepainting business. As a story of decline, the personal and the historical come together. The novel begins in the era of Woodrow Wilson's prosperity and ends in the era of Herbert Hoover's depression. The historical slide parallels the personal slide. Studs can find nothing of substance to which to commit his life: home, church, school, and playground—all prove inadequate, and he drifts to gangs and the pool hall. When he works, it is as a housepainter in his father's business; but his ability to work is compromised by his growing alcoholism and declining health, until he dies at the age of twenty-seven from pneumonia. In his own account of the novel, Farrell discusses how Prohibition alcohol, often harmfully toxic, led to the kind of ending that befell Studs. This is a novel where hope for a future turns to memories of a past, the present perpetually empty.

Farrell's answer to the story of Studs involves his own story, told in the person of Danny O'Neill, who from the age of three to his manhood lived with his grandmother's family because his own parents were too strapped to take care of him. Minor intrigue provides the backdrop of the novel: an uncle who strived for success; an aunt who was carrying on an affair with a successful businessman-politician and who was stealing money from the hotel register where she worked as a clerk; and the story of Danny's natural father, an express truck driver, who could never make enough money to properly support his growing family. But the focus is on Danny O'Neill himself, who is able to break the cycle of financial and intellectual poverty within which his family is trapped by entering the University of Chicago and planning a career as a writer.

Danny's plans are realized in the third cycle of novels that take him to New York. There he engages the intellectual struggle that results in his repudiating the absolutes of his Catholic religion for the absolutes of the Communist party, before he rejects both for the absolutes of art. The absolutism he ascribes to art is eventually tempered by a growing affinity for John Dewey's pragmatism and the belief that truth is a function of empirical-experiential testing.

The reference to John Dewey, the note on which the *Bernard Carr* trilogy ends, was the note that Farrell brought to his writing in all of these fictional cycles. Farrell's view deviated from traditional naturalism: he did not stress nature as much as nurture—that is, he emphasized how the workings of society and the forces of the environment determined his protagonist's life. Even Stud's degeneration was more a social process than a moral decline. Like John Dewey, Farrell believed that modern institutions were not supplying the needs of a new generation and that individual failure in America was inseparable from the social failure of the nation itself.

As Farrell progressed in these works, he increasingly began to tell the story from the point of view of the characters themselves, and the novels became more impressionistic than the strict naturalistic novel with its "scientific" observer. He also began to set the stories against the background of the events of the day, using, for example, newspaper headlines, as did Dos Passos in his *USA* trilogy. His use of the more personal point of view was not always successful. Curtailing the perspective to the juvenile minds of Studs and Danny limited what could be said to a diminished awareness. That the novels were overwritten, going on for hundreds of pages, did not help matters. Theme was more important than telling. Farrell had significant insight into the meaning of an industrialized America and its psychic toll on the poor and near poor, but his aesthetic sense was limited. Despite these flaws, these stories add up to a cautionary tale, a representative depiction of success and failure in America.

Along with Farrell, Willard Motley, Nelson Algren, William Kennedy, and Joyce Carol Oates were still working literary naturalism after World War II. The achievement here is mixed. None of these writers approaches the accomplishment of Dreiser in *An American Tragedy*, although a number of them sought to imitate it. But they share the sympathy of the earlier naturalists for the urban hobo, the itinerant worker, or just the general drifter. Henry Miller and Jack Kerouac would give us a more romantic version of this world.

Willard Motley (1912–1965) was a black American novelist, whose best work was *Knock on Any Door* (1947). Motley's novel tells the story of Nick Romano, a child of Italian immigrant parents, who starts out as an ambitious, obedient, and deeply religious, young man, and ends up a criminal. The novel brings two forces into play—the family and the gang, the latter displacing the former. Nick repudiates his stern father who cannot hold a job, his weak and overly religious mother, his older siblings who turn hostile, and he gives his allegiance to his antisocial friends, who draw him into the world of crime. Part of the novel is seen through the eyes of Emma Schultz, whose father dies when she is eight and who is raised in poverty by a stern, immigrant mother, a background that parallels Nick's. Their love affair and marriage ends with her suicide. In the meantime, Nick has run the gamut from petty theft, to armed robbery, to killing a policeman—a criminal career that takes him from reform school, to prison, to death row. Social institutions—the family, the church, public schools, and the justice system—fail him, and his end in the electric chair seems inevitable.

Nick's story is inseparable from his poverty. Class differences create different laws and institutions for each class. *Knock on Any Door* carries on the narrative tradition of Crane's *Maggie* (1893). It owes even more to both Dreiser's *An American Tragedy* and Richard Wright's *Native Son*. All three novels recount stories of young men shaped by their environment, each defying a hostile legal system and suffering the ultimate penalty. Each novel has a courtroom scene in which lawyers argue the case for and against Clyde, Bigger, and Nick, the defense maintaining their innocence on the grounds that each character was the product of social forces that determined his fate. Nick did not kill the policeman—society did. Nick's outrage at the forces that have shaped his life is so extreme—and he is so angered by police brutality—that he boasts of killing the policeman at his trial and seals his fate. The meaning of the novel is summarized near the end by his defense attorney. He tells the jury, "I accuse—you and me—this precious thing we call Society—of being the guilty parties who have brought Nick Romano, innocent, here in this courtroom before us!"[17]

As in *Native Son*, a racial theme runs through many narratives by African American authors in which characters, including white ethnic ones like Nick, can only be released from cultural restraints by acts of violence. Motley absolves Nick of murder because he is the victim of his ethnic poverty, just as African Americans are, and the closed doors of opportunity that went with that condition. Weaned on the Horatio Alger formula of the poor boy struggling to rise above his humble circumstances and winning success through luck and pluck, a new audience was willing to entertain the opposite claim, extreme as it was. Society created Clyde, Bigger, and Nick and then destroyed them to protect itself. As the title suggests, a Nick Romano can be found behind any door in the urban slum.

Motley's world is that of Chicago's skid row, as in *Let No Man Write My Epitaph* (1958). Very seldom does Motley take us outside this world. His narrative realm is surrounded by Nelson Algren's world to the north, Saul Bellow's to the west, and James T. Farrell's to the south. He comes closest to a larger look at Chicago in *We Fished All Night* (1951), which deals primarily with the disillusionment of war but also with the city's corrupt machine politics. It has been argued that Motley avoids black life, populating his novels instead with second-generation Italians, Poles, and Jews working toward assimilation. In *We Fished All Night,* his principal character is a Polish Catholic named Chet Kosinski, who changes his name to Don Lockwood and tries to pass as a WASP. Motley seems more interested in class than race, showing the similarities between blacks and whites trapped by poverty. In *Let Noon Be Fair* (1963), for example, his Italian American characters have many of the characteristics of Richard Wright's black characters. Motley's writing, a combination of Wright's violence and John Steinbeck's sentimentality, was more appreciated in the forties and fifties than it is today.

Along with James T. Farrell and Richard Wright, Nelson Algren also offered a naturalistic version of Chicago. His best works include *The Man with the Golden Arm* (1949), dealing with drug addiction, and *A Walk on the Wild Side* (1956). His affair with Simone de Beauvoir is described fictionally in her *The Mandarins* (1956) and in his autobiography. Algren began his career as a journalist, but during the Depression he became a drifter, traveling throughout the Southwest. For a brief time, he was involved with the American Communist Party. Ross Macdonald has referred to him as the "poet of the sad metropolis that underlies our North American cities."[18] Algren depicts a world that upper- and middle-class America denies exists: life on the road, life in the slums, and life in the poorer working-class neighborhoods, especially in the Polish section of Chicago, where Algren grew up. Hoboes, prostitutes, criminals, fighters, drug addicts, and drunks populate his novels. Poverty is the source of most wrongdoing: it drives men to crime and women to prostitution. Evil thus comes from environmental conditioning, not innate traits.

Somebody in Boots (1935), Algren's first novel, is the story of Cass McKay, a poor illiterate Texan, who drifts through America in the Depression. The novel is in the tradition of vagabond literature similar to that featuring the tramps of Jack London, the homeless or itinerant workers of John Steinbeck and John Dos Passos, and the seekers in Jack Kerouac's novels. *Never Come Morning* (1942), his second novel, deals with the destruction of Bruno Lefty Bicek, who betrays both himself in his desire for a boxing career and his girlfriend when he surrenders her to his friends in order to comply with the code of the gang. *The Man With the Golden Arm*, panoramic in scope, has been called the *Winesburg, Ohio* (1919) of the slums. Like Crane, Norris, and Dreiser, Algren is concerned with the dispossessed who are products of both biology and society. His story is about a morphine addict, Frankie Majcinek, who works as a card dealer in Schwiefka's gambling house: he is called Frankie Machine because he deals with the accuracy of a machine. *A Walk on the Wild Side* is a reworking of *Somebody in Boots*. A drifter, similar to Cass McKay, is beaten blind after becoming involved with criminals in New Orleans. Algren is here working the same vein of American literature in which we find Jack Kerouac's outcasts, who in turn look back to Kenneth Rexroth's and Henry Miller's outsiders. *A Walk on the Wild Side* marks a break in the social protest novel: Algren postulates that we must either realistically accept the lower depths or turn its inhabitants into the sentimental primitives found in Steinbeck and Henry Miller.

Another depiction of down-and-out life is the Albany cycle by William Kennedy composed of *Legs* (1976), *Billy Phelan's Greatest Game* (1978), and *Ironweed* (1983)—all of which take place in Depression-era Albany and depict politicians, journalists, and general low-life. Perhaps the best of Kennedy's novels is *Ironweed*. It is the story of Billy Phelan's father, Francis Phelan, a skid-row bum and his companion, Helen Archer. Francis returns to Albany twenty-two years after he abandoned his family. A former major-league third baseman, Francis was an employee on the Albany trolley line when he threw a stone that killed a strikebreaker. Several years later—the year is 1916—he accidentally dropped and killed his thirteen-day-old baby. Overcome by guilt, he took to the road, abandoning his wife and his nine-year old son, taking up the life of a hobo.

Kennedy explores both sin and guilt. His sympathies are with outcasts, vagabonds, and derelicts. He writes about them from the inside: they do not know they are outsiders. He wants to touch what is human inside the bum's life. Helen, who has had a year at Vassar, becomes Francis's soul mate. When her family money dried up, she married unhappily, at which time she ran away to pursue a singing career. She finds Francis instead, and together they live by their wits, until Helen dies of cancer. Twenty-two years later—the year is 1938 and Francis is now fifty-eight—he returns to Albany on the boxcar Ulysses (a Homeric-Joycean touch) and gets a job digging graves in Saint Agnes Cemetery, where the dead speak to him (a device surely derived from Edgar Lee Master's *Spoon River Anthology*). He talks to his dead parents, gamblers, baseball players, strikebreakers, and hoboes. No voice comes, however, from the grave of his son, Gerald Michael Phelan, who died in 1916 of a broken neck.

Kennedy is really working two stories in this novel: that of Francis's early glorious days as a ballplayer, and his later hobo exis-tence. But the two stories cannot come together: there is no center. There is no common ground among the stories of Harold Allen, the scab Francis killed with the stone, Francis's nine years on the road with Helen, or the death of his friend Rudy, killed by a mob of Le-gionnaires out to destroy a hobo jungle. The common denominator in his life, what holds it all together, is remorse: guilt is what Francis has left after a life that began in glory but ended in burnt-out regret.

While her later works represent a kind of modern American gothic, critics correctly connected Joyce Carol Oates's early novels and stories with literary naturalism, especially with the naturalism of Dreiser.[19] Her background—Irish-Catholic working class—can be compared to Dreiser's German-Catholic background. For her,

history, as it unfolds, is an overwhelming force, leaving lost innocence and anomie or purposelessness. Her characters fight to survive
in an amoral world, and her novels deal with the social violence of
lower-class Americans living through terrifying events that they do
not understand. Her plots often begin with a naturalistic treatment
of poverty in the Depression era before breaking into forms of violence: arson, riot, murder, and rape. Her early novels are set in an
imaginary place, ironically called Eden. But Eden, what one critic described as "violent, transient, massive, ugly, corrupt, vulgar, hysteri-
cal, and insanely rigid,"[20] becomes America. Stated differently, her
America comprises farmhouses, gas stations, dirt roads, and empty
shacks. Cities are transitory—places situated between past and future. And down the road always awaits violence.

Oates reveals a savagery beneath the veneer of civilized life. She
depicts the fear of sudden eruptions of hidden psychic forces that lie
within but cannot be controlled. If Wright and Motley's characters
involve the outsider, Oates's characters fear it—fear being cut off
from others and from the human race, fear being locked out of love
and forced to face on their own an alien world beyond understanding. Her novels reveal the shifting line between the individual and the
mass—the realm of "them." She depicts causation without cause: a
world where convention and tradition have been transformed and
things do not connect, the result of which is drift and deterioration.
She reverses the modernist trust in redemption through high art.

Oates is extremely prolific, sometimes writing two novels a year.
Her early work, *A Garden of Earthly Delights* (1967), a trilogy, depicts
the life of migrant workers in rural Eden County, based on Erie
County, where Oates grew up. *Expensive People* (1967) treats the op-
posite world: the suburban rich. *them* (1969) portrays an inner city
Detroit family. *Wonderland* (1971) details the degeneration of a sur-
geon who is brilliant in his profession but helpless at home. *Do with
Me What You Will* (1973) deals with lawyers (instead of doctors). *As-
sassins* (1975) is a story of the assassination of a conservative politician and the effect it has on his widow and his two brothers. *Son of
Morning* (1978) is a study of religious zealotry. And "Where are You
Going, Where Have You Been" (1974) involves the sexual awakening
of a romantic young girl by a mysterious man, who may be a sex fiend
(if the story is read realistically) or the devil (if read symbolically).

Oates's place in the realist/naturalist tradition is best represented by the novel *them*. The novel depicts the Wendall family over
a thirty-year period, from 1937 to 1967, focusing on Loretta, the
mother; Jules, the son and brother; and Maureen, the daughter, who
becomes the principal character. Loretta finally accepts her place in
the ghetto, becomes one of "them." Jules joins a group of anarchists;
denied love and material goods, he turns his lack into a symbolic way
of life when he becomes intent on burning America down. Maureen
refuses to give up hope, as did Loretta, and seeks more from life than
Jules, even as all the Wendalls seemed doomed by the poverty that
has led to emotional deformity. *them* is a novel that depicts history as
shards, reflecting characters whose lives are in pieces. As in naturalistic fiction, time overpowers the helpless and character becomes fate
in this linear tale about realistic people, spiritually and materially deprived. Oates's later fiction—*Bellefleur* (1980), *A Bloodless Romance*
(1982), and *Mysteries of Winterthurn* (1984)—represents a gothic departure from her earlier naturalistic writing; it approaches the symbolic, depicting fantasy-like situations, although violence, especially
crimes against women and children, is a narrative constant.

Despite the persistence of naturalism even after World War II, it
thinned and then eventually disappeared altogether. Critics accused
naturalism of being reductive, of explaining the complex in terms
of the simple: society in terms of the self, humanity in terms of the
animal, the organic in terms of the inorganic (mechanistic). Many
naturalistic assumptions came close to affirming racial theories long
repudiated. To equate humanity with a beast of prey or to chemical
compounds was more metaphorical than scientific. Naturalism was
devoid of literary meaning in its reduction of humanity to case his-
tories. The life struggle became ironic rather than tragic: Crane's
oiler fights the sea only to die in sight of land; Dresier's Carrie fails
when she is most conventional, succeeds when she sells her virtue;
Clyde Griffiths's desire for the good life leads to death. After World
War II, naturalism undermined itself with its predictability.

Literary realism/naturalism was essentially the end product of the
division between nineteenth-century philosophy and science. Philosophy concentrated primarily on theories of the mind; science on
theories of matter. This division gave way in the face of modernism—
especially Heisenberg's declaration that scientific experiment

involved its own mode of subjectivity, that the participant's subjectivity could not be separated from the experiment. This resulted in what he called the Uncertainty Principle in quantum mechanics, the belief that we cannot measure the precise location and momentum of a particle at any given time. When coupled with Einstein's theory of relativity, the impossibility of an observer in one system to measure the other, this idea challenged strict causality (since if we can't know both the position and the momentum of a particle at any given time we cannot predict its future position and momentum) and reinforced the earlier philosophy of Bergson, out of which came the basic tenets of modernism. Bertrand Russell's *Icarus* (1924), J. B. S. Haldane's *Daedalus* (1924), and Alfred North Whitehead's *Science and the Modern World* (1925) all bore witness to this transformation.

9

Critical Transformations

1

In the last generation there have been radical changes in the assumptions governing our sense of the novel. Postmodern criticism has attempted to bridge the distinction between elitist and popular culture. Individual consciousness, whether that of the author or his characters, is inseparable from the world of which it is a part. Artistic consciousness cannot be divorced from an all-encompassing commercialism. Such readings challenged the naturalistic emphasis on the biological while delimiting the notion of environment to a system of institutions held together by constructed forms of power.

A major postmodern assumption is that reality is bracketed—that language or some other semiotic system mediates between human beings and nature and by extension history. We thus know nature and history through the systems we use to explain them to ourselves. Physical reality is no longer a reflective mirror; historical time does not unfold meaningfully. All elements within these systems are self-referential: they are no longer a reservoir of meaning that is a function of the relationship between language and reality but are endowed only with the meaning of the system itself. Consciousness is enfolded into the systems we use to explain reality, not into reality. Postmodernism thus begins where Nietzsche left off, postulating a universe without either subject or subjectivity, intelligible only in terms of the way we choose to talk about it.

Under the influence of structuralism and poststructuralism, the idea of the mimetic was seriously challenged. One no longer referred to literature as a reflection of reality in nature, governed by principles of revelation, symbolic unfolding, or evolutionary process. Roland Barthes (1915–1980) contended that a realistic story like Balzac's "Sarrasine" was just as conventional as more self-conscious literary works and that a realistic text drew no more directly on "life" than any other kind of writing. Barthes maintained that narrative functions as part of a language system controlled by its own inner grammar. Instead of discussing Balzac in terms of theme, character, setting, plot, symbols, and point of view, Barthes divided the text into what he called "lexies," and then proceeded to read the text word by word, producing over two hundred pages of commentary on a thirty-page story.

His assumption is that the world is apprehended only through language, which in turn encodes our understanding of reality. There are five such codes: the proairetic or code of action, the hermeneutic or code of puzzles, the cultural or code of fashions, the connotative or code of themes, and the symbolic or code of tropes. At first glance, this looks as if Barthes is simply bringing the old categories of theme, plot, and symbol in by the backdoor—but this is not the case. For we understand character, setting, and plot in terms of the idea of individuals, places, and actions in the real world, but Barthes's codes refer to language, which is an encoded barrier to reality.

Whereas Zola believed that the author of the experimental novel was comparable to the scientist in the laboratory, describing objectively the reality of the historical moment, Barthes insisted that all writers functioned within self-enclosed language systems. Such encoding leads to two kinds of texts: the writerly text that a reader can rewrite by reading because the codes are still active and alive, and a readerly text that cannot be rewritten in the process of reading because the codes are no longer historically relevant. Barthes thus emptied literary realism of meaning by cutting it off from a physical reality that it embodied and by seeing it as encoding signs from a dead and empty past.

2

A change in critical paradigm brought about new ways of reading modern texts—both realist and modernist. The fusion of high and low literature and a concern with the new consumerism put the emphasis on the relation between literature and culture. And then there are the studies that attempt to redefine the whole realist/naturalist movement. A book that questions the usefulness of realism and naturalism as descriptive terms is Michael Davitt Bell's *The Problem of American Realism* (1993). Bell is interested in the way realist and naturalist authors themselves define these terms in their own critical writing. Howells's limitations stemmed from the difficulty of reconciling realism and aestheticism. Despite such limitations, Bell uses Howells's desire to depict "the smiling aspects of life" as the benchmark of literary realism and finds both Twain and James wanting as realists. Bell dismantles literary naturalism by employing the same method. Using Norris's theory as the basis for defining literary naturalism, Bell argues that Crane's more mannered style distanced him from both Norris's naturalism and Howells's realism. Bell repudiates the idea that Dreiser was a naturalist on the grounds that Dreiser's omniscient narrator, slipping into an untutored style that often sounds like the voice of his characters, fails to establish a distance between author and characters.

Bell belongs to the group of recent critics who have substituted "textuality" for "reality"—that is, who limit the heuristic context by reducing realistic and naturalistic texts to purely literary matters (usually style and language), denying the idea that such texts are historical representations. While good at presenting a survey of narrative theory, Bell arrives at broad conclusions based on limited literary evidence: he treats no novels by Howells and only one or two by the other authors, often in a context marginal to realism/naturalism as a way of depicting reality. Moving in a different direction from Bell is Rachel Bowlby's *Just Looking* (1985), a study of the connection between literary naturalism and consumerism. Bowlby argues that we determine our identity by what we consume. But soon one becomes consumed by consumption: the goods possess the buyer and not the other way around. Narcissus fell in love with himself. Bowlby sees the consumer, especially the female consumer, as Narcissus—hooked on goods connected with one's own sense of self. But at some point the mannequin in the window becomes a second self, an "other," someone one could be if one could pay the price.

A study that deals with the connections between the novel and American history is Philip Fisher's *Hard Facts* (1985). Fisher deal with

three "hard facts": possessing the land necessitated killing or displacing Native Americans; the Jeffersonian vision excluded slaves; and
the rise of capitalism brought with it an urban culture. The fate of
the Native American was played out in the wilderness as depicted in
Cooper's *Leatherstocking Tales* (1823–41); the Jeffersonian vision gave
rise to the farm and the yeoman farmer who tilled the land for himself, a life from which African Americans were excluded as in Stowe's
Uncle Tom's Cabin (1851); and the new city accommodated an individualism that flourished at the expense of the family as depicted in
Dreiser's *Sister Carrie* (1900). As we moved from wilderness to farm
to city, each setting shaped the form of the representative novel. In
Sister Carrie, New York, according to Fisher, is an extended stage; the
emphasis is on how everyday objects and places—such as clothes and
public spaces (e.g., hotels)—create the social reality. The newspaper
gives an account after the event, supplying a record separate from
the event itself—that is, supplying the "facts" of a fiction. New York
gives off more energy than Chicago and, in effect, accelerates time.
Hurstwood—while only thirty-nine—begins to act as if he is sixty:
he seems to age quicker in New York. In moving back and forth
between what is "real" in New York and what is "fictional" in Dreiser's novel, Fisher creates an overlap between fiction and reality.

Fisher's critical method approaches those of the new historicism.
This movement is to be applauded for restoring history to the critical
equation. But the new historicists' concept of history is vastly different from the traditional one. Instead of thinking of history as "reality" and the text as fiction, the new historicist sees both history and
texts as fiction—that is, as constructs that determine the consciousness of an era (or episteme, to use Michel Foucault's term). History
becomes a form of discourse, analogous to a language system that
creates its own reality. The term "new historicism" is thus a mis-
nomer, both inexact and redundant, since the new historicist does
not believe that each age contains a geist or core meaning waiting to
be uncovered by the historian.

The new historicist shares a kinship with the idea of pragmatic reality and emphasizes the relativity of the present as a way into the past.
Central to the new historicism is a belief in constructs. The past is unknowable, except as a form of discourse. Such ideas are consistent

with poststructuralist theory and superficially sound right. Who can deny the inventive, self-interested aspect of history? And how can we see the past except through the distortions of the present? Put simply, the critic sees each culture subject to a set of self-generated constructs held in place by forms of power.

But in reducing history to a construct, the new historicist often fails to distinguish between differing orders of constructs—between, for example, the constructs supplied by an age and their own. Every era offers up its version of reality based upon the prevailing ideas of the times, which is frequently vastly different from the historicized version supplied by the contemporary critic. Secondly, the new historicists often fail to distinguish between constructs that look "out" at a historical moment (the Civil War or the Holocaust) and those that look "in" to an imaginary reality (such as their own economic paradigms or their version of Renaissance self-fashioning). Lastly, the new historicists seldom distinguish between physical reality and mental constructs. Entropy, for example, is a physical law, not a cultural construct; it functions the same in North America as in South Africa. If it did not operate universally, we would not just live in a different culture; we would live in a different universe. Their failure to distinguish between these "realities" results in their conflating the real and unreal, the historical and the ahistorical—and is a bit schizophrenic.

Like most critical methods, the new historicism is privileged and judgmental. It creates its own canon and determines how that canon will be read. The critic decides what aspects of the past will serve as a prism through which the meaning of the canonical works the movement has established will be gleaned. While the formalist critic gives primary attention to the way the artistic imagination shapes a text, the new historicist sees the text as a product of cultural forces, albeit arbitrary. The formalist stresses the writing process behind naturalism; the new historicist stresses the reading process, linking it to the pragmatism of reader-response theory. While the formalist stresses the way the individual imagination creates his or her own brand of naturalism, the new historicist does away with the idea of naturalism altogether and collapses it into cultural forms held together by institutional forms of power, an aspect of the method once again influenced by Michael Foucault.

My critique here is not meant to demean the new historicism as much as to suggest the impediments it puts in the way of other critical methods. By insisting that history is a construct, by denying its linear nature, and by rejecting history's distinct capacity, the new historicism cuts the text off from its historical origins and substitutes an arbitrary element of history for something like the workings of an era; misleading in name, it is really ahistorical, despite its claim to supplying a cultural poetics.

An example of a new historicist reading is Walter Benn Michaels's *The Gold Standard and the Logic of Naturalism* (1987). Like Bowlby and Fisher, Michaels reduces naturalism to the product of a commodity culture. He believes that consumerism and a money economy create the prism through which literary naturalism must be viewed. Michaels believes that the gold standard locked naturalism into place as a monetary system, despite the fact that most of the naturalists repudiated the gold standard.

Michaels argues that sex, art, and economics are all a part of the same process. A more "naturalistic" reading would see them as distinct activities, as three different ways of relating to nature, existing in a hierarchy from those closest to nature (sex), to those most abstractly separated from nature (economics), to those that can give us an insight into the relationship between the former and the latter (art).

Michaels reads Zerkow's obsession with gold in *McTeague* (1902) as an equation that links gold, language, and junk. Zerkow does substitute the story Maria tells for the reality of the gold dinner plates. But Norris does not equate these elements as much as show how a greed that goes beyond natural necessity creates a pathological state of mind in which one is willing to murder for an illusion, a mirage.

In Michaels's discussion of the economy, the crowd as an aggregate has a legal status that equates with the constructed reality of the corporation and not with any physical reality. In Michaels's readings, we not only lose the connection between human beings and nature, but the philosophical subject is collapsed into the money economy, which in turn becomes an extended form of textuality.

Such textuality is grounded, as in most new historicist criticism, in a trope that connects both text and culture. Michaels's trope involves production, consumption, and exchange, and these ideas are equated in pinwheel fashion to a string of cultural matters: the body, mind, desire, love, writing, feminine theory, utopian fantasy, and much more. The trope allows discussion of the way economic reality—money, interest, contracts, corporate structure—anticipates human reality. Relationships among characters become a form of exchange; the fiction of literature finds its equivalent in the fiction of money systems. Michaels reduces both systems to a given from which author and reader cannot escape because, whether they know it or not, they are inside, not outside, these systems, as a fish is to water.

But such a restriction seemingly does not apply to Michaels himself who is able to move outside these "fictions" to discuss the idea of identity between money and human systems. He concludes that just as the value of money cannot be reduced to its composition (paper), the value of the economy cannot be reduced to a person: "The economy . . . is still not a person. . . . But precisely because there is no such person . . . it provides a singularly compelling image of the naturalist distinction between material and identity. Failing to be a person, it images by the way it isn't a person the condition in naturalism of the possibility of persons."[1] This passage—with its slippery, convoluted language—is representative of the writing in the book as a whole. Much of what passes for complexity stems from obscurity. As for the conclusion, it is contrived: a naturalist like Dreiser has a theory of money and a theory of self, but they are neither identical nor interchangeable.

Another privileged reading of literary naturalism is June Howard's *Form and History in American Literary Naturalism* (1985). Howard's book is different in what it attempts and in its scope from the Michaels's book. Her concern is with the nature of naturalism in relation to history. The book comprises three elements—a theoretical discussion, a discussion of economic and social matters, and a series of critical readings of Dreiser, London, Norris, and Upton Sinclair. The main assumption of this book is somewhat ambiguously stated: "my task is not to set literary texts against a 'history' or 'reality' . . . but rather to trace how naturalism is shaped by and imaginatively reshapes a historical experience."[2]

As with Michaels, the writing here becomes vague. How can we separate naturalistic texts from history when "naturalism is shaped by . . . historical experience," unless the unstated premise is that history influences the text less than the text history, the text becoming the prism through which we interpret our world. If that is what Howard means, her argument would seem at least in part to derive from Fredric Jameson's idea of the political unconscious. Such a conclusion is suggested—but not clarified—when she tells us, "Naturalism does not provide a window into reality. Rather it reveals history indirectly in revealing itself" (29).

For Howard, the "historical" and the "real" seem to be different matters. Despite the fact that she has told us that she will not set literary texts against history or reality, she does both. Her book works the belief that historical matters such as immigration, poverty, and the radicalizing of America are both "real" and the basis for literary naturalism, and ends up reducing naturalism to radical history.

Another book that reads realistic texts against a new paradigm is Mark Seltzer's *Bodies and Machines* (1992), a study of how the machine has influenced the way we think of bodily functions and vice versa. Seltzer distinguishes between the natural and the mechanical— between the woman bringing forth a child and a machine bringing forth a product. Whereas more traditional readings of naturalism present it as invoking natural processes, Seltzer sees naturalism as a by-product of the machine age in which human beings are represented as an extension of the machine.

Daniel H. Borus's *Writing Realism* (1989) is one of the few studies that attempts to reconcile the novel and history, although he does not believe that the literary text is "a direct reflection of the history in which it was written," and the historical is deemed "elusive." Concentrating on Howells, James, and Norris, Borus is less concerned with the workings of history than with the way the historical determines how a text is written—how it determines "the way the narration is formed, the language deployed, the particular stance toward events."[3] The emphasis, in other words, is on literary technique, not the way that realism is informed by and the product of an historical moment. In its emphasis on a mass market, Borus's book moves us toward another category of critical study.

As even the most cursory survey reveals, recent studies of realism and naturalism have followed the pioneering work of Fredric

Jameson, treating these movements as exercises in constructed reality—that is, as transformations, both dialectical and nonsystematic, of capitalism with its mass markets and emphasis on consumption. Amy Kaplan's *The Social Construction of American Realism* (1988) and Phillip Barrish's *American Literary Realism, Critical Theory, and Intellectual Prestige, 1880–1995* (2001) embody such a critical approach. Barrish believes "the 'real' is only . . . available via mediating contexts and constructions." He is primarily concerned with the rise of a middle-class reality and "the role that literary realism played in helping the new middle classes differentiate themselves from people of 'lower' and . . . 'higher' socioeconomic status," as revealed by the conflicts within the class itself.[4]

Kaplan makes claim to the same territory: she is concerned with social change, class difference, and mass culture, as constructed reality, arguing that the writers themselves "[construct] the reality their novels represent." Kaplan's focus is "on narrative process, on how realism works to construct a social world out of the raw materials of unreality, conflict, and change" (8). The fiction is thus the source of the historical, the prism through which reality is seen, rather than vice versa. Kaplan ponders why some endings are deemed realistic and others unrealistic, and she concludes: "The 'unrealistic' endings of realistic novels . . . posit an alternative reality which cannot be fully contained in the novels' construction of the real. . . . As the endings lay bare the unresolved debates with competing versions of reality, we are better able to see the social construction of realism" (160). But another way of looking at this problem is to see the variations of realism/naturalism as part of what is pretextualized—as part of the complexity of the mode. The primitive can thus be looked on as both redemptive and destructive, and Conrad and London can offer radically different conclusions to the same narrative problem.

A critic who resisted the expanded critical claims of textuality is the late Edward Said. He saw that textuality—lacking agency and grounding—displaced a history of which it was an inseparable part: "Even if we accept . . . that there is no way to get past texts to apprehend 'real' history directly[,] . . . it is still possible to say that such a claim need not eliminate interest in the events and circumstances entailed by and expressed in the texts themselves. . . . My position is that texts are worldly, to some degree they are events, and, even when they appear to deny it, they are themselves a part of the social world, human life, and of course the historical moments in which they are located and interpreted."[5]

Said goes on to speak of the difference between "filiation" and "affiliation"—the first being connected with the natural processes of birth and family, the second being a product of cultural institutions and critical authority. The process of affiliation—the desire to "possess" a culture and to define its "reality," a reality that is critically generated and passed down to future generations—provides new ways of reading, new paradigms or constructs, and new conclusions, held in place by power, most often by controlling publishing or media outlets, by what is included and excluded from anthologies and journals, and by academic curriculum. Said here is referring to the way that Western culture preempted Oriental culture, but his point applies as well to literary movements like realism and naturalism: "filiation gives birth to affiliation" (23). "Affiliation then becomes," he explains, "in effect a literal form of *re-presentation*, by which ours is good . . . and what is not ours in this ultimately provincial sense is simply left out" (21–22).[6]

3

As George Becker has asserted, "the subject of realism is not especially congenial to the critics of our day. . . . Some critics have gone so far as to deny there was such a thing as a realistic *movement* in literature; others deny the possibility of a realistic work . . . and of a realistic aesthetic"(3). As a survey of recent literary criticism also reveals, there has been a tendency to ignore the fact that realism and naturalism were international movements (see Cady, Pizer, Walcutt, Sundquist), to read realist/naturalist novels independently of any generic context (see Michael Davitt Bell and Yves Chevrel), and to reduce narrative consciousness to forms of language or to cultural tropes (the result of Roland Barthes' and Michel Foucault's influence on the new historicism). And yet, as Becker continues, "there was a realistic movement, an innovation and an aspiration that shook the academies and the public more deeply than any other literary movement in history" (3). Realism was initially a reaction to romanticism, which presumed an ideal reality that the realists believed was out of touch with everyday life (5).

But if realism emerged out of the need to go beyond romanticism, it succumbed in turn to modernist transformations of romantic assumptions. Formal and postmodern criticism deny that naturalism had a narrative reality that was informed by historical reality, which distinguished it from other forms of fiction. By seeing realism and naturalism as primarily a matter of language, recent critics have de-emphasized its representational aspect. If it all comes down to language, and language does not provide a textual outlet to a physical reality, then how can there be realism?

The argument here has its origins in the tail end of romanticism, in the aesthetic movement, the belief in art for art's sake, which claimed that a poem (that is, language) was its own justification. Such doctrine has been disputed by critics like Emmanuel Levinas, who in rejecting Heidegger's homage to the aesthetics of Hölderlin, argued, "Art for art's sake . . . is false inasmuch as it situates art above reality."[7] Even T. S. Eliot may have been repudiating his formalist origins when he declared near the end of his career, "poetry is only poetry so long as . . . the subject matter is valued for its own sake."[8] But despite such caveats, recent theory has exalted language to the exclusion of content, and having done so, it has been able to extend the canon. There is now no narrative model that has to be accommodated and, as a result, many ethnic works—novels about slavery or Native American culture—are read as part of the realist/naturalist canon.[9]

Another reason that recent critics have abandoned the *idea* of realism/naturalism stems from postmodern criticism's professed distrust of master narratives. Such criticism has been obsessive in its attempt to "decenter" reality, to reject a tendency to totalize. Recent criticism has thus questioned Plato's Idea, Hegel's *Geist*, Kant's *Noumenon*, Husserl's Consciousness, and Heidegger's Being. Added to this trend is the distrust of megaorganizations like the International Monetary Fund or the World Bank that implement new forms of imperialism. Also rejected is any center—for example, the idea of Europe or male sexuality—that could preserve the current configuration of power. But these matters are hardly relevant to a discussion of realism and naturalism as conceptualized by their original practitioners. Further, these critics create their own master narrative out of postmodern theory. Here the center is denied, leading to a substitute master narrative based on *no* center as the *new* center.[10]

Once a text is denied a provisional center, there is no way of recommending one interpretation of a work over another or indeed of recommending the work itself over another.[11] A casualty in this power game has been the advocate of narrative typology, even when such theory demonstrably has heuristic value, allowing the critic to demonstrate textual connections, make comparative judgments, and bear witness to the evolution of genre. Carried to its absurd conclusion, such an argument makes it impossible to compare texts by the same author, given the fact that, say, Crane's *Maggie* (1893) is different from *The Red Badge of Courage* (1895), and Dreiser's *Sister Carrie* (1900) is different from *An American Tragedy* (1925).

Despite critical resistance to totalization, it is only when we can abstract from a larger idea of "realism" or "naturalism" that we begin to see how the works that comprise the tradition are connected. Zola and Dreiser in *Nana* (1884) and *Sister Carrie* write novels that are independent of each other but that nevertheless enjoy numerous similarities. Both depict human beings as only one remove from the animals, maintaining that underneath the veneer of civilization lurks the beast. Both assume that humanity is determined by forces, chemical and atavistic, that negate free will. And both assume that there are forces within the individual as well as environmental forces outside of the individual that determine one's fate. Heuristic terms that allow such comparisons are critically useful.

To reject realism/naturalism as descriptive terminology also means one cannot take into account the modality of an individual work. Dickens's comic realism is different from Melville's romantic realism, and each in turn is different from naturalism, as naturalism is different from literary modernism. Each text creates its own "reality," but such reality is general enough to be shared by other literary works within the same narrative mode. The way we respond to reality depends greatly on how we conceptualize that reality. Understanding how realism/naturalism works generically helps us better to read these works and to assess their individual strengths and limitations.

Perhaps another way of conceptualizing literary naturalism is synoptically (that is, as comprising texts having a common view). For example, the first three Gospels of the New Testament have elements in common at the same time as each text has aspects that preserve its own uniqueness and difference. And yet another way would be to adopt Darwin's own thinking on the relationship between the general and the particular or what he referred to as genotype and phenotype. As we saw, the genotype is the sum total of inherited possibilities of a species; the phenotype describes the individual traits that emerge from the play between genotype and environment. Applied to fictional forms, the genotype is the narrative mode or sum total of a narrative model, while the phenotype is the individual traits of a specific novel. Naturalism is the end product of interplay between its genotype and the expression of a historical moment and an author's sensibility.

4

Despite recent trends, the first wave of contemporary criticism saw a correspondence between American and French naturalism. In one of the early influential books, Lars Anhebrink argued in *The Beginnings of Naturalism in American Fiction, 1891–1903* (1950) that a close correspondence obtained between the works of Zola and those of Hamlin Garland, Stephen Crane, and Frank Norris. Anhebrink's book not only argued influence, but he insisted that there was such a thing as literary naturalism.

We are unlikely to see a critical return to such an "originist" theory of naturalism, but recent works suggest that the *idea* of literary naturalism may not be dead. For example, despite their caveats, Yves Chevrel's *Le Naturalisme* (1982) and David Baguley's *Naturalistic Fiction* (1990) are books from which one can abstract a definition of French literary naturalism. Chevrel is very much the product of recent French thought, and his method argues for a discrete and individual treatment of representative works. But buried in his book is a broad definition of naturalism, and so also in David Baguley's.

Despite Baguley's belief that generic study is reductive, his book offers a rather straightforward definition of naturalism as a generic literary movement. He discusses the concept of history as it applies to naturalism, representing naturalism as a conscious international literary movement by the "groupe de Médan" (Zola invited his literary associates to Thursday dinners in Médan, the village twenty-five miles outside Paris where he had a country home).

Baguley believes that, despite the presence of Spencer and the importation of Comte, who attracted some interest, scientific determinism never caught on in England, although he argues that Hardy's interest in Zola "was more pronounced than he [Hardy] liked to admit."[12] In his chapter "The Founding Texts," he engages an "originist" theory, asserting that *Madame Bovary* (1857), *Germinie Lacerteux* (1864), *Thérèse Raquin* (1867), and *L'Education sentimentale* (1869) were the texts out of which the movement grew. He concludes that naturalism involves an "entropic vision": "at the heart of the naturalistic vision," he maintains, "there is a poetics of disintegration, dissipation, death, with its endless repertory of wasted lives, of destructive forces, of spent energies . . . [with] time . . . presented as a process of constant erosion" (222). While reluctant to define naturalism, Baguley nevertheless does so, and his conclusion catches us by surprise. As in the Howard book discussed above, theory and practice are not in sync with each other.

As suggested by this study, a theory of modes helps to explain the parameters within which the literary imagination works: it moves the focus away from the idea of creative genius, away from theories of literary form, and away from the total subjectivity of the critic to the idea of a literary "reality" that precedes the text. Once a theory of modes is in place, one can study the way one mode transforms another.

A full-length book that performs this important task is Paul Civello's *American Literary Naturalism and its Twentieth Century Transformations* (1994). Civello convincingly demonstrates how the naturalism of Frank Norris was transformed by Ernest Hemingway, and that of Hemingway transformed by Don DeLillo. Norris, his starting point, makes, like Zola, traditional use of evolutionary ideas from Darwin and Spencer, modifying them in light of his reading of Asa Gray and Joseph Le Conte, bringing a life force into play in opposition to the play of human animality and degeneration. Hemingway's cosmic indifference separates his fiction from Norris's: in Hemingway what has changed is not so much the naturalistic world as the state of mind one brings to it. Jake Barnes and Lt. Henry redefine naturalism by engaging their worlds rather than responding passively. It is Don DeLillo who totally reconceptualizes naturalism as a literary method.

Civello persuasively argues that this transformation stems as much from changes in scientific theory as from literary or cultural change. Along with other critics, Civello charts the movement from Newtonian certainty and knowability to uncertainty and indeterminacy in the realm of physics. Gödel's Incompleteness Theorem is important in this transition, as is Einstein's Theory of Relativity, but most important is the quantum theory of Planck, Bohr, and Heisenberg. Heisenberg's *Physics and Philosophy* (1958) is especially relevant. Beginning with Planck's discovery that light, thought of as electromagnetic wave, sometimes behaves like energy particles or quanta, the waves were reinterpreted as "probability waves"—as indicators that quantum was present on the wave.

Heisenberg (1901–1976) is, of course, talking about subatomic physics and not about the meaning of fiction to its readers. But his theory led to the Uncertainty Principle: the impossibility of measuring both the position and velocity of a particle. Heisenberg took his theory of uncertainty even further, maintaining the impossibility of a subject separate from the experiment, thus the impossibility of separating subject from object and therefore the ability to observe objectively. We only find what we are looking for. Heisenberg concluded that what we observe is not nature but our questions about nature.

DeLillo puts an end to Zola's experimental novel. The author must interact with his fictional world and can no longer stand apart from that world as the scientist in the laboratory seemingly stands apart from his experiment. Civello applies these ideas to a reading of Don DeLillo's *Libra* (1988), a novel dealing with the assassination of President Kennedy. In *Libra*, DeLillo becomes a part of the historical events, his fiction serving as another interpretation of the assassination. But the author cannot grasp this realm objectively, as could Norris, or create his own version of reality, as could Hemingway.[13] Not only are novels written in different modes, but key ideas also undergo transformation between modes. The naturalist's obsession with degeneration, for example, gave way to the modernist's emphasis upon decadence, and in turn decadence gave way to the postmodernist's concern with entropy—a transition that reveals how historical modes contain different versions of the same idea.

Conclusion

In this study, we have examined the text as historical representation to see in what way a changing culture entailed a changing novel, to explore how representational change becomes inseparable from historical change. Realism came into being simultaneously with a new commercial-industrial order. From More's *Utopia* (1516) to Bacon's *New Atlantis* (1627), we have idealized attempts to come to terms with this New World. The utopia was the subform that projected possible versions of the new society, and almost all of the utopias gave new status to the individual. In fiction, the focus was on an individual character: titles became a character's name and story (Robinson Crusoe, Moll Flanders, Joseph Andrews, Tom Jones, Clarissa Harlowe, Oliver Twist, David Copperfield).

This emphasis further advanced the cause of realism. Out of it came shared experiences that led to similarities of plot: the decline of the estate, the loss of community, the journey to the city, the pitfalls of courtship, the threat of the mob, the rise of a consumer and smokestack culture, the perils of imperial adventure, the lonesome tasks of the western cowboy or the urban detective. Realism came into being when the romantic view, with its idealized concept of nature, found itself incapable of coming to terms with a new urban reality. Realism portrayed an individual in a changing world confronting personal and communal crises. For every protagonist there was an antagonist. While the realist character often found himself or herself bereft of a moral frame of reference, there was usually more free will available than in literary naturalism, where the character was determined by heredity, environment, or historical, political, social, or cosmic forces.

A major claim of this study is that naturalism evolved out of literary realism and functioned as a narrative mode, creating its own version of reality. It shares narrative themes in works that came from both sides of the Atlantic, and these narrative patterns led to plots that highlighted the individual at a moment of cosmic peril or natural crisis: the shipwreck ("The Open Boat" [1897]); the transition from civilization to primitive conditions (*Captains Courageous* [1797], *The Sea Wolf* [1904], *Moran of the Lady Letty* [1898]); love-gone-awry (*Germinie Lacerteux* [1864], *Thérèse Raquin* [1867], *Madame Bovary* [1865], *Anna Karenina* [1877], *Jude the Obscure* [1894]); love-turned-violent (*An American Tragedy* [1925], *Native Son* [1940], *Knock on Any Door* [1947]); the novel of political or business intrigue (*The Pit* [1903], *The Financier* [1912], *The Titan* [1914]).

As we have seen, Aristotle thought of tragedy as involving a flawed persona whose actions lead to self-destruction. The naturalists thought of tragedy as involving a determined reality that set limits beyond which a character could not safely go. Each character brings a proclivity to a given situation that predisposed choice, thus negating a strict sense of free will. A novelist like Dreiser reduced experience to this idea: he saw his characters becoming tragic outsiders by breaking conventions (Hurstwood stealing the money, Cowperwood manipulating the money markets, Clyde plotting to murder Roberta). All of the transgressions were anticipated, had to do with money, and were criminal acts. Dreiser himself, in a less extreme way, tested conventions when he went beyond what was narratively acceptable in *Sister Carrie* (1900), *The Titan,* and *The "Genius"* (1915), expanding the limits of fiction, and making a new novel possible for writers like John Dos Passos and Norman Mailer.

While a particular ideology was never a part of the theory itself, some naturalistic writers (e.g., London and Sinclair) turned to socialism for a political answer, while others (Dreiser, Wright, Algren) turned to communism, and still others (Farrell, H.G. Wells) to pragmatist or utopian theory. Put differently, there is a realm (really a sequence) of events that the naturalistic novel took as its own, which it attempted to depict with historical and scientific objectivity.

Repetition led to a predictability of plot, and literary naturalism as a mode thinned. But at its height it gave voice to worldly ideas that still have currency. These novels rewrote the romance, producing less elevated characters and situating them in a more amoral world. A moral imperative that remained stemmed from the outrage at a money system that allowed profit at the expense of a helpless public: Twain's and Norris's angry response to land grabs by the railroads, Dreiser's rebuke of big developers for their manipulation of public utilities, Sinclair's repugnancy at rat dung in the sausage.

And yet there is no good and evil per se—only power, an authority that either works for or against us. When that power is working *for* us, we consider it a good; when it is working *against* us, we consider it evil. Reality becomes contingent, defined in terms of *them* versus *us*, subject to personal observation and experience in a world where individual temperament predetermines choice (a different concept of temperament is often the difference between realism and naturalism).

Realist/naturalist fiction primarily depicted ordinary people, often financially strapped, compulsively driven by desires for love (sex), power, or money. They confronted, usually with limited understanding, cosmic and social forces that were almost always hostile. They made disastrous mistakes in love or with respect to social relationships and usually paid a supreme price for their misjudgments. They were tested by the reality they encountered, which exploited the weaknesses they brought to it. Their world lacked a moral center: there was no central character to resolve the conflict in sentimental/ moral terms. Realism/naturalism usually presented the dark side of reality, highlighting a spiritual, sexual, and intellectual malaise that was inseparable from a process of degeneration.

Literary naturalism challenged the shibboleths of a previous era—questioned the idea of heroism, the Horatio Alger formula for success, the Christian sense of sin and punishment, and the reality of a beneficent Maker. It challenged the glory of war, the myth of the West; it questioned the existence of love and the constancy of friendship. In an age of runaway capitalism, it questioned the belief that the market created financial reality, viewing more realistically the effects of political corruption and the boundless working of chicanery and greed on the money system. It looked suspiciously at long-sacred institutions: the church, the legal and justice system, the stock exchange, and Congress. It helped focus on the defects of an industrial economy and exposed the raw contradictions that were basic to human nature.

Much idealized pretense was blown away by the idea of submerged social and cosmic forces, forces that explained why urban order could give way so quickly to riot and mayhem. Naturalism depicted repressed sexuality that led to forms of the grotesque, to the inversion of natural instinct, and to the uncanny transformation of the familiar into the strange. Literary naturalism is an exercise in the exploration of a second self, the double, or what I have been calling "the stranger in the mirror." The idea here stems from the evolutionary belief in a human divide—the assumption that we are both rational and irrational, human and animal. Such a dualism naturally brings oppositions into play: the sublime and ugly, the regenerative and degenerative, the predictable and the unpredictable, repose and violence. The idea of a second self is also given metaphorical expression in the fact of generational change—the transformation of hereditary stock between generations.

Literary naturalism was primarily an ironic mode, creating a discrepancy between what the characters knew and what would befall them. It was materialistic, mechanistic, empirical, and relativistic, bringing natural explanations to human experience. The naturalist often identified with the downtrodden or the underdog, but questioned the sentiment of a Dickens: a character adapted to his or her environment or was destroyed by it. Social change could be legislated, but only to a point. If there was anything to bewail, it was life itself. When the naturalist did appeal to sentiment, it was to elicit reader sympathy for the social situation that produced the deprived, misplaced characters that made up the naturalist world rather than to suggest the innate goodness of human beings. Realism/naturalism addressed a spectrum of humanity, taking us from the heightened sensibility of James's characters to the more insensate forms of humanity we find at times in Norris, Sinclair, Farrell, and H. G. Wells. That characters so extreme could occupy the same world testified to the narrative diversity of the mode—evolutionary difference in literature as well as in nature.

When in fashion these narrative modes supplied a literary context for understanding the movement from land to city, the exploitation of natural resources, the contradictory nature of financial institutions, and the abuses of a smokestack economy and its effect on the human psyche. Much of the rejection of realism and naturalism as descriptive terms stems from an inability today to see the whole picture—the failure to see the way a fictional and historical world coalesced to produce varied but related texts.

We have, for example, Twain on one end of the spectrum and James on the other. When they are reduced to their styles, their differences seem insurmountable. But narratively-speaking each is concerned with the meaning of a new America—one from the perspective of a changing America, the other from the perspective of a declining Europe, and both from the perspective of a defining and defined individualism. The realistic/naturalistic novel has been read novel by novel for the last fifty years and has been primarily thought of as merely representing a variety of styles, not susceptible to definition. Appreciating stylistic differences but not disregarding the historical circumstances that gave rise to realism/naturalism helps in retrieving the authorial intention that first brought these movements into being. For too long, we have reduced these novels to their literary components and missed the forest for the trees.

In delineating the idea of self and in codifying the historical moment, realism/naturalism defined the parameters of a new age. More than any other literary form, such works illuminated an historical era that began in nineteenth-century Europe and ended in the middle of the twentieth century in America. In the twentieth century, realism/naturalism was attacked for presenting a too deterministic and overly behaviorist view of human nature. But by 1953 a theory of genes and of DNA led to an understanding of heredity and human development as a predisposed physical reality. Coupled with a belief that genetic inclination was influenced by varied response to environment, such aspects of human biology amounted to another form of determinism and led back to mechanistic assumptions that were closer to the ideas of naturalism than its detractors ever anticipated or liked to admit.

Notes

Chapter 1: Realism and Naturalism as an Expression of an Era

1. David Graham Phillips (1867–1911) was assassinated by the disgruntled subject of one of his attacks. Other works that fall within the category of muckraker reporting are Samuel Hopkins Adams's book on patent medicines (*The Great American Fraud,* 1906); and Ray Stannard Baker's treatise on racial discrimination (*Following the Color Line,* 1908; New York: Harper and Row, 1963). The word "muckraker," a term from Bunyan's *Pilgrim's Progress,* was used by Theodore Roosevelt, who was sympathetic to the aims of reform within limits.

2. For a more extended discussion of heat-death, see Michael H. Whitworth, *Einstein's Wake: Relativity, Metaphor, and Modernist Literature* (Oxford, U.K.: Oxford University Press, 2001), 62–63.

3. Nordau's division of urban humanity into an emotionally drained overclass and bestial underclass may be the basis for H. G. Wells's division of humanity into the Eloi and the Morlocks in the *Time Machine* (1895). In *Buddenbrooks* (1901) Thomas Mann humanized this division a bit, but still divided his family into those who had become dysfunctionally aestheticized or overly materialized. For a series of essays on the theme of degeneration, see Edward Chamberlin and Sander L. Gilman, eds., *Degeneration: The Dark Side of Progress* (New York: Columbia University Press, 1985).

4. George L. Mosse, *The Culture of Western Europe: The Nineteenth and Twentieth Centuries* (New York: Rand McNally, 1961), 78–81. Eugenics with its theory of human "improvement" is usually associated with Nazi programs of sterilization. But during the early part of the twentieth century,

eugenics flourished in many countries, including Great Britain and the
United States, where it was aimed at curbing the perpetuation of physical
and mental deficiencies. In Great Britain, there were several forms of eugenics. Negative eugenics (the desire to eliminate "inferior" breeds of humanity) was sponsored by George Bernard Shaw, H. G. Wells, and D. H.
Lawrence. Positive eugenics (the desire to create a "superior" breed of humanity) was promulgated by Aldous Huxley, J. M. Synge, and Arnold Bennett. A plea for both negative and positive eugenics came from W. B. Yeats,
Virginia Woolf, and T. S. Eliot. For a discussion of this activity in Great
Britain, see Donald J. Childs, *Modernism and Eugenics: Woolf, Eliot, Yeats
and the Culture of Degeneration* (Cambridge, U.K.: Cambridge University
Press, 2001). In America, the eugenics movement was sponsored by the
Carnegie Institution of Washington and the Rockefeller Foundation. The
drive influenced the Immigration Act of 1924, which restricted immigration from eastern and southern Europe and outlawed in some states interracial marriage. The case of Bucks vs. Bell in 1927 saw the United States
Supreme Court uphold by an eight to one vote the constitutionality of Virginia's eugenic sterilization law. For a full-length study of this movement,
see Edwin Black, *War Against the Weak: Eugenics and America's Campaign
to Create a Master Race* (New York: Four Walls and Eight Windows, 2003).

   5. David Barash, *Sociobiology: The Whispering Within* (New York: Souvenir Press, 1979), 153.

   6. Georg Lukács, *Essays on Realism*, ed. Rodney Livingstone, trans. David
Fernbach (Cambridge, Mass.: The MIT Press, 1981); see also George Licht-
heim, *George Lukács*, ed. Frank Kermode (New York: Viking Press, 1970).

   7. Johns Hopkins, a Baltimore merchant, began a philanthropic tradition by dedicating his fortune to the building of a new university, which
opened in 1876, at a time when the idea of a university was undergoing radical change. Charles W. Eliot, president of Harvard, had totally revised the
idea of a university curriculum, moving it away from classical studies toward modern science, the professions, and an elective system that encouraged individual research and study. The faculty for the new university was
often recruited from Europe, especially from Germany. In return, many
young American scholars ventured to Germany to learn the methods of
historicism. From New England, for example, came George Ticknor, Edward Everett, and Joseph Green Cogswell, who spent a year or more at
Göttingen: Ticknor was to become the father of modern language studies;
Everett helped promote the study of Greek mythology and culture in
America; and Cogswell was a founder of the modern library system. For a
discussion of the transformations in higher education, see Charles A. and

Mary R. Beard, *The Rise of American Civilization* (New York: Macmillan, 1930), 467–77. For a more detailed account of German postgraduate studies, see Van Wyck Brooks, *The Flowering of New England* (1936; New York: E. P. Dutton, 1952), 75–91.

8. For a more detailed discussion of what amounts to the transition from naturalistic to modernist history, see J. H. Hexter, *On Historians: Reappraisals of Some of the Makers of Modern History* (Cambridge, Mass.: Harvard University Press, 1979). And for a summary of history as a profession see John Higham, *History: Professional Scholarship in America* (Baltimore: Johns Hopkins University Press, 1983).

9. John B. Wolf, *France 1814–1919* (New York: Harper and Row, 1963), 71.

10. Ibid., 281, 113, 31.

11. For a more detailed discussion of the urban background of French literature, see Richard Lehan, *The City in Literature: An Intellectual and Cultural History* (Berkeley: University of California Press, 1998), 59–61.

12. Elizabeth Stuart Phelps, for example, sympathetically depicted the plight of mill workers in *The Silent Partner* (1871). Other novels that treat the poor are Thomas Bailey Aldrich's *The Stillwater Tragedy* (1880), Amanda Douglas's *Hope Mills* (1880), Mary Hallock Foote's *Coeur d' Alene* (1894), and Francis Hopkinson Smith's *Tom Grogan* (1896). Novels which depict the rise of speculative finance and industrial wealth are Henry Francis Keenan's *The Money-Makers* (1885), Charles Dudley Warner's *That Fortune* (1899), Garrett P. Serviss's *The Moon Metal* (1900), David Graham Phillips's *The Great God Success* (1901), Robert Barr's *The Victors* (1901), Will Payne's *The Money Captain* (1898) and *On Fortune's Road* (1902), H. K. Webster's *The Banker and the Bear* (1900), Samuel Merwin's *The Honey Bee* (1901), Merwin and Webster's *Calumet "K"* (1901) and *The Short Line War* (1899), and Harold Frederic's *The Lawton Girl* (1890) and *The Market-place* (1899). And novels that depicted the corruptive effect of the new economy, either on the system or the individual, are Rebecca Harding Davis's *John Anderson* (1874), J. W. De Forest's *Honest John Vane* (1875), J. G. Holland's *Sevenoaks* (1875), Edgar Fawcett's *An Ambitious Woman* (1883), F. Marion Crawford's *An America Politician* (1885), Thomas Stewart Denison's *An Iron Crown* (1885), Paul Leicester Ford's *The Honorable Peter Stirling* (1894), Hamlin Garland's *A Spoil of Office* (1892), Henry Blake Fuller's *The Cliff-Dwellers* (1893) and *With the Procession* (1895), and almost all of the novels of Robert Herrick, but especially *The Gospel of Freedom* (1898), *The Web of Life* (1900), *The Real World* (1901), *The Common Lot* (1904), *The Memoirs of an American Citizen* (1905), *Together* (1908), and *One Woman's Life* (1913).

13. Walter Fuller Taylor, *The Economic Novel in America* (Chapel Hill: University of North Carolina Press, 1942), 25. Taylor bases his statement on statistics derived from Ernest Ludlow Bogart, *The Economic History of the United States* (New York: Longmans, Green 1907), 381–82, 400–402.

14. It is interesting that Bryan should be the anti-Darwinian spokesman in the Scopes trial, connected with outlawing the teaching of evolution in Tennessee. While supporting the farmer and while claiming the superiority of the country over the city, the populists also tended to support evangelical religious beliefs.

15. The Tammany Society, formed in 1786 after the American Revolution, was originally a fraternal order dedicated to social, ceremonial, and patriotic activities. But by 1854 the society became a leading political force. Under such city bosses as W. M. Tweed and Richard Croker, the society controlled New York City politics. While claiming to operate in the name of the common man, the organization was involved in blatant political corruption. Dreiser's brother-in-law, L. A. Hopkins (the model for Hurstwood), was connected to the Tammany organization at the end of the nineteenth century. In 1932 the Tammany group was badly defeated at the polls and never recovered its political power.

16. Henry Adams, *The Education of Henry Adams* (1907, 1918; New York: Modern Library, 1999). The connection between Adams and literary naturalism is the subject of Harold Kaplan's *Power and Order: Henry Adams and the Naturalist Tradition in American Fiction* (Chicago: University of Chicago Press, 1981).

17. Louis Menand, *The Metaphysical Club* (New York: Farrar, Straus and Giroux, 2002).

18. John Dewey, in *The Influence of Darwin on Philosophy, and Other Essays in Contemporary Thought* (New York: Holt, 1910), reprinted in *Darwin,* ed. Philip Appleman (New York: W. W. Norton, 1970), 402, hereafter cited in the text.

19. Ernest Hemingway, *The Sun Also Rises* (New York: Scribners, 1926), 148.

20. See Amy Kaplan's *The Social Construction of American Realism* (Chicago: University of Chicago Press, 1988), 2, hereafter cited in the text. Kaplan makes the interesting point that Chase's emphasis on romance diminished critical interest in realism. She believes this emphasis stemmed from Chase's New Critical interest in the lyric and the influence of Lionel Trilling's repudiation, the product of his antiliberalism, of critics like V. L. Parrington and F. O. Matthiessen. Trilling's distinction between "mind" and "reality," along with the New Criticism, encouraged a spate of formalist studies in the Sixties that divorced realism from its social context. She believes that the

more socially oriented critics like Warner Berthoff and Jay Martin "missed the mark" when it came to "mimetic accuracy." Her own study substitutes the "reality" abstracted from the fiction for the reality of history.

21. Richard Chase, *The American Novel and its Tradition* (New York: Doubleday, 1957), 12–13, 25–28.

22. Charles Child Walcutt, *American Literary Naturalism: A Divided Stream* (Minneapolis: University of Minnesota Press, 1956).

23. Eric Sundquist, "The Country of the Blue," in *American Realism: New Essays*, ed. Eric Sundquist (Baltimore: Johns Hopkins University Press, 1982).

24. The romance and gothic fiction have long been conflated. See, for example, Elizabeth MacAndrew, *The Gothic Tradition in Fiction* (New York: Columbia University Press, 1979); David Punter, *The Literature of Terror: A History of Gothic Fictions from 1765 to the Present Day* (London: Longman, 1980); and William Patrick Day, *In the Circles of Fear and Desire: A Study of Gothic Fantasy* (Chicago: Chicago University Press, 1985). See also Kathryn Hume, *Fantasy and Mimesis: Responses to Reality in Western Literature* (New York: Methuen, 1984), and *The English Hero, 1660–1800*, ed. Robert Folkenflik (Newark: University of Delaware Press, 1982), especially the essays by Robert Hume and Arthur Lindley. Recently there has been an attempt to treat the romance as an early expression of modernism. See Nicholas Daly, *Modernism, Romance, and the Fin de Siècle: Popular Fiction and British Culture, 1880–1914* (Cambridge, U.K.: Cambridge University Press, 1999), 8–24. The argument here is that the romance opens up a primitive world analogous to that which we find in the modernist novel, a world involving a realm of elemental consciousness. But it is exactly this aspect of the romance that has linked it with literary naturalism. Moreover, the modern novel makes more conscious use of myth than does the romance. But the links among novels from Stoker-Haggard to Kipling-Stevenson to Norris-London to Hemingway-Dos Passos to Cain and Chandler form a narrative chain (as we shall see in chapters 3 and 8) that reflects gradations in an evolutionary line from fantasy to realism.

25. This scheme is taken from George J. Becker, ed., *Documents of Modern Literary Realism* (Princeton: Princeton University Press, 1963), 36, hereafter cited in the text.

26. Laurence Lerner, *The Frontiers of Literature* (Oxford, U.K.: Basil Blackwell, 1988), 60–68. Lerner restates the argument of R. G. Collingwood in *The Idea of History,* 246. In his essay, "Politics and the English Language," now a classic, George Orwell demonstrated how political reality informs language. In an essay that pushes this argument to its limit, "The Hollow Miracle," George Steiner contends that "Nazism found in the [German]

language what it needed to give voice to its savagery," indicting language itself for the criminal activity of the Nazis (see *Language and Silence: Essays on Language, Literature, and the Inhuman, 1958–1966* [Harmondsworth, U.K.: Penguin Books, 1979]). A more moderate argument might connect political reality and language, seeing one informed by the other. Such an argument would preserve the notion of human agency, making each a product of a physical reality that it represents but does not initiate.

27. Saree Makdisi, *Romantic Imperialism: Universal Empire and the Culture of Modernity* (Cambridge, U.K.: Cambridge University Press, 1998), 24.

Chapter 2: Realism as Narrative Mode

1. In Part 2, Quixote sees the folly and the impracticality of his ideals. When Quixote renounces the chivalric ideals, he reconciles the knight-errant with the caballero. The worldly journey has been completed; the spiritual journey waits. Cervantes died on April 23, 1616, and was buried in the Trinitarian Convent in the Calle de Contararnas.

2. For an extended discussion of the natural-supernatural connection in romantic literature, see M. H. Abrams, *Natural Supernaturalism: Tradition and Revolution in Romantic Literature* (New York, W. W. Norton, 1971), 65–70.

3. Ian Watt, *The Rise of the Novel: Studies in Defoe, Richardson, and Fielding* (Berkeley: University of California Press, 1957), 14, 24, 26.

4. Leo Bersani, *Balzac to Beckett: Center and Circumference in French Fiction* (New York: Oxford University Press, 1970), 1–90.

5. Michael Harrington, *The Accidental Century* (New York: Macmillan, 1965), 157.

6. Twain's *Pudd'nhead Wilson* was inspired by the Plessy vs. Ferguson case (1893–96) in which Plessy, a light-skinned mulatto, provoked his own arrest by riding in the railroad car reserved for whites. Since he could pass for white, the case foregrounded the silliness of the color line. Nevertheless, the Supreme Court failed to uphold Plessy's claim to equal rights. For a detailed discussion of the case and its relationship to Twain's novel, see Eric J. Sundquist, "Mark Twain and Homer Plessy," in *The New American Studies: Essays from* Representations, ed. Philip Fisher (Berkeley: University of California Press, 1991), 112–38.

7. Twain's *Life on the Mississippi* reworked a Rip Van Winkle–like approach to American ideals, a tendency to locate ideals in a world that cannot accommodate them. We have dozens of Rip Van Winkle books—works like James's *The American Scene,* Dreiser's *Hoosier Holiday,* Pound's "Patria Mia," Eliot's *After Strange Gods,* Fitzgerald's "My Lost City," and Henry

Miller's *Remember to Remember*. In these works a writer returns to an American scene, usually after an absence of twenty years, to find that world sadly transformed and the values it embodied changed as well. Such an experience, of course, is in great part subjective, since one man's diminished world becomes the basis for another's ideal. Yet in each case the writer conveys a vivid sense of a moment of possibility that will never come again having been used up—a sense of the promises of the past having been betrayed.

8. Mark Twain, *A Connecticut Yankee in King Arthur's Court* (1889; New York: Morrow, 1988), 33.

9. William Dean Howells, *A Modern Instance* (Boston: J. R. Osgood, 1881), 394.

10. Granville Hicks, *The Great Tradition: An Interpretation of American Literature since the Civil War* (New York: International Publishers, 1935), 77.

11. Henry James, *The House of Fiction: Essays on the Novel*, ed. Leon Edel (Westport, Conn.: Greenwood Press, 1973), quoted in Hicks, 108.

12. Edmund Wilson, "The Pilgrimage of Henry James," *The Shores of Light: A Literary Chronicle of the Twenties and Thirties* (New York: Farrar, Straus and Young, 1952), 222, reprinted in *The Portable Edmund Wilson*, ed. Lewis M. Dabney (New York: Viking Penguin Books, 1983), 129.

Chapter 3: Realism, Narrative Subforms, and Historical Process

1. Watt, *The Rise of the Novel*, 48–49.

2. In the western, the hero usually comes from the East, confronts an evil in the West, and then wins the shootout that advances life on the land. Fitzgerald inverts this formula in *The Great Gatsby*. The main characters come from the West, Gatsby and Tom Buchanan confront each other in a verbal shootout at the Plaza Hotel, and Tom's amoral power prevails.

3. For a book-length study on this theme, see Tony Tanner, *Adultery in the Novel: Contract and Transgression* (Baltimore: Johns Hopkins University Press, 1979).

4. For various definitions of the crowd see Gustave Le Bon's *The Crowd: A Study of the Popular Mind* (1896); a useful commentary on Le Bon is Robert Nye's *The Origins of Crowd Psychology: Gustave Le Bon and the Crisis of Mass Democracy in the Third Republic* (London: Sage Publications, 1975); Sigmund Freud, *Group Psychology and the Analysis of the Ego*, trans. James Strachey (New York: Boni and Liveright, 1922); and Elias Canetti, *Crowds and Power*, trans. Carol Stewart (New York: Viking Press, 1962).

5. For a different reading of James's *Casamassima*, see Mark Seltzer's "*The Princess Casamassima*: Realism and the Fantasy of Surveillance," in

American Realism 95 –118. Seltzer argues that James's use of realistic technique parallels the surveillance techniques of the police. In rejecting that
kind of surveillance, James also rejected the realist method at this point in
his career—and moved toward the modern novel.

6. Edmund Wilson, "The Kipling that Nobody Read," in *The Wound and
the Bow: Seven Studies in Literature* (New York: Oxford University Press,
1965), 143.

7. Edmund Wilson, "Hemingway: Gauge of Morale," in *The Wound and
the Bow*, 174.

8. Mary Lawlor, *Recalling the Wild: Naturalism and the Closing of the
American West* (New Brunswick: Rutgers University Press, 2000).

9. For a detailed discussion of noir, see *Shades of Noir: A Reader*, ed. Joan
Copjec (New York: Verso, 1993), especially "Strange Pursuit: Cornell Wool-
rich and the Abandoned City" by David Reed and Jayne L. Walker, 57 –96, and
"Democracy's Turn: On the Homeless Noir" by Dean MacCannell, 279 –97.

10. Michael Davitt Bell, *The Problem of American Realism: Studies in the
Cultural History of a Literary Idea* (Chicago: University of Chicago Press,
1993), 169 –204.

11. For the need to break with the genteel tradition and the part played by
"local color," see Malcolm Cowley, ed., *After the Genteel Tradition: American
Writers, 1910–1930* (Carbondale: Southern Illinois University Press, 1964),
171–73. Cowley argues that elements of the bleakness that characterize this
writing stemmed from the emotional disposition of the writers themselves.

12. For a discussion of the Puritan versus Pioneer idea in Anderson, see
Susan Hegeman, *Patterns for America: Modernism and the Concept of Culture* (Princeton: Princeton University Press, 1999), 120–25.

Chapter 4: A Field of Force: The Biological Model

1. Loren Eiseley, *Darwin's Century: Evolution and the Men Who Discovered It* (New York: Anchor, 1961); Ernst Mayr, *The Growth of Biological
Thought: Diversity, Evolution, and Inheritance* (Cambridge, U.K.: Cambridge University Press, 1982).

2. Peter J. Bowler, *Biology and Social Thought 1850–1914* (Berkeley: Office
for History of Science and Technology, University of California at Berkeley,
1993), 7.

3. Two important books on the background of literary realism are Ro-
land E. Martin's *American Literature and the Universe of Force* (Durham,
N.C.: Duke University Press, 1981) and John J. Conder's *Naturalism in
American Fiction: The Classic Phase* (Lexington: University of Kentucky
Press, 1984). The Martin book sees physical force as the primary aspect of
literary naturalism, while the Conder book sees philosophical determinism

as the defining quality of literary naturalism. One book gives us a useful history of physics and the working of force, the other of philosophy and the meaning of determinism. The books share common ground, however, in the belief that physical force gives way to evolution in the writings of Herbert Spencer and John Fiske, which would then, I suggest, call for a biological explanation of the meaning behind literary naturalism. See also Louis J. Zanine, *Mechanism and Mysticism: The Influence of Science on the Thought and Work of Theodore Dreiser* (Philadelphia: University of Pennsylvania Press, 1993).

4. John Butler Yeats, *Essays, Irish and American* (Dublin, Ireland: The Talbot Press,1918), quoted in Basil Willey, *Darwin and Butler: Two Versions of Evolution* (London: Chatto and Windus, 1960), 63.

5. Published in the *Press* (Christchurch, N.Z., March 14, 1863, and July 26, 1865); both reprinted in *A First Year in Canterbury Settlement, with Other Early Essays*, ed. R. R. Streatfeild (London: A. C. Fifield, 1914) and in *The Note-books of Samuel Butler, ed. Henry Festing Jones* (London: A.C. Fifield, 1912).

6. Samuel Butler, *Life and Habit* (London: A. C. Fifield, 1910), 261, hereafter cited in the text.

7. Samuel Butler, *Evolution, Old and New* (New York: E. P. Dutton, 1911), 346, hereafter cited in the text.

8. Samuel Butler, *The Way of All Flesh* (1903; New York: Penguin Books, 1966), 211, hereafter cited in the text.

9. Samuel Butler, *Erewhon* (1872; New York: Modern Library, 1927), 274, hereafter cited in the text.

10. Frederick Brown, *Zola: A Life* (New York: Farrar, Straus and Giroux, 1995), 152.

11. Emile Zola, "The Experimental Novel," in *Documents of Modern Literary Realism*, 162–96.

12. Quoted in Bettina L. Knapp, *Emile Zola* (New York: Ungar, 1980), 21. For other books on Zola see Matthew Josephson, *Zola and His Time: The History of His Martial Career in Letters* (New York: Garden City Publishing, 1928); Elliot M. Grant, *Emile Zola* (New York: Twayne, 1966); Joanna Richardson, *Zola* (London: Weidenfeld and Nicolson, 1978); Graham King, *Garden of Zola: Emile Zola and his Novels for English Readers* (New York: Barnes and Noble, 1978); Brian Nelson, *Zola and the Bourgeoisie: A Study of Themes and Techniques in les Rougon-Macquart* (London: Macmillan, 1983). Two important essays on Zola are by Georg Lukács in *Studies in European Realism*, with an introduction by Alfred Kazin (New York: Grosset and Dunlap, 1964), 85–96, and Harry Levin in *The Gates of Horn: A Study of Five French Realists* (New York: Oxford University Press, 1963), 305–71. The Brown

biography, cited above, is the most complete study that we have of Zola's life.

13. Emile Zola, *The Fortune of the Rougons,* trans. E. Vizetelly (London: Vizetelly, 1886), 77–78.

14. The novels that treat the peasant world are *La Fortune des Rougon* (1871), *La Conquête Plassans* (1874), *La Faute de l'abbé Mouret* (1876), and *La Terre* (1887). The Paris novels are *La Curée* (1872), *Le Ventre de Paris* (1873) *Son Excellence Eugène Rougon* (1876), *L'Assommoir* (1877), *Nana* (1878), *Potbouille* (1882), *Au Bonheur des Dames* (1883) *La Joie de vivre* (1884), *L'Oeuvre* (1886), *La Bête humaine* (1890), and *L'Argent* (1891). The bridge between the provincial and city novels are *Germinal* (1885) and *La Débâcle* (1892), which depict provincial events that have their origins in the economic and political system of the city.

15. Emile Zola, *L'Assommoir,* trans. Leonard Tancock (New York: Penguin Books, 1970), 21.

16. Emile Zola, *Nana,* trans. E. Vizetelly (New York: Modern Library, 1927), 246, hereafter cited in the text.

17. Jacques Ellul, *The Technological Society,* trans. John Wilkinson (New York: Vintage, 1964).

18. Karl Beckson, *London in the 1890s: A Cultural History* (New York: W. W. Norton, 1992), 300–306.

19. William B. Dillingham, *Frank Norris: Instinct and Art* (Lincoln: University of Nebraska Press, 1969).

20. Frank Norris, *The Octopus* (Boston: Houghton Mifflin, 1958), 448, hereafter cited in the text.

21. Frank Norris, "The Frontier Gone at Last," in *The Responsibilities of the Novelist, and Other Literary Essays* (New York: Doubleday, Page, 1903), 71, 74, 77. Norris restates this thesis in *The Octopus* (1901; New York: New American Library, 1964), 227–28. There are two studies of Zola's influence on Norris: Marius Biencourt, *Une Influence du naturlisme français en Amerique* (Paris: Marcel Girard, 1933), and Lars Ahnebrink, "The Influence of Emile Zola on Frank Norris," in *The Influence of Emile Zola on Frank Norris,* Essays and Studies on American Language and Literature 5 (Uppsala, Sweden: A.-B. Lundequistska Bokhandeln, 1947).

22. Howard Horwitz finds a parallel between speculative finance and romantic love in *The Pit.* Laura's flirtations are a form of speculation and need to be curbed before she can see to the heart of Jadwin's and her own desire for love. See Howard Horwitz, "To Find the Value of X: *The Pit* as a Renunciation of Romance," in *American Realism,* 226–31.

23. Frank Norris, *The Pit* (New York: Grove Press, n.d.), 62, 120; cf. 189, hereafter cited in text.

24. Theodore Dreiser, *A Book About Myself* (New York: Boni and Liveright, 1922), 457.

25. Theodore Dreiser, *Sister Carrie,* ed. Donald Pizer (1900; New York: W. W. Norton, 1970), 7, hereafter cited in the text.

26. When Dreiser was working on *Sister Carrie,* Elmer Gates sent him a manuscript in which he explained his theory of anastates and katastates. Dreiser read the manuscript with interest and requested a bibliography of other mechanistic material, which Gates sent him. Dreiser was corresponding with Gates as late as December 11, 1901 regarding Gates's theories of anastates/katastates and other mechanistic assumptions. Dreiser long retained his interest in the polarities of life, what he later referred to as human "positives and negatives of energy." For a more detailed discussion of the influence of Elmer Gates on Dreiser, see Richard Lehan, *Theodore Dreiser: His World and His Novels* (Carbondale: Southern Illinois University Press, 1969), 66–67.

27. Theodore Dreiser, *The Financier* (1912; New York: Dell, 1961), 526.

28. Jacques Loeb was an American physiologist, born in Germany, whose work at the Rockefeller Institute involved the study of tropism (the response, positive or negative, of an organism to stimuli) and the regeneration of plants through chemical stimuli. Dreiser corresponded with him from 1915 on, and Loeb's theories—based on the assumption that human life functions primarily as a response to immediate stimuli—influenced Dreiser's middle and late work, although Dreiser had anticipated ideas similar to Loeb's, perhaps through the influence of Elmer Gates, as early as *Sister Carrie*. For a more detailed discussion of the influence of Jacques Loeb on Dreiser, see Lehan, *Theodore Dreiser* 160. Loeb was depicted in Sinclair Lewis's novel *Arrowsmith*.

29. Theodore Dreiser, *An American Tragedy* (1925; New York: New American Library, 1964), 489, hereafter cited in the text.

30. Theodore Dreiser, "Notes on Life," quoted in Lehan's *Thedore Dreiser,* 165.

31. Eliseo Vivas, "Dreiser, An Inconsistent Mechanist," *Ethics* 48.4 (1938): 498–508.

32. Dreiser's friendship with Charles Fort dated from 1905. Dreiser tried (unsuccessfully) to get Fort's science fiction published. Fort believed that life was a "superdream"; he claimed that blood had rained from the sky and insisted on other preternatural events, including visits from extraterrestrial aliens. Between 1914 and 1919, Fort collected over forty thousand notes from newspapers and popular journals involving strange phenomena; these he arranged under thirteen hundred headings. When Dreiser put pressure on Boni and Liveright, this collection was published under the title *The*

Book of the Damned (1919) and became a commercial success. The book clearly influenced Dreiser's collection of scientific notes, gathered over the last twenty years of his life and published posthumously as *Notes on Life*, ed. Marguerite Tjader and John J. McAleer (Tuscaloosa: University of Alabama Press, 1974). Despite the antiscience basis of Fort's work, Dreiser never disparaged it. In fact, Dreiser supposedly made use of Fort's unpublished novel "X" in his play *The Dream.*

33. Theodore Dreiser, *Chains* (New York: Boni and Liveright, 1927), 247.

34. Lionel Trilling, "Reality in America," in *The Liberal Imagination: Essays on Literature and Society* (New York: Viking, 1953), 7–21.

35. Jack London, "To Build a Fire," in *The Call of the Wild and Selected Stories* (New York: New American Library, 1960), 143, hereafter cited in the text.

36. Jack London, "Love of Life," in *The Call of the Wild and Selected Stories*, 170.

37. Van Wyck Brooks, "Upton Sinclair and His Novels," in *Sketches in Criticism* (New York: E. P. Dutton, 1932), 291–98. Robert Cantwell, "Upton Sinclair," in *After the Genteel Tradition*, ed. Malcolm Cowley (New York: W. W. Norton, 1937; Carbondale: Southern Illinois University Press, 1964), 37–47.

Chapter 5: A Field of Force: The Cosmic Model

1. Joseph Conrad, *Tales of Land and Sea* (Garden City, N.Y.: Doubleday, 1916), 612, hereafter cited in the text.

2. John W. Griffith, *Joseph Conrad and the Anthropological Dilemma: "Bewildered Traveller"* (Oxford, U.K.: Oxford University Press, 1995), see especially 153–78.

3. Ian Watt, *Conrad in the Nineteenth Century* (Berkeley: University of California Press, 1979), 153, hereafter cited in the text.

4. J. Hillis Miller, *Poets of Reality: Six Twentieth-Century Writers* (Cambridge, Mass.: Harvard University Press, 1965), 7, hereafter cited in the text.

5. In a densely argued psychoanalytical study, Beth Sharon Ash maintains that Conrad's novel suffers from Wait being a stereotypical character. By "stereotypical," I assume that she means that he represents the black race in simplistic ways. But Wait's function in the novel is to embody the limitations of humanity, and to this extent he takes on a symbolic reality that goes beyond race. See *Writing in Between: Modernity and the Psychosocial Dilemma in the Novels of Joseph Conrad* (London: Macmillan, 1999), 19–58.

6. Joseph Conrad, *Notes on Life and Letters,* quoted in Allan Hunter, *Joseph Conrad and the Ethics of Darwinism: The Challenges of Science* (London: Croom Helm, 1983), 11.

7. Joseph Conrad, *Heart of Darkness,* ed. Robert Kimbrough (1902; New York: W. W. Norton, 1988), 50, hereafter cited in the text.

8. Chinua Achebe, "An Image of Africa: Racism in Conrad's *Heart of Darkness,*" *The Massachusetts Review* 18 (1977): 782–94.

9. An opposite view of the debased savage involves the myth of the noble savage. We know now that this myth did not originate with Jean Jacques Rousseau. Ter Ellingson believes that it stemmed from the eighteenth-century anthropologist John Crawfurd and was a romantic construct intended to contrast the pristine savage with decadent civilization. As Conrad's novel suggests, the idea of both civilized and savage nobility belied true human nature and were historical constructs, not realities. For a history of savage nobility see Ter Ellingson, *The Myth of the Noble Savage* (Berkeley: University of California Press, 2001).

10. In an introduction to his edited collection of essays on Achebe's novel, *Things Fall Apart* (Philadelphia: Chelsea House, 2002), Harold Bloom diverges from the multiculturism of his contributors and argues that Achebe's novel draws on an idea of tragedy that is not historicized but that goes to the heart of what is universally human: "I submit," Bloom writes, "that Okonkwo's tragedy is universal, despite its Nigerian circumstancing. It is . . . a universal sorrow, and therefore can only be secondarily illuminated by the ordinances of Multiculturism, African conscious-raising, and new-mode canonizers. . . . [This book] owes nothing to the Four Horsemen of Resentment: Fanon, Foucault, Derrida, and Lacan" (2). Bloom's comment, which represents a remarkable departure from his earlier pronouncements, is directly relevant to the civilization versus culture dispute.

11. Joseph Conrad, *Nostromo* (1904; New York: New American Library, 1960), 396, 399.

12. Stephen Crane, *Stories and Tales,* ed. Robert Stallman (New York: Vintage Books, 1955), 233.

Chapter 6: A Field of Force: The Social/Political Model

1. The connection between technological power and science fiction is treated in the following fiction: Mark Adler's *Interface, Volteface,* and *Multiface;* Isaac Asimov's *Foundation, Foundation and Empire,* and *Second Foundation;* Arthur Clark's *Childhood's End* and *The City and the Stars;* Samuel R. Delaney's *The Fall of the Towers* and *Dhalgren;* Jonathan Fast's *The Secrets of Synchronicity;* Jane Gaskell's *A Sweet, Sweet Summer;* Mark S. Geston's *The Siege of Wonder;* Robert A. Heinlein's *Stranger in Strange Land* and *The Moon is a Harsh Mistress;* Ursula Le Guin's *The Word for World Is Forest* and *The Dispossessed;* Stanislaw Lem's *The Cyberiad* and *Solaris* (on knowledge

and information as power); Walter M. Miller's *A Canticle for Leibowitz;* Frederick Pohl and C. M. Kornbluth's *The Space Merchants* and *Gladiator-at-Law;* Mack Reynold's *Black Man's Burden, Boarder, Breed, Nor Birth, The Best Ye Breed,* and *Mercenary from Tomorrow;* Robert Silverberg's *A Time of Change;* Clifford D. Simak's *City;* and Norman Spinard's *The Men in the Jungle* and *The Iron Dream.*

2. H. G. Wells, *A Modern Utopia* (New York: Scribners, 1905), 79 –80.

3. H. G. Wells, *Mind at the End of its Tether* (London: William Heinemann, 1945), 30.

4. George Orwell, *Nineteen Eighty-Four* (New York: New American Library, 1949), 216 –17. Orwell saw power embodied in totalitarian figures like O'Brien as the greatest threat to liberal democracy. Today the threat comes from terrorist organizations, whose multilateral formations take us beyond the nation state. This new political reality is based on international threats from power-driven cult leaders whose desire for control is semi-religious and who work beyond the restrictions of the military. We have thus moved from Orwell's Winston to Ian Fleming's James Bond.

5. There are often contradictions between Nazi theory and practice. For a more detailed discussion of the ideas and practices that forms of fascism held in common see Robert O. Paxton, *The Anatomy of Fascism* (New York: Alfred A. Knopf, 2004).

6. Robert Ferguson, *Enigma: The Life of Knut Hamsun* (London: Hutchinson, 1987).

7. For a more detailed discussion of Dreiser's politics see Lehan, *Theodore Dreiser: His World and His Novels,* 170–208.

Chapter 7: Thematics and the Conventions of the Novel

1. Arnold Hauser, *The Social History of Art,* trans. Stanley Godman (London: Routledge and Kegan Paul, 1951), 81.

2. The question of illness and health in Dreiser and Gilman is treated at length by Hildegard Hoeller in "Herland and Hisland: Illness and 'Health' in the Writings of Charlotte Perkins Gilman and Theodore Dreiser," *Dreiser Studies* 34.2 (Winter 2003): 24 –43.

3. For a discussion of mental illness as a late-nineteenth- and early-twentieth-century phenomenon, see Tom Lutz, *American Nervousness, 1903: An Anecdotal History* (Ithaca: Cornell University Press, 1991). For a discussion of this problem as filtered through more contemporary thought, see John S. Haller and Robin M. Haller, *The Physician and Sexuality in Victorian America* (Westport, Conn.: Greenwood Press, 1978); Diane Price Herndl, *Invalid Women: Figuring Feminine Illness in American Fiction and*

Culture, 1840–1940 (Chapel Hill: University of North Carolina Press, 1993); Sandra M. Gilbert and Susan Gubar, *The Madwoman in the Attic: The Woman Writer and the Nineteenth-Century Literary Imagination* (New Haven: Yale University Press, 1979); and Susan Sontag, *Illness as Metaphor; and, AIDS and Its Metaphors* (New York: Anchor Books, 1990).

4. For an account of this theory of gender, see Judith Butler, *Gender Trouble: Feminism and the Subversion of Identity* (London: Routledge, 1990). For a discussion of gender theory more specific to literary naturalism, see Irene Gammel, "Sexualizing the Female Body: Dreiser, Feminism, and Foucault," in *Theodore Dreiser: Beyond Naturalism*, 31–51, ed. Miriam Gogol (New York: New York University Press, 1995).

5. For a discussion of how realism shifted emphasis from a feminine to masculine perspective in fiction, see Hildegard Hoeller, *Edith Wharton's Dialogue with Realism and Sentimental Fiction* (Gainesville: University of Florida Press, 2000).

6. William Bellamy, *The Novels of Wells, Bennett and Galsworthy: 1890–1910* (New York: Barnes and Noble, 1971) argues for a radical difference between the end-of-the-century novels (*The Time Machine*, 1895; *A Man from the North*, 1898; *Jocelyn*, 1898) and their Edwardian counterparts (*Tono-Bungay*, 1909; *The Old Wives' Tale*, 1908; *The Man of Property*, 1906), seeing the first order as pessimistic and the second as optimistic, or "therapeutic," to use his term. As we move away from naturalistic assumptions, the narrative world does become less troubled—but perhaps not to the extent that Bellamy contends.

7. *The Years* involves the Pargiter family as seen through several generations. The oldest daughter, Eleanor, is the one fixed presence against whom this span of time is measured. She is the Mrs. Dalloway-Mrs. Ramsay-Percival figure, aware of each generation as they come and go. Eleanor asks the ever-present Woolfian question: is there a meaning behind their lives, a pattern to time? The answer appears to be no. When it comes to time, change rather than a meaning built into time is at work. There was no spokesperson of modernity more critical of the old realism than Virginia Woolf. She was particularly hard on the Arnold Bennett-like novels of saturation, told chronologically, covering generational life rather than the highlights of time. Her fiction shifted emphasis away from the physical event, making it essentially either a part of history or of memory, transforming it from physical to mental reality. Like the vitalists, she transformed time-bound reality by allowing it to be changed by the mind.

8. For a general discussion of the idea of culture and a more specific discussion of Van Wyck Brooks's idea of Puritan and Pioneer, see Hegeman, *Patterns of America*, 71–81, 153–57.

Chapter 8: Literary Transformations

1. Charles Ferrall, *Modernist Writings and Reactionary Politics* (Cambridge, U.K: Cambridge University Press, 2001), 1–8.

2. Marcel Proust, *Remembrance of Things Past* (New York: Random House, 1925).

3. F. Scott Fitzgerald, *The Great Gatsby* (New York: Scribners, 1925; Simon & Schuster, 1995), 169.

4. Henry Adams, *The Education of Henry Adams* (Boston: Houghton Mifflin, 1946), 382.

5. Harry Levin, *The Gates of Horn*, 32.

6. Peter Brooks, *The Melodramatic Imagination: Balzac, Henry James, Melodrama, and the Mode of Excess* (New Haven: Yale University Press, 1976). See also Christopher Prendergast, *Balzac: Fiction and Melodrama* (London: Edward Arnold, 1978).

7. *The Deer Hunter,* portraying both domestic reality and the Vietnam War, is really about courage and friendship in a hostile world. Set in a fictional Pennsylvania coal-and-steel town made up of mainly Slovakian immigrants, the principal characters bond (symbolized by the deer hunt) in ways that see them through wartime, crippling ordeals, and a self-destructive friend's death. As in naturalistic fiction, the intense action and violence of the story is set against an ethnic background so ordinary in its lower-class concerns that the film has a static quality. There are other remnants of literary naturalism—the music, for example, of Johnny Cash. Born into poverty in Arkansas at the height of the Depression, Cash sang about the lives of coal miners and sharecroppers, convicts and cowboys, railroad workers and laborers. Cash began his career as a rockabilly singer in Memphis, where country and the blues mixed. His music, infused with naturalistic themes, bridged storytelling and life experience—a tradition maintained by Bob Dylan, Willie Nelson, and Waylon Jennings.

8. Edmund Wilson, "The Boys in the Back Room," *Classics and Commercials: A Literary Chronicle of the Forties* (New York: Farrar, Straus, 1950), reprinted in *A Literary Chronicle: 1920–1950* (New York; Doubleday, 1956), 245.

9. Edmund Wilson, "The All-Star Literary Vaudeville," *The Shores of Light,* reprinted in *A Literary Chronicle,* 80.

10. Dos Passos's aestheticism stemmed from his exposure to this movement when he was a student at Harvard. Many of his Harvard contemporaries—for example, E. E. Cummings—wrote out of an aesthetic tradition that had its origins in Pater and Wilde in England and Huysmans in France. Malcolm Cowley discusses the Harvard connection in *Think*

Back on Us, ed. Henry Dan Piper (Carbondale: Southern Illinois University Press, 1967), 212–18, 298–300, 203–7.

11. For a discussion of the difference between naturalism and classical tragedy, see Joseph Wood Krutch, *The Modern Temper: A Study and a Confession* (New York: Harcourt, Brace, 1929) and Herbert J. Muller, *The Spirit of Tragedy* (New York: Knopf, 1956).

12. Paul Bowles, *The Sheltering Sky* (New York: Vintage Books, 1949).

13. Norman Mailer, *The Naked and the Dead* (New York: Holt, 1948).

14. Richard Wright, *Native Son* (New York: Harpers and Brothers, 1940), 335, hereafter cited in the text.

15. For a slightly different assessment of Wright's use of Bigger Thomas, see Alfred Kazin, *On Native Grounds: An Interpretation of Modern American Prose Literature* (1942; New York: Doubleday, 1956), 301–2. Kazin argues that Wright justified terror to break through white, middle-class indifference to Bigger's problem: "Bigger Thomas 'found' himself in jail as Wright 'found' himself, after much personal suffering and confusion, in the Communist Party. . . . Once the point had been made, the reader's apathy destroyed, the moment's urgent release effected, there was nothing left but to go round and round in the same vindictive circle."

16. Bellow's *Augie March* was a product of Humboldt Park, a Jewish neighborhood in Chicago. Bellow redefines the heroic, discounting the pioneers' settling the West in favor of a city kid fighting his way out of the slums. Bellow softens the deterministic aspect of naturalistic environment. Despite his cramped circumstances, Augie finds opportunities that allow him to escape his poverty. For a discussion of the ways in which Bellow departs from literary naturalism, see Richard Lehan, *A Dangerous Crossing* (Carbondale: Southern Illinois University Press, 1973), 108–33.

17. Willard Motley, *Knock on Any Door* (New York: New American Library, 1947), 450.

18. Ross Macdonald, composite review of Nelson Algren's novels, *New York Times Book Review*, December 4, 1977.

19. See Brian P. Hayes, composite review of Joyce Carol Oates's novels, *Saturday Review*, October 9, 1971, 38.

20. Ellen Hope Meyer, Omnibus review featuring Oates's *Garden of Earthly Delights*, *Mediterranean Review* (Spring 1972): 50–55.

Chapter 9: Critical Transformations

1. Walter Benn Michaels, *The Gold Standard and the Logic of Naturalism: American Literature at the Turn of the Century* (Berkeley: University of California Press, 1987), 179–80.

2. June Howard, *Form and History in American Literary Naturalism* (Chapel Hill: University of North Carolina Press, 1985), 70, hereafter cited in the text.

3. Daniel H. Borus, *Writing Realism: Howells, James, and Norris in the Mass Market* (Chapel Hill: University of North Carolina Press, 1989), 4, 8.

4. Phillip Barrish, *American Literary Realism, Critical Theory, and Intellectual Prestige, 1880–1995* (Cambridge, U.K.: Cambridge University Press, 2001), 8, 4.

5. Edward W. Said, *The World, the Text, and the Critic* (Cambridge, Mass.: Harvard University Press, 1983), 4, hereafter cited in the text.

6. The impetus for critical change often comes from the most prestigious universities. In the past Yale has led the way. First, there was the rise of the New Criticism under the auspices of Brooks and Warren, and then later French deconstruction under the influence of Jacques Derrida, Hillis Miller, Geoffrey Hartman, and Harold Bloom, who only recently has distanced himself from his earlier pronouncements. The new historicism had its origins at the University of California at Berkeley before Stephen Greenblatt left for Harvard. Once in the profession, the Ph.D. trained at a leading graduate school is in a position to make that training count at other universities. Doctrine is spread by professors who influence faculty hiring, revise academic curriculums, control conferences, create critical journals, or serve on important editorial and other professional committees. University presses go along in order to avoid the charge of not being *au courant*. Such critical influence brings in recruits from elsewhere, creates its own authority. We live in an age of rankism, especially evident in an academic environment. When the typical assistant professor realizes that he or she will not get tenure—that is, not get published—if one goes against prevailing authority, he or she skews the work to accommodate such authority. The resulting academic publication is as predictable as if it were controlled by censorship, which indeed it is.

7. Emmanuel Levinas, *Collected Philosophical Papers*, trans. Alphonso Lingis (Pittsburgh: Duquesne University Press, 1998), 2.

8. T. S. Eliot, *To Criticize the Critic, and Other Writings* (London: Faber and Faber, 1965), 38 –39.

9. For an example of such reading between borders, see Elizabeth Ammons, "Expanding the Canon of American Realism," in *The Cambridge Companion to American Realism and Naturalism,* ed. Donald Pizer (Cambridge, U.K.: Cambridge University Press, 1995), 95 –114. Ammons would include within the revised canon such works as W. E. B. Du Bois's *The Souls of Black Folk,* Charles W. Chesnutt's *The Conjure Woman,* and Zitkala Sua's

Old Indian Legends. While questioning realism/naturalism as a literary category, Ammons creates literary categories based on ethnicity. Ammons's revised canon is implemented by Kenneth K. Warren in the same volume, 263–77.

10. While the formalist critic looks for elements that unify the text, the deconstructionist looks for elements that disrupt such unity. Despite their opposed intentions, their methodology is remarkably similar: each critic searches for the element in the text that gives coherence—for the idea of textual disunity depends on coherence as much as the idea of textual unity does—to his or her pregiven assumptions of how the text works. In both cases, the procedure is circular: the pregiven assumptions anticipate the conclusions, and the conclusions validate the pregiven assumptions. A resolution to this problem involves intelligent choice, based on the weight of evidence.

11. The denial of judgmental ability is contradicted when the practitioners give grades in their college courses, recommend or reject manuscripts as readers for university presses, and select one candidate's grant application over another when acting as judges for national foundations.

12. David Baguley, *Naturalistic Fiction: The Entropic Vision* (Cambridge, U.K.: Cambridge University Press, 1990), 37, hereafter cited in the text.

13. Paul Civello, *American Literary Naturalism and its Twentieth-Century Transformations: Frank Norris, Ernest Hemingway, and Don DeLillo* (Athens: University of Georgia Press, 1994), 122–23.

Selected Bibliography

The bibliography here is mostly composed of secondary sources, given the fact that most of the novels discussed in this study appear in many different editions and are listed in the chronology. There has been no attempt on my part to suggest a preference of one edition over another, although quoted material is documented to the edition used in the endnotes. The same principle applies to readily available historical sources, such as Nietzsche's *The Birth of Tragedy* and Freud's *Civilization and Its Discontents*.

Ahnebrink, Lars. *The Beginnings of Naturalism in American Fiction: A Study of the Works of Hamlin Garland, Stephen Crane, and Frank Norris, with special reference to Some European Influences, 1891–1903.* Cambridge, Mass.: Harvard University Press, 1950.

Baguley, David. *Naturalistic Fiction: An Entropic Vision.* Cambridge, U.K.: Cambridge University Press, 1990.

Bakhtin, Mikhail. *The Dialogic Imagination.* Edited by Michael Holquist. Translated by Caryl Emerson and Michael Holquist. Austin: University of Texas Press, 1981.

———. *Problems of Dostoevsky's Poetics.* Translated by R. W. Rostel. N. p.: Ardis, 1973.

Bannister, Robert. *Social Darwinism: Science and Myth in Anglo-American Thought.* Philadelphia: Temple University Press, 1979.

Barash, David. *Sociobiology: The Whispering Within.* New York: Souvenir Press, 1979.

Barzun, Jacques. *Darwin, Marx, Wagner: Critique of a Heritage.* 1941. Rev. 2nd ed., New York: Doubleday, 1958.

Becker, George. *Realism in Modern Literature.* New York: Ungar, 1963.

——, ed. *Documents of Modern Literary Realism,* Princeton: Princeton University Press, 1963.

Beckson, Karl. *London in the 1890s: A Cultural History.* New York: W. W. Norton, 1992.

Beer, Gillian. *Darwin's Plots: Evolutionary Narrative in Darwin, George Eliot, and Nineteenth Century Fiction.* London: Ark, 1983.

Bell, Michael Davitt. *The Problems of American Realism: Studies in the Cultural History of a Literary Idea.* Chicago: University of Chicago Press, 1993.

Bellamy, William. *The Novels of Wells, Bennett, and Galsworthy: 1890–1910.* New York: Barnes and Noble, 1971.

Bellos, David. *Balzac Criticism in France 1850–1900: The Making of a Reputation.* Oxford, U.K.: Clarendon, 1976.

Benjamin, Walter. *Charles Baudelaire: A Lyric Poet in the Era of High Capitalism.* Translated by Harry Zohn. London: New Left Books, 1973.

Bentley, Eric. *The Cult of the Superman: A Study of the Idea of Heroism in Carlyle and Nietzsche.* Gloucester, Mass.: Peter Smith, 1969.

Berthoff, Warner. *The Ferment of Realism: American Literature, 1884–1919.* New York: Free Press, 1965.

Block, Haskel M. *Naturalistic Triptych: The Fictive and the Real in Zola, Mann, and Dreiser.* New York: Random House, 1970.

Borus, Daniel H. *Writing Realism: Howells, James, and Norris in the Mass Market.* Chapel Hill: University of North Carolina Press, 1989.

Bowlby, Rachel. *Just Looking: Consumer Culture in Dreiser, Gissing, and Zola.* New York: Methuen, 1985.

Bowler, Peter J. *Biology and Social Thought 1850–1914.* Berkeley: Office for History of Science and Technology, University of California at Berkeley, 1993.

Brombert, Victor. *The Novels of Flaubert: A Study of Themes and Technique.* Princeton: Princeton University Press, 1966.

Brooks, Peter. *The Melodramatic Imagination: Balzac, Henry James, Melodrama, and the Mode of Excess.* New Haven: Yale University Press, 1976.

Brooks, Van Wyck. *The Flowering of New England.* 1936. Reprint, New York: E. P. Dutton, 1952.

Brown, Frederick. *Zola: A Life.* New York: Farrar, Straus and Giroux, 1995.

Cady, Edwin H. *The Light of Common Day: Realism in American Fiction.* Bloomington: Indiana University Press, 1971.

Cantor, Norman F. *The American Century: Varieties of Culture in Modern Times.* New York: Harper Collins, 1997.

Carter, A. E. *The Idea of Decadence in French Literature, 1830–1900.* Toronto: University of Toronto Press, 1958

Carter, Everett. *Howells and the Age of Realism.* Philadelphia: Lippincott, 1954.

Chamberlin, Edward J., and Sander L. Gilman, eds. *Degeneration: The Dark Side of Progress.* New York: Columbia University Press, 1985.

Chase, Richard. *The American Novel and Its Tradition.* Garden City, N.Y.: Doubleday, 1957.

Chevrel, Yves. *Le Naturalisme.* Paris: Presses universitaires de France, 1982.

Civello, Paul. *American Literary Naturalism and its Twentieth-Century Transformations: Frank Norris, Ernest Hemingway, and Don DeLillo.* Athens: University of Georgia Press, 1994.

Conder, John J. *Naturalism in American Fiction: The Classic Phase.* Lexington: University Press of Kentucky, 1984.

Conn, Peter. *The Divided Mind: Ideology and Imagination in America, 1898–1917.* Cambridge, U.K.: Cambridge University Press, 1983.

Cowley, Malcolm. "'Not Men': A Natural History of American Naturalism." *Kenyon Review* 9 (1947): 414–35. Reprinted in *Evolutionary Thought in America,* ed. Stow Persons. New Haven: Yale University Press, 1950.

———. *Think Back on Us: A Contemporary Chronicle of the 1930's.* Edited by Henry Dan Piper. Carbondale: Southern Illinois University Press, 1967.

———, ed. *After the Genteel Tradition: American Writers since 1910.* 1937. Reprint, Carbondale: Southern Illinois University Press, 1964.

Darwin, Charles. *Darwin: A Norton Critical Edition.* New York: W. W. Norton, 1979.

Dembo, L. S. *Detotalized Totalities: Synthesis and Disintegration in Naturalist, Existential, and Socialist Fiction.* Madison: University of Wisconsin Press, 1989.

Den Tandt, Christophe. *The Urban Sublime in American Literary Naturalism.* Urbana: University of Illinois Press, 1998.

Dillingham, William B. *Frank Norris: Instinct and Art.* Lincoln: University of Nebraska Press, 1969.

Eiseley, Loren. *Darwin's Century: Evolution and the Men Who Discovered It.* New York: Doubleday, 1961.

Ellul, Jaques. *The Technological Society.* Translated by John Wilkinson. New York: Knopf, 1964.

Fanger, Donald. *Dostoyevsky and Romantic Realism: Balzac, Dickens, and Gogol.* Cambridge, Mass.: Harvard University Press, 1965.

Fisher, Philip. *Hard Facts: Setting and Form in the American Novel.* New York: Oxford University Press, 1985.

Fishkin, Shelley Fisher. *From Fact to Fiction: Journalism and Imaginative Writing in America.* Baltimore: Johns Hopkins University Press, 1985.

Furst, Lillian R., and Peter N. Skrine. *Naturalism.* London: Methuen, 1971.

Geismar, Maxwell. *Rebels and Ancestors: The American Novel, 1890–1915.* Boston: Houghton Mifflin, 1953.

Gogol, Miriam, ed. *Theodore Dreiser: Beyond Naturalism.* New York: New York University Press, 1995.

Graham, Don. *The Fiction of Frank Norris: The Aesthetic Context.* Columbia: University of Missouri Press, 1978.

Greene, John C. *Darwin and the Modern World View.* Baton Rouge: Louisiana State University Press, 1961.

———. *The Death of Adam: Evolution and Its Impact on Western Thought.* Ames: Iowa State University Press, 1959.

———. *Science, Ideology, and World View: Essays in the History of Evolutionary Ideas.* Berkeley: University of California Press, 1981.

Griffith, John W. *Joseph Conrad and the Anthropological Dilemma: "Bewildered Traveller."* Oxford, U.K.: Oxford University Press, 1995.

Guerard, Albert. *The Triumph of the Novel: Dickens, Dostoyevsky, Faulkner.* New York: Oxford University Press, 1976.

Habegger, Alfred. *Gender, Fantasy, and Realism in American Literature.* New York: Columbia University Press, 1982.

Halperin, John. *Gissing: A Life in Books.* New York: Oxford University Press, 1982.

Hauser, Arnold. *The Social History of Art.* Translated by Stanley Godman. London: Routledge and Kegan Paul, 1951.

Hegeman, Susan. *Patterns for America: Modernism and the Concept of Culture.* Princeton: Princeton University Press, 1999.

Hemmings, F. W. J., ed. *The Age of Realism.* New Jersey: Humanities Press, 1978.

Henderson, Harry B., III. *Versions of the Past: The Historical Imagination in American Fiction.* New York: Oxford University Press, 1974.

Hernadi, Paul. *Beyond Genre: New Directions in Literary Classification.* Ithaca: Cornell University Press, 1972.

Himmelfarb, Gertrude. *Darwin and the Darwinian Revolution.* New York: W. W. Norton, 1962.

Hofstadter, Richard. *Social Darwinism in American Thought.* 1944. Rev. ed., Boston: Beacon Press, 1955.

Howard, June. *Form and History in American Literary Naturalism.* Chapel Hill: University of North Carolina Press, 1985.

Hunter, Allan. *Joseph Conrad and the Ethics of Darwinism: The Challenges of Science.* London: Croom Helm, 1983.

Jackson, Holbrook. *The Eighteen Nineties: A Review of Arts and Ideas at the Close of the Nineteenth Century.* 1913. Reprint, Harmondsworth, U.K.: Penguin Books, 1950.

Jouve, Nicole Ward. *Baudelaire: A Fire to Conquer Darkness.* London: Macmillan, 1980.

Kaplan, Amy. *The Social Construction of American Realism.* Chicago: University of Chicago Press, 1988.

Kaplan, Harold. *Power and Order: Henry Adams and the Naturalistic Tradition in American Fiction.* Chicago: University of Chicago Press, 1981.

Kazin, Alfred. *On Native Grounds: An Interpretation of Modern American Prose Literature.* 1942. Abr. ed., New York: Doubleday, 1956.

Knapp, Bettina L. *Emile Zola.* New York: Frederick Ungar, 1980.

Kolb, Harold H., Jr. *The Illusion of Life: American Realism as a Literary Form.* Charlottesville: University Press of Virginia, 1969.

Le Bon, Gustave. *The Crowd: A Study of the Popular Mind.* 1895. Reprint, Harmondsworth, U.K.: Penguin Books, 1964.

Lehan, Richard. "American Literary Naturalism: The French Connection." *Nineteenth-Century Fiction* 38 (1984): 529–57.

———. *The City in Literature: An Intellectual and Cultural History.* Berkeley: University of California Press, 1998.

———. "Realism/Naturalism: The European Background." In *The Cambridge Companion to American Realism and Naturalism,* edited by Donald Pizer, 47–73. Cambridge, U.K.: Cambridge University Press, 1995.

———. *Sister Carrie.* Gale Masterworks Series. Detroit: Gale Research, 2000.

———. "*Sister Carrie:* The City, the Self, and the Modes of Narrative Discourse." In *New Essays on Sister Carrie,* edited by Donald Pizer, 65–85. Cambridge, U.K.: Cambridge University Press, 1991.

———. *Theodore Dreiser: His World and His Novels.* Carbondale: Southern Illinois University Press, 1969.

Lerner, Laurence. *The Frontiers of Literature.* Oxford, U.K.: Basil Blackwell, 1988.

Levin, Harry. *The Gates of Horn: A Study of Five French Realists.* New York: Oxford University Press, 1963.

Lukács, Georg. *Essays on Realism.* Edited by Rodney Livingstone. Translated by David Fernbach. Cambridge, Mass.: MIT Press, 1981.

———. *Studies in European Realism: A Sociological Survey of the Writings of Balzac, Stendhal, Zola, Tolstoy, Gorki, and Others.* Translated by Edith Bone. London: Hillway, 1950.

Martin, Jay. *Harvests of Change: American Literature 1865–1914.* Englewood Cliffs, N.J.: Prentice Hall, 1967.

Martin, Ronald E. *American Literature and the Universe of Force.* Durham, N.C.: Duke University Press, 1981.

Marx, Karl. *The Holy Family, or, Critique of Critical Critique.* Moscow: Foreign Languages Publishing House, 1956.

Masur, Gerhard. *Prophets of Yesterday: Studies in European Culture, 1890–1914.* New York: Macmillan, 1961.

Matthiessen, F. O. *Theodore Dreiser.* New York: William Sloane, 1951.

Mayr, Ernst. *The Growth of Biological Thought: Diversity, Evolution, and Inheritance.* Cambridge, U.K.: Cambridge University Press, 1982.

McElrath, Joseph R., Jr. *Frank Norris Revisited.* New York: Twayne, 1992.

McKay, Janet H. *Narration and Discourse in American Realistic Fiction.* Philadelphia: University of Pennsylvania Press, 1982.

McKeon, Michael. *The Origins of the English Novel, 1600–1740.* Baltimore: Johns Hopkins University Press, 1987.

Michaels, Walter Benn. *The Gold Standard and the Logic of Naturalism.* Berkeley: University of California Press, 1987.

Miller, J. Hillis. *Poets of Reality: Six Twentieth-Century Writers.* Cambridge, Mass.: Harvard University Press, 1965.

Mitchell, Lee Clark. *Determined Fictions: American Literary Naturalism.* New York: Columbia University Press, 1989.

Mosse, George L. *The Culture of Western Europe: The Nineteenth and Twentieth Centuries.* New York: McNally, 1961.

Nelson, Brian, ed. *Naturalism in the European Novel: New Critical Perspectives.* New York: Berg, 1992.

Newlin, Keith, ed. *A Theodore Dreiser Encyclopedia.* Westport, Conn.: Greenwood Press, 2003.

Nordau, Max. *Entartung.* 1892. Published in English as *Degeneration.* New York: Appleton, 1895; reprint, New York: H. Fertig, 1968.

Parrington, Vernon Louis. *The Beginnings of Critical Realism in America, 1860–1920.* Vol. 3, *Main Currents in American Thought.* New York: Harcourt, Brace, 1932.

Peck, Daniel. *Faces of Degeneration: A European Disorder, 1848–1919.* Cambridge, U.K.: Cambridge University Press, 1989.

Perosa, Sergio. *American Theories of the Novel, 1793–1903.* New York: New York University Press, 1983.

Pizer, Donald. *The Novels of Frank Norris.* Bloomington, Indiana University Press, 1966.

———. *The Novels of Theodore Dreiser.* Minneapolis: University of Minnesota Press, 1976.

———. *Realism and Naturalism in Nineteenth Century America.* 1966. Rev. ed., Carbondale: Southern Illinois University Press, 1984.

———. *The Theory and Practice of American Literary Naturalism: Selected Essays and Reviews.* Carbondale: Southern Illinois University Press, 1993.

———. *Twentieth-Century American Literary Naturalism: An Interpretation.* Carbondale, Southern Illinois University Press, 1982.

———, ed. *The Cambridge Companion to American Realism: Howells to London.* Cambridge, U.K.: Cambridge University Press, 1995.

———, ed. *Documents of American Realism and Naturalism.* Carbondale: Southern Illinois University, 1998.

Pizer, Donald, and Earl N. Harbert, eds. *American Realists and Naturalists.* Vol. 12, *Dictionary of Literary Biography.* Detroit: Gale Research, 1982.

Poirier, Richard. *A World Elsewhere: The Place of Style in American Literature.* New York: Oxford University Press, 1966.

Prendergast, Christopher. *Balzac: Fiction and Melodrama.* London: Edward Arnold, 1978.

Quirk, Tom, and Gary Scharnhorst, eds. *American Realism and the Canon.* Newark: University of Delaware Press, 1994.

Rahv, Philip. "Notes on the Decline of Naturalism." *Partisan Review* 9 (1942): 483–931. Reprinted in *Image and Idea.* Norfolk, Conn.: New Directions, 1949.

Rosenfield, Israel. *The Invention of Memory: A New View of the Brain.* New York: Basic Books, 1988.

Said, Edward W. *The World, the Text, and the Critic.* Cambridge, Mass.: Harvard University Press, 1983.

Schilling, Bernard, N. *The Hero as Failure: Balzac and the Rubempré Cycle.* Chicago: University of Chicago Press, 1968.

Seltzer, Mark. *Bodies and Machines.* New York: Routledge, 1992.

Shi, David. *Facing Facts: Realism in American Thought and Culture, 1850–1920.* New York: Oxford University Press, 1995.

Simmons, Ernst, J. *Introduction to Russian Realism.* Bloomington: Indiana University Press, 1965.

Sklar, Martin, *The Corporate Reconstruction of American Capitalism, 1890–1916.* Cambridge, U.K.: Cambridge University Press, 1988.

Stromberg, Roland N., ed. *Realism, Naturalism and Symbolism: Modes of Thought and Expression in Europe, 1848–1914.* New York: Harper and Row, 1968.

Sundquist, Eric J., ed. *American Realism: New Essays*. Baltimore: Johns Hopkins University Press, 1982.

Sypher, Wylie. *Loss of Self in Modern Literature and Art*. Westport, Conn.: Greenwood Press, 1979.

Thorp, Willard. *American Writing in the Twentieth Century*. Cambridge, Mass.: Harvard University Press, 1960.

Trachtenberg, Alan. *The Incorporation of America: Culture and Society in the Gilded Age*. New York: Hill and Wang, 1982.

Trilling, Lionel. "Reality in America." In *The Liberal Imagination: Essays on Literature and Society*. New York: Viking, 1950.

Vivas, Eliseo. "Dreiser, An Inconsistent Mechanist." *Ethics* 48.4 (1938): 498–508.

Walcutt, Charles Child. *American Literary Naturalism: A Divided Stream*. 1956. Reprint, Westport, Conn.: Greenwood Press, 1973.

Warren, Robert Penn. *Homage to Theodore Dreiser, August 27, 1871–December 28, 1945, on the Centennial of His Birth*. New York: Random House, 1971.

Watt, Ian. *Conrad in the Nineteenth Century*. Berkeley: University of California Press, 1979.

———. *The Rise of the Novel: Studies in Defoe, Richardson, and Fielding*. Berkeley: University of California Press, 1957.

Whitworth, Michael H. *Einstein's Wake: Relativity, Metaphor, and Modernist Literature*. Oxford, U.K.: Oxford University Press, 2001.

Wilson, Angus. *Emile Zola: An Introductory Study of His Novels*. 1952. Reprint, London: Mercury Books, 1965.

Wilson, Edmund. *Classics and Commercials: A Literary Chronicle of the Forties*. New York: Farrar, Straus, 1950.

———. *A Literary Chronicle: 1920–1950*. New York: Doubleday Anchor, 1956.

———. "The Pilgrimage of Henry James." *The Portable Edmund Wilson*, edited by Lewis M. Dabney. New York: Viking Press, 1983.

———. *The Shores of Light: A Literary Chronicle of the Twenties and Thirties*. New York: Farrar, Straus and Young, 1952.

———. *The Wound and the Bow: Seven Studies in Literature*. 1941. Reprint, New York: Oxford University Press, 1965.

Winner, Anthony. *Characters in the Twilight: Hardy, Zola, and Chekhov*. Charlottesville: University Press of Virginia, 1981.

Zanine, Louis J. *Mechanism and Mysticism: The Influence of Science on the Thought and Work of Theodore Dreiser*. Philadelphia: University of Pennsylvania Press, 1993.

Ziff, Larzer. *The American 1890s: Life and Times of a Lost Generation*. New York: Viking, 1966.

Index